African peace

Manchester University Press

African peace

Regional norms from the Organization of African Unity to the African Union

Kathryn Nash

MANCHESTER UNIVERSITY PRESS

Published by Manchester University Press
Altrincham Street, Manchester M1 7JA

www.manchesteruniversitypress.co.uk

British Library Cataloguing-in-Publication Data
A catalogue record for this book is available from the British Library

ISBN 978 1 5261 5281 7 hardback

First published 2021

Typeset by
Servis Filmsetting Ltd, Stockport, Cheshire

To Mom, Dad, Dustin, Jessica, and Collin

Contents

Figures

Acknowledgments

While researching and writing this book I became indebted to a large number of people. I would like to thank my colleagues at the School of Oriental and African Studies and the University of Edinburgh for their steadfast support and valuable feedback throughout this process. In particular, Leslie Vinjamuri, Stephan Chan, and Christine Bell provided unwavering mentorship. I would also like to thank the entire Political Settlements Research Programme for feedback on earlier drafts of the introduction and encouragement throughout this process. I am particularly indebted to Laura Wise, Robert Wilson, and Sean Molloy, who gave substantial feedback on several drafts, as well as several anonymous reviewers for their constructive and robust engagement with my manuscript. Finally, I would like to thank my editor and the whole team at Manchester University Press, who helped shepherd this work through the publication process.

I collected evidence for this book from the African Union Commission Archives, and I would like to thank Chedza Molefe, Sirak Tesfaye, and Stephen Mayega for their invaluable assistance in facilitating my visit and navigating the archives. They were incredibly hospitable to me and all visiting scholars and ensured I had access to the wealth of material available at the archive. Citations of the archival documents use the title and information as shown on the original document. This does lead to some inconsistency in the formatting of citations but is done to ensure readers can trace the documents used.

I would like to thank the UK Foreign, Commonwealth and Development Office (FCDO) for the funding of my current position as part of the Political Settlements Research Programme at the University of Edinburgh. However, the information and views set out in this publication are mine and do not necessarily reflect the official position of FCDO. Neither FCDO nor any person acting on their behalf may be held responsible for the use of the information contained therein. In addition, some material from Chapters 4 and 5 appears in a chapter of the edited volume *Visions of African Unity: New Perspectives on the History of Pan-Africanism and African Unification*

Projects edited by Matteo Grilli and Frank Gertis, reproduced with the permission of the editors and Manchester University Press.

Finally, I would like to thank my family and several close friends near and afar, including Jennifer Roggio, Caryl Tuma, Bethany Haworth, and Greg O'Keefe, for their support through the long process to research, write, and publish this volume.

Abbreviations

ALF	African Leadership Forum
AMIB	African Union Mission in Burundi
AMIS	African Union Mission in Sudan
APSA	African Peace and Security Architecture
ASEAN	Association of Southeast Asian Nations
CAR	Central African Republic
CSSDCA	Conference on Security, Stability, Development and Cooperation in Africa
ECOMOG	Economic Community of West African States Monitoring Group
ECOWAS	Economic Community of West African States
FLN	Front de Libération Nationale
ICC	International Criminal Court
ICISS	International Commission on Intervention and State Sovereignty
NATO	North Atlantic Treaty Organization
NGOs	non-governmental organizations
OMIC	Observer Mission in the Comoros
PSC	(AU) Peace and Security Council
R2P	Responsibility to Protect
RPF	Rwandan Patriotic Front
SADC	Southern African Development Community
SMC	Standing Mediation Committee
UDHR	Universal Declaration of Human Rights
UNAMIR	United Nations Assistance Mission for Rwanda
UNDPKO	United Nations Department of Peacekeeping Operations
UNECA	United Nations Economic Commission for Africa
UNITAF	Unified Task Force
UNOSOM	United Nations Operation in Somalia
UNPROFOR	United Nations Protection Force
UNSC	United Nations Security Council

1

Introduction

Who contributes to the ideas or norms that govern the international system? The literature has explored the role of norm entrepreneurs, international institutions, courts, transnational networks, and states to create and promote norms that set expectations for how global society should work.[1] However, there is often a piece of the puzzle that is missing. Regional organizations have defined regional priorities, created norms and policies, and contributed to international norms. Yet, despite their impact at both the regional and international levels, the contributions of regional institutions as norm creators and promoters, particularly in marginalized regions, is under-examined. This book analyzes how African regional organizations created peace and security norms in order to better understand the role regional organizations play in shaping international society. It argues that the Organization of African Unity (OAU) and then the African Union (AU) uniquely adapted existing international norms as well as created new peace and security norms within their regional sphere and largely independent of international pressure.

Norms are collective expectations for appropriate behavior.[2] They are vital because they can provide legitimacy in the international system. They can prescribe standards, and they can be both an instrument of power and an obstacle to its use.[3] For instance, norms can constrain power by limiting the types of weapons that can be used in war.[4] But they can be an instrument of power when they are used to promote a system that is beneficial to certain actors. While it is important to understand how powerful states have created and used norms to enhance and maintain power, it is equally important to investigate how norms have been created and used by less powerful actors. This volume not only explores the specific processes and strategies used by African regional organizations to create norms but also how African regional bodies then used their norms to enhance African legitimacy and power. In examining these issues, this book illuminates the influence of regional organizations in the Global South and adds to an emerging and overdue literature on the global governance contributions of these organizations.⁵ It also contributes to our understanding of norm creation within the specific spaces of regional organizations. As such, it has implications both for the role that regional organizations play in shaping norms in their own spheres and also the role they play in shaping and promoting international norms.

Specifically, I ask why the OAU chose norms in 1963 that underpinned a non-interference conflict management policy and why the AU chose very different norms in the early 2000s that led to a non-indifference conflict management policy. I argue that African regional organizations created norms for their own purposes and based on their own experiences, and international influence was not a determinant factor in the evolving peace and security norms within Africa. As Chapter 4 will demonstrate, the OAU adopted norms of non-interference in the internal affairs of member states, protection of state sovereignty and territorial integrity, and regional primacy that led to a conflict management policy of non-interference even in the face of conflicts that threatened atrocities or regional stability. However, norms are not static, and they evolved in the regional context so much so that the AU adopted norms that emphasized human security and allowed for intervention in the internal affairs of member states in some circumstances. These norms led to a new conflict management policy of non-indifference. Chapters 6–9 explore the evolution of these norms while Chapter 11 discusses the creation of the AU. While the AU has not always been able to prevent or stop conflict, the non-indifference policy has meant that the African regional organization is far more willing and capable of engaging in conflict management on the continent. I argue that the shift from non-interference to non-indifference was incremental, began as early as the 1970s, and was largely internally driven within Africa. Norm creation and evolution was predicated on advocacy by leaders, mutually constituted regional ideas and interests, and experiences. Understanding processes of norm creation and evolution within the OAU and now the AU is a starting point for demonstrating how norms crafted by African regional institutions contribute to norms that are adopted more widely in the international system.

Contrary to interpretations that focus on the role of global events or influence, the emergence of norms that supported the shift from non-interference to non-indifference does not begin in the context of the post-Cold War world. Instead it begins in the context of the immediate post-independence world. The adoption of norms that underpinned non-interference was the starting point for norm creation by African regional institutions, and scholars can only understand the emergence of norms that underpin non-indifference by understanding norm creation in the post-colonial period and its progression over time. The process of evolution was not perfectly linear, and the transition should be seen as a slow institutional progression interspersed with failures, multiple phases, and several factors pushing it forward as well as back.

The larger implication is that theories of international relations that chiefly attribute changes in domestic and regional norms to international dynamics or the influence of powerful states are underdetermining. They neglect key motors of change, which are found in ideas, values, experiences, and both material and non-material interests. The idea of pan-Africanism and how it shaped regional interests along with the collective experience of the African region under colonialism and immediately after independence, in addition to advocacy by African leaders, played a major role in determining the norms chosen at the advent of the OAU. Likewise, the normative shifts within Africa cannot be seen as largely attributable to shifts in global politics or the influence of major states or international institutions. The transformation of the understanding of pan-Africanism, the experiences of African states with conflicts and atrocities, advocacy by key leaders, and regional interests were the main drivers.

This book focuses on regional organizations because these institutions are the framework through which all of these factors are channeled to culminate in norm creation. It also focuses specifically on African regional organizations. However, this is not an argument that Africa is unique in its ability to construct norms and influence international norms. Rather it is an in-depth study of African regional organizations that puts forward a theoretical framework on norm creation that could potentially be applied to other regional organizations. As an overview of the existing literature will show, norm creation is often assumed to have arisen at the international or domestic levels. However, it is important to show how norms are created and promoted by Global South regional organizations that are often understood to predominantly be the recipients of norms, in order to understand how those regions emerged from decolonization struggles and sought to contribute and continue to contribute to the ideas that govern the international system.

Evidence and approach

This book employs a process-tracing methodology using archival documents collected from the AU Commission Archives. Sources include speeches from African leaders at the OAU founding conference, verbatim meeting records, administrative reports and budgets, reports prepared for the Council of Ministers and Heads of State and Government, and summit agendas and outcome documents. As a general methodology, process-tracing focuses on tracing theoretical causal-mechanisms. It looks at events over time, and sequencing is very important. This makes it uniquely suited to analyzing the creation and evolution of norms over a 40–year period between the creation of the OAU to the AU.

There are different types of process-tracing that are used at different junctures in this study. Theory-testing process-tracing takes theory from existing literature and then tests whether evidence demonstrates that the hypothesized causal mechanisms are present in a case. Theory-building process-tracing attempts to build theoretical explanations from empirical evidence.[6] In this book, the change in norms in the constitutive documents of African regional organizations is the dependent variable that is investigated. I test whether the creation and evolution of norms in Africa fits within existing theories of institutional change and norm creation. As will be discussed, I do find that the evolution from the OAU to the AU fits within Mark Blyth's institutional change theory, which is critical for explaining the timing of the formal institutional and normative shift from the OAU to the AU. However, I demonstrate that existing norm creation theories do not fit this case. Therefore, I also use theory-building process-tracing to explain the theoretical causal mechanisms by which the OAU and AU chose specific norms, and this theory can be applied in other regional contexts. The nature of theory is a contested concept in international relations. I do not claim that my theory has predictive power but rather that it explains a phenomenon of norm development within regional organizations and can be applied and tested across different contexts.

While process-tracing is valuable, there are cautions and critiques of the method. Notably, there are multiple causal paths that may lead to the same outcome.[7] The normative shift from the OAU to the AU is widely explored in the literature, and I explore alternative explanations later in this chapter and demonstrate how archival evidence disproves existing explanations. Other dominant explanations focus on the period immediately surrounding the change in the constitutive document in the transition from the OAU to the AU. This has led to a focus on international pressure or changing global dynamics in the post-Cold War period. The value of this book is that the starting point is the creation of the OAU, so it includes analysis of the creation and breakdown of OAU norms as well as the construction of a new system that includes periods of progression and regression. In short, my study starts with the events that fed into the change, analyzing and understanding each distinct period but also viewing them temporally. It is through this analysis that I am able to show that the change began well before the end of the Cold War and thus challenge explanations that focus on international pressure and global dynamics due to the sequencing of events. Furthermore, I sought to triangulate my evidence by finding multiple sources to prove my argument. I began by consulting the primary sources and then compared these sources to diplomatic and academic accounts. I also compared speeches and debate records against the actions, funding priorities, and policies of the OAU. I also used very limited interviews with AU officials, primarily around the interpretation of recent events and evolving AU peace and security mechanisms.

Finally, given that the methodology is process-tracing, this volume does rely on internal documents, which of course have biases as they are produced by the organization being studied. However, the purpose of this book is not to critically examine the utility or effectiveness of African regional organizations but rather to analyze the process that led to a change in norms between the OAU and AU. In doing so, it adds to the literature on the history of the OAU, but fundamentally, it is a challenge and contribution to international relations literature on the creation of norms and the role of regional organizations.

Overview of argument

The history of African regional organizations can be split into the two phases of the OAU period from 1963–2002 and the AU period from 2002 onward. This book does provide some vital context around decolonization struggles and the emergence of pan-Africanism, but the focus is on the period around the creation of the OAU and the period between the OAU and the AU. This focus allows me to concentrate on why and how particular norms were chosen at the advent of both the OAU and AU. Chapter 2 presents an overview of the legal, institutional, policy, and practice differences between the OAU and AU. While these two distinct organizations can be viewed on a continuum, the differences between each organization's approach to peace and security is clear. At the creation of the OAU, the organization chose a set of norms, including non-interference in the internal affairs of member states, a commitment to enhancing the sovereignty and territorial integrity of African states, and regional primacy. These norms governed interactions between states and the management of violent conflict on the continent, and they manifested in a peace and security policy of non-interference, which meant the OAU was largely powerless to effectively address violent conflict. When the AU officially replaced the OAU, the organization embraced a very different set of norms premised on human security and sovereignty as responsibility that led to a policy of non-indifference, which allowed more forceful action to prevent and manage violent conflict even if AU norms and capacities are still very much developing. However, significant analysis of how norms may be continuing to evolve in the AU era because of modern events and changing interests is outside the scope of this volume.

The central argument of this book is that the shift from non-interference to non-indifference was a multi-stage process that was underpinned by ideas and largely internally driven. The first stage, and the starting point for understanding norms in the African regional context, is the adoption of norms that underpinned the non-interference policy at the founding of the OAU. The second stage was a period in the 1960s and 1970s of catastrophic conflicts and atrocities that had a traumatic impact on Africa's global reputation and internal development and pushed some African leaders to re-evaluate strict non-interference. The third stage of the process is seen in the late 1970s and early 1980s when there is the beginning of a shift away from strict non-interference with the adoption of human security-oriented policies and protocols. The fourth stage is the period of the 1990s wherein African leaders created new institutions but still tried to underpin them with the same OAU era norms, and the fifth stage is the complete break from the OAU era with the establishment of the AU.

The transformation of African regional norms was spurred on by critical events in Africa, the influence of respected leaders, and evolving regional interests, and was underpinned by pan-Africanist ideas. The conflicts and atrocities that shocked many African leaders, and threatened African interests during the 1960s–1970s, included the Nigerian-Biafran war from 1967–1970 in which an estimated 600,000 civilians died, the atrocities of Uganda's Idi Amin, and the human rights abuses of Emperor Bokassa of Central African Empire. Beyond key events and regional interests, pan-Africanism and ideas around human security and sovereignty as responsibility helped to theoretically underpin regional security cooperation and humanitarian intervention. It is these factors that led to an evolution from non-interference under the OAU to non-indifference under the AU. The shift began in the 1970s and was gradual, culminating in the AU Constitutive Act that was negotiated beginning in 1999 and adopted in July 2000. Explanations that focus primarily on the influence of the international cannot explain the shift in African policies and practices that milestones indicate began to happen before the end of the Cold War as well as before the emergence of international intervention norms.

The indications of shifting regional norms before the end of the Cold War include the lack of robust condemnation for the Tanzanian invasion of Uganda in 1979, which eventually led to the overthrow of Idi Amin, the Nigerian engagement to end conflict in Chad from 1979–1982 leading to Africa's first multi-lateral peacekeeping mission, the proposal for an OAU Peace and Security Council in the early 1980s, and the Economic Community of West African States (ECOWAS) intervention in Liberia

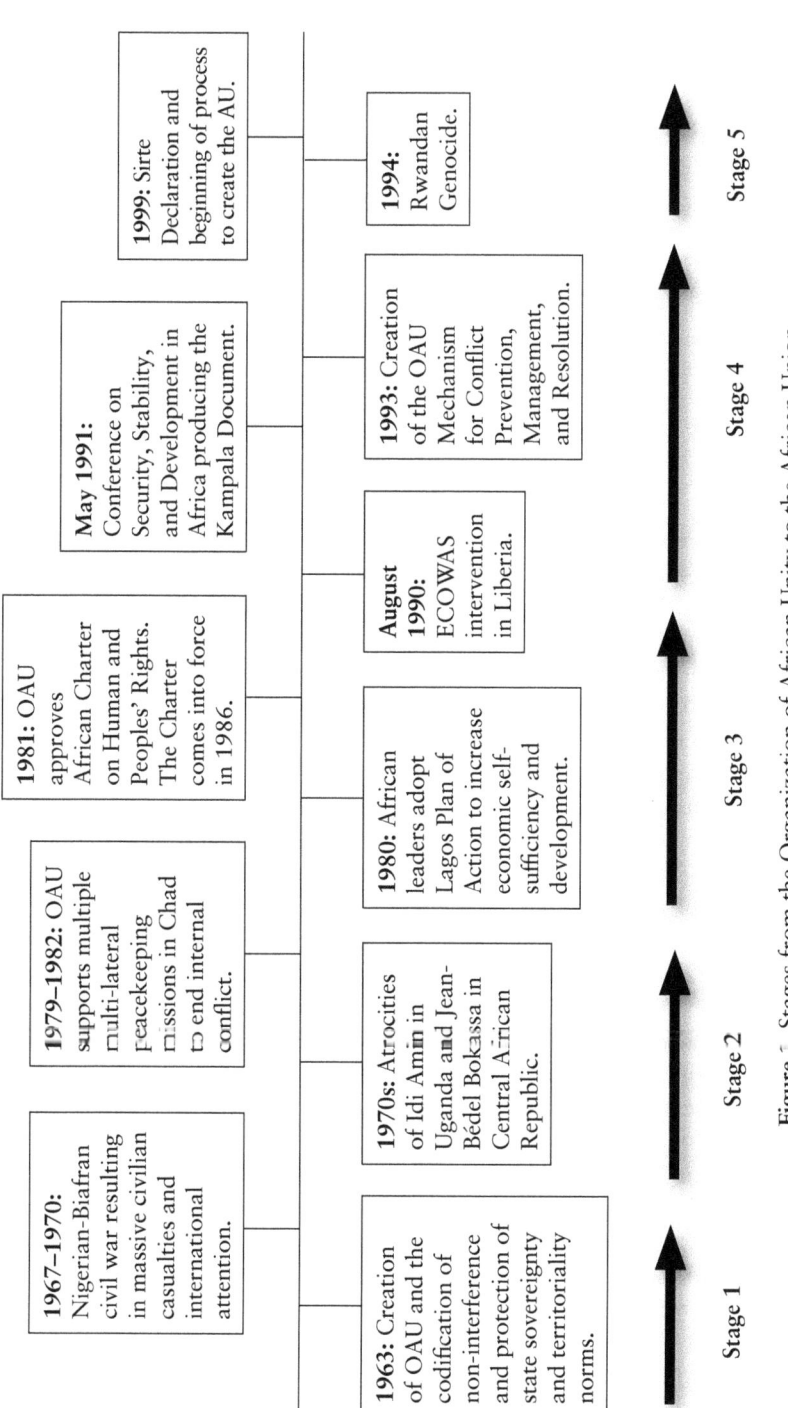

1963: Creation of OAU and the codification of non-interference and protection of state sovereignty and territoriality norms.

1967–1970: Nigerian-Biafran civil war resulting in massive civilian casualties and international attention.

1970s: Atrocities of Idi Amin in Uganda and Jean-Bédel Bokassa in Central African Republic.

1979–1982: OAU supports multiple multi-lateral peacekeeping missions in Chad to end internal conflict.

1980: African leaders adopt Lagos Plan of Action to increase economic self-sufficiency and development.

1981: OAU approves African Charter on Human and Peoples' Rights. The Charter comes into force in 1986.

August 1990: ECOWAS intervention in Liberia.

May 1991: Conference on Security, Stability, and Development in Africa producing the Kampala Document.

1993: Creation of the OAU Mechanism for Conflict Prevention, Management, and Resolution.

1994: Rwandan Genocide.

1999: Sirte Declaration and beginning of process to create the AU.

Stage 1   Stage 2   Stage 3   Stage 4   Stage 5

Figure 1 Stages from the Organization of African Unity to the African Union

in 1990. These milestones were indications of changing ideas and practices within Africa about intervention and the role of the region in conflict
management. Furthermore, they often preceded notable international
milestones that pushed forward intervention norms at the global level.
These events and a more robust comparison of international and regional
developments is elaborated on in Chapter 10. While international actors
can certainly influence regional norms and practices, in the case of African
peace and security norms, international influence was not a primary factor
in their creation and evolution, and new intervention ideas and practices
were often seen first in African regional institutions.

Norm creation and promotion

Dominance of the Global North

International relations and international law theory have extensively explored
the construction, evolution, and dispersion of political and legal norms.
Within international relations, constructivist theorists in particular focus
on the role of ideas in shaping global governance. However, constructivist
accounts of norm creation and promotion tend to fall into categories that
focus on norm creation by norm entrepreneurs and dispersion through institutions and states or norms that emerge in domestic spheres and dispersion
through transnational networks. Within this literature there is also often an
assumption that international norms emerge in powerful states in the Global
North and then are diffused to states in the Global South through emulation,
coercion, or other processes.[8] This leads to norm creation and evolution that
is geographically concentrated and either coming from the top-down or the
bottom-up, leaving little if any room to explore the role of regional organizations to create their own norms and contribute to global norms.

Finnemore and Sikkink argue that norm creation and dispersion happen
in a three-stage process. First there is the emergence of the norm. This
happens when norm entrepreneurs, individuals, or organizations that have
a strong sense of appropriate behavior work to convince states to adopt a
norm and then promote it. When a critical mass of states adopts the norm,
it is said to reach a tipping point, which is hopefully followed by a norm
cascade as more and more states adopt the norm. The final stage is internalization wherein the behavior prescribed by the norm becomes almost taken
for granted.[9] In this conception, the desirability of the norm and the quality
of the states promoting it largely determine why certain norms take hold and
others do not.[10] This process can encompass both a bottom-up approach
with norm entrepreneurs pushing for change and a top-down approach with
the international community then supporting certain norms.

If there is an unwillingness to accept a particular norm, states can be subject to both domestic and international pressure. The spiral model sets out five stages of typically non-western countries adopting international norms. The first stage is repression, wherein the norm-violating state represses its population, and transnational advocacy networks seek to gather enough information on the state's repressive practices to draw attention at the international level. The second stage is denial. At this stage, the repressive state typically denies any charges that it violates international norms and offsets criticism by making arguments about illegitimate outside interference. If sufficient pressure is applied then the norm-violating state enters stage three where it makes tactical concessions. These concessions are typically cosmetic or temporary. At this point domestic actors must link with international actors and apply pressure from above and below. The increasing pressure from domestic populations and the international community create a situation where leaders in the norm-violating state face either continuing to resist change and being removed from power or undertaking controlled liberalization. Indications of this stage are the ratification of human rights agreements and their subsequent institutionalization in domestic law. Finally, the last stage is rule-consistent behavior where the previously norm-violating state has adopted and now complies with international human rights norms.[11] Here again, it is advocacy by domestic actors and transnational networks with pressure from the international community that forces a change.

One instance of a Global North state supporting the creation and promotion of norms is Canada, which has supported norms rooted in human security.[12] Taking the example of seeking to ban landmines, six non-governmental organizations (NGOs) organized the International Campaign to Ban Landmines in 1992. This group grew to over 1,200 organizations in over 60 countries acting as norm entrepreneurs by lobbying governments in their respective countries. Canada became involved in 1996 when it offered to host a strategy conference.[13] In doing so, Canada sought to use its position in the international system to directly lobby other states and use its resources to amplify the discussions. Canada also played a central role in supporting the creation of the Responsibility to Protect (R2P) norm, discussed later in this chapter, as it hosted and sponsored the International Commission on Intervention and State Sovereignty (ICISS), which is the body that produced the R2P report.[14]

There are also scholars who highlight the dominance of Global North actors in norm creation by highlighting how norms have been used to maintain a system of dominance by particular states. Third World Approaches to International Law have developed a substantive challenge to some of the premises of international law.[15] For instance, Anghie argues that the foundations of international law, and notably the doctrine of sovereignty, were created to manage the relationship between European and non-European spheres during the colonial era.[16] Upon independence, new states tried to revise old international law doctrines, which furthered western interests, or even create new doctrines to further the interests of newly independent states. For example, new states pushed for permanent sovereignty over natural resources.[17] This is a doctrine that argues the natural resources of a territory belong to the people of a territory; therefore people who lived in formerly colonized territories could assert sovereignty over those resources because their sovereignty preceded colonialism. In this way new states were asserting a right against state responsibility and respecting the obligations of predecessor states in a manner that would have enhanced their economic and political sovereignty.[18] This challenge to the international system did not result in significant changes to how sovereignty was practiced. However, as this volume will show, there are instances where actors in the Global South have contributed substantially to international norms, and these contributions are underacknowledged. Overall, the totality of political and legal norm scholarship begs further questions on the role actors in the Global South play in norm creation and promotion.

Contributions of Global South actors

There is an emerging literature on the active role that actors in the Global South play in constructing and promoting norms. This literature does not seek to negate power disparities in the international system but rather it is to highlight instances where Global South actors have been influential but perhaps unacknowledged. Sikkink demonstrates this disparity between influence and acknowledgment in her work on the role of Latin American protagonists in the creation of global human rights norms. Latin American countries drafted the American Declaration of the Rights and Duties of Man (American Declaration) eight months before the Universal Declaration of Human Rights (UDHR) was passed by the UN General Assembly in December 1948.[19] During negotiations to draft the UDHR, Latin American delegations, particularly Mexico, Cuba, and Chile, drew on their own constitutional traditions and experience with the American Declaration to almost singlehandedly insert language into the UDHR on rights to justice.[20]

Coleman and Tieku have identified four pathways through which African actors have developed African norms and at times contributed to international norms.[21] First, African individuals, organizations, and networks have shaped global norm creation processes. For instance, Boutros Boutros Ghali, Francis Deng, and Kofi Annan were all instrumental in distinct ways in pushing forward a norm of humanitarian intervention.[22] The second pathway is through a deliberate African regional subsidiarity push. Through the process of subsidiarity, Global South actors adopt norms in a bid to preserve their autonomy and protect themselves from outside domination. One such norm in the African context was the norm of pan-African solidarity, which has recently been utilized to shield some African leaders from prosecution by the International Criminal Court (ICC).[23] Third, distinctive norms may emerge from a coalition of African states that develop a norm to address a common problem. And fourth, norms may emerge from the efforts of nonstate actors who advocate for particular norms through their governments or institutions.[24]

Expanding on the example of African contributions to intervention norms, the UN Secretary General Kofi Annan issued a challenge at the UN General Assembly in September 1999 for the international community to reflect on human security and intervention. As discussed above, the Canadian government responded by announcing the establishment of the ICISS in September 2000.[25] The Commission was asked to reconcile the tensions between upholding state sovereignty and the humanitarian necessity of protecting civilians after the atrocities in Rwanda and Kosovo.[26] It was comprised of a group of academics, diplomats, and policy-makers from across the globe and co-chaired by Gareth Evans and Mohamed Sahnoun. The ICISS report was released in December 2001.

There are numerous examples of ideas and practices originating in African institutions that pushed forward thinking on responding to crises and humanitarian intervention prior to the release of the ICISS report. For instance, ECOWAS sought to impose a ceasefire in a civil war through a non-consensual military intervention in August 1990.[27] Francis Deng proposed the initial concept of sovereignty as responsibility in a book chapter and then further elaborated on the concept in a 1996 book.[28] And of course, the AU codified Article 4(h) asserting the right of a regional organization to intervene in the internal affairs of a member state in response to atrocities in their Constitutive Act that was adopted in 2000 and entered into force in May 2001. Given the significant development of humanitarian intervention ideas and practices originating in Africa in the 1990s, Darkwa, Acharya, and other scholars have sought to draw out the contributions of African institutions and scholars to the creation of the R2P norm and the advancement of intervention practices,[29] but other R2P scholarship as well as the ICISS report itself focus on the NATO intervention in Kosovo in 1999 and the UN interventions in Somalia and Iraq in the early 1990s coupled with the 1994 tragedy of the genocide in Rwanda without engaging with the practices of African institutions that pushed forward a humanitarian intervention norm.[30] Too often these discourses are dominant, and Africa

African peace

becomes a space where tragedies on its soil spur action but ideas and practices from African institutions are not seen as contributing to the response.

Regional organizations in norm creation and promotion

There is some literature that considers the role of regional organizations in the Global South in norm creation. Acharya argues that regions are part of a legitimate normative order and have agency when choosing how to receive international norms. Constitutive localization is the active construction (through discourse, framing, grafting, and cultural selection) of foreign ideas by local actors, which results in a norm developing significant congruence with local beliefs and practices.[31] The Association of Southeast Asian Nations (ASEAN) drew on cognitive priors, which can include cultural beliefs, religious traditions, and the principled ideas of elites, when determining which norms ASEAN nations adopted. In particular, and much like the OAU, a deep distrust of western intentions among the founding leaders of many Asian Pacific nations led to strong support for sovereignty and non-intervention norms and skepticism of robust regional collective security organizations.[32]

Norm subsidiarity describes a process where, "local actors develop new rules, offer new understandings of global rules, or reaffirm rules in the regional context in order to preserve their autonomy from dominance, neglect, violation, or abuse by more powerful central actors."[33] It differs from localization in several key ways. Localization is inward looking and explains how local actors adopt foreign norms whereas subsidiarity is outward looking. The main focus with subsidiarity is the relationship between local actors and external powers, and this relationship is defined by local actor's fear of domination. With localization, local actors are norm-takers while in subsidiarity they are norm-rejecters and norm-makers that can export local norms which support a struggle against powerful actors. While localization can apply to any country or region that is adopting an outside norm, subsidiarity by its definition is specific to less powerful states most likely in the Global South.[34]

Subsidiarity emerged out of the post-World War II system in which states in the Global South were marginalized from major decision-making structures within the international community. The post-World War II international organizations were and still are dominated by major powers and can often neglect the interests and views of weaker states. Weaker states are concerned with ensuring that powerful states do not set regional agendas and that regional solutions are first sought for regional problems. In addition to marginalization, Global South states are also concerned with the blatant hypocrisy present in the international system that allows powerful states to flout long-held norms of sovereignty and non-intervention, particularly during the post-colonial and Cold War periods.[35]

In this interplay between localization and subsidiarity, Acharya argues that localization was at play in ASEAN's adoption of non-intervention norms. However, in the African context, I argue in Chapter 4 that subsidiarity cannot fully explain why the OAU codified norms in 1963 that promoted non-intervention, sovereignty, territorial integrity, and regional primacy. Subsidiarity focuses on regions choosing norms from fear of outside domination. In the case of the OAU, the organization adapted international norms in innovative ways to protect their newly independent states from outside domination but also from interference from within Africa. There were other options available to African leaders. Kwame Nkrumah proposed a radical African unity project that would have involved some pooling of state sovereignty to create a regional bloc to push back against international actors and guard against neo-colonialism.[36] As speeches and records from the OAU founding conference will demonstrate, this model was not adopted due to fears of subversion from within and outside Africa coupled with the calculation that conforming to the international system and adopting non-intervention norms was the best way to ensure political independence and achieve political liberation for all African countries. In embracing non-intervention and state security, the OAU was conforming to the prevailing international system that prioritizes state sovereignty. However, African leaders were doing so because of their fear of outside domination and interference from other African states and believed that a non-intervention framework was the best way to protect their nascent states and build their credibility in the international system.

Furthermore, African leaders worked to develop non-interference and regional primacy norms in ways that would shore up independent African state sovereignty while diminishing the legitimacy of colonial and white-minority regimes. As analysis of the Lusaka Manifesto and the work of the OAU Liberation Committee in subsequent chapters will demonstrate, African states linked adherence to non-interference to accepting, in principle, norms of racial equality and self-determination.[37] This linking justified intervention in some states while protecting newly independent African states. Additionally, African states pushed a norm of regional primacy that went beyond the norm codified in Chapter VIII of the UN Charter that allows regions a place in the global order. The OAU actively sought to restrict and dictate the terms of international involvement in continental affairs and expand its influence in the UN and other international institutions.[38] The OAU norms that were chosen not only reflect the status quo but rather reflect the beliefs of African leaders about which norms would help them accomplish their goals of shoring up African sovereignty and statehood, liberating the continent, and securing Africa's place in the world. The chosen norms were also adapted to shore up the legitimacy of African independent states whilst denigrating the credibility of colonial and white-minority regimes and interference in internal African affairs. Overall, there must be more consideration of contestation of norms within regions and the agency of regional organizations to create and promote norms, and the norm literature must also more fully consider why marginalized and formerly colonized regions may adopt specific norms not because of outside pressure but because of calculations based on their unique experiences, interests, and values.

Explaining the shift from the OAU to the AU

There has long been debate about how Africa should manage conflicts within its borders. Mazrui proposed the concept of Pax Africana in 1967, described as a peace that was assured by Africans within the bounds of Africa.[39] The question has always been how to achieve peace in Africa, and the norms OAU and AU led to very different answers. The central question of this volume is: why were different peace and security norms chosen at the advent of the OAU and the AU. Williams wrote a seminal piece on the transition norms that supported non-intervention under the OAU to norms that supported non-indifference under the AU. In Williams' analysis, the central tenets of the AU's current security culture are outlined in the AU Constitutive Act or other protocols and include:

(1) Sovereign equality of members (Article 4a).
(2) Non-intervention by member states (Article 4g).
(3) Anti-imperialism/African Solutions first.
(4) Uti possidetis (Article 4b).
(5) Non-use of force/peaceful settlement of disputes (Articles 4e, 4f, 4i).
(6) Condemnation of unconstitutional changes of governments (Article 4p).
(7) The Union's right to intervene in a member state in grave circumstances (Article 4h).

> Paul D. Williams, "From Non-Intervention to Non-Indifference: The Origins and Development of the African Union's Security Culture," *African Affairs* 106, no.423 (2007): 261.

Norms six and seven are recent while norms one to five date back to the OAU period and were chosen because of discourses about African identity and pan-Africanism, and the debates over how to pursue African unity following the decolonization period.[40] Williams argues that the new AU norms concerning unconstitutional changes of government and allowing humanitarian intervention developed in response to internal and external factors, the most important of which were, "contradictions within the OAU's own principles and the growing pressure on African governments to be seen to conform to transnational norms on liberal democracy and human rights."[41] Specifically, the contradictory OAU stances on secession, non-intervention, and African autonomy and pressure from western funders, international organizations, and local NGOs pushed the OAU to adopt human rights and democratic reforms.[42]

Koga analyzed regional security institutions in Africa and Asia and demonstrated that institutional literature has a bias toward western states and has failed to focus on regional security institutions developed by non-Great Powers.[43] Koga's comparative volume analyzes institutional shifts in ASEAN, ECOWAS, and OAU/AU. For the OAU/AU case, Koga focuses on the OAU peacekeeping efforts in Chad from 1979–1982 and the period from 1989–2002. The institutional shift occurred during the second period, and the most notable factors in the shift are the changing strategic environment, member states' expectations, and internal ideas with the OAU.[44] Walraven contends that African experiences with conflict fed into the normative and institutional changes that took place within the OAU in the early 1990s, and these changes formed the basis of the reforms that created the AU. While there are some new organs under the AU, Walraven views the continuing lack of a regional hegemon and an emphasis on African elites as factors that contributed to the malfunctioning of the OAU and continue to impede the functioning of the AU.[45]

Jeng has also examined the normative transition from the OAU to the AU as part of a wider study on peacebuilding. Jeng emphasizes the importance of pan-Africanism as an ideology that has been a constant presence in Africa's norm- and institution-building processes while recognizing that the concept has been reinterpreted over time.[46] Jeng emphasizes the end of the Cold War in the timing of reform effort and argues that the end of the Cold War freed Africa from the negative impacts of the superpower rivalry while also exposing challenges the continent would face in a changing and increasingly globalized world.[47] There is significant work on the impact of the Cold War in Africa, not only in terms of the superpower rivalry fueling conflict but also influencing ideologies and politics that have endured during and long after the end of the Cold War.[48] Arguments around the timing of the transition from the OAU to the AU after the end of the Cold War will be dealt with throughout this volume as one possible alternative explanation.

My argument adds to and at points diverges from these analyses. While other scholars acknowledge past events in the reforms that took place in the 1990s and 2000s, the emphasis is on the post-Cold War era. This volume uses detailed archival records to discuss the creation of the norms at the advent of the OAU and their slow evolution over time. The breakdown of non-interference began decades before the replacement of the OAU with the AU, and international pressure was not a determinant factor in the evolution of norms within the African regional institution. Non-interference was challenged throughout the tenure of the OAU, and there was a decreasing tendency amongst OAU member states to criticize African states that intervened in internal conflicts while there were increasing criticisms of strict non-interference. In the coming chapters, this will be evidenced through analysis of the Nigerian-Biafran civil war, atrocities and conflict during the 1970s, OAU peacekeeping in Chad in the early 1980s, OAU reform attempts in the 1980s and 1990s, and precedents set by African sub-regional organizations. Overall, I argue that both the OAU and the AU adopted norms which were underpinned by pan-Africanist ideas that helped to shape regional interests and values and were influenced by key events and leaders. This book demonstrates how regions create norms in the regional context, distinct from international pressure. By doing so I seek to add to our understanding of how regional organizations contribute to international society, both by showing agency in their own spheres and pointing to instances where norms originating in regional organizations may have contributed to international norms.

Institutional evolution

In addition to providing an argument for how African leaders and the impact of events underpinned by ideas and interests shaped norms and subsequently policies, this book also needs an argument to explain the timing and nature of institutional change from the OAU to the AU. Blyth argues for a model of institutional change that sees ideas and interests as embedded elements of institutional change.[49] He constructed a five-point hypothesis about institutional change. First, during a crisis it is ideas (not institutions) that reduce uncertainty because ideas provide the basis on which to understand the crisis and the parameters for response. Second, ideas make collective action and coalition building possible. Third, when restructuring an institution, you must first delegitimize the ideas the underline the existing institution. Fourth, after the old institution has been discredited, ideas provide the blueprint for a new institution. Finally, the fifth hypothesis is that ideas make institutional stability possible.[50]

Blyth uses economic ideas to illustrate his model and argues that the transformations in economic and regulatory institutions that took place in the 1920s–1930s and the 1970s–1980s show the relationship between ideas, interests, and institutions. Importantly, while outside factors, such as economic shocks or the failure of economic policies, may help to explain why an economic institution becomes unstable it cannot explain how a new structure is created.[51] In the case of African regional institutions, we see several outside factors impact the OAU and diminish its stability. The 1967–1970 Nigerian-Biafran war with its tremendous humanitarian impact divided OAU member states and brought international attention. The atrocities of the 1970s from Emperor Bokassa in CAR to Idi Amin in Uganda again shocked many member states and brought internal criticisms of the OAU's inability to address peace and security issues in Africa. Finally, the 1994 Rwandan Genocide appalled Africa and the international community after there was a collective failure to act, and African leaders realized that the UN could not be counted on to intervene in Africa to stop large-scale crises or atrocities.

After each of these crises, there were efforts to reform OAU mechanisms to manage conflict, indicating that African states were still trying to work within the existing set of ideas that prioritized state security even though there were indicators and acknowledgments of institutional ineffectiveness. In the late 1970s there are indications of a turning point in the shift away from strict non-interference. President Nyerere of Tanzania makes the case that atrocities are undermining respect for Africa and the ability of the region to push for the eradication of white-minority regimes on the continent, which are seen as a fundamental security threat to African states.[52] Beyond securing the continent from outside political domination, new interests are beginning to emerge, notably promoting economic development.[53] The crisis of conflict and atrocities in Africa are seen as negatively impacting the regions' vital interests of freeing the continent from the last remnants of colonization and delivering on living standard improvements for Africans through effective development.

Following Blyth's model for institutional change we see the crisis of an ineffective conflict management system take form in the late 1960s–1970s. At first the existing ideas around conflict management – strict non-interference, protection of state sovereignty, peaceful settlement of disputes amongst African states, and internal diplomatic processes – formed the basis of legitimate responses. There were attempts to fix and empower the Commission of Mediation, Conciliation and Arbitration, and when this body was not utilized, ad hoc commissions comprised of Heads of States were formed to address conflicts. However, as the conflicts persisted and turned to atrocities, these crises began to undermine the main interests of the OAU. It was at this point that new approaches and structures to manage conflict were explored as the crisis deepened. These efforts floundered though because there were no coherent ideas to underpin the creation of a new peace and security approach. In this way the OAU was delegitimized, and the next step was to identify a blueprint for a new institution. This is where political and intellectual elites with principled ideas entered the picture. Francis Deng laid the groundwork with his conceptions of security as responsibility,[54] and sub-regional organizations as well as individual actors push forward ideas linking security with stability and development.[55] Finally, OAU Secretary General Salim Ahmed Salim supported these ideas and proposed new institutional frameworks.

Contributions to the literature

This book contributes to the existing literature in several ways. First, it provides a theory of how a regional organization created norms through contestation of ideas amongst elites being pushed forward by events, advocacy by key leaders, and interests and values. While it acknowledges the impact of major geo-political shifts and international and domestic pressure it sees these as secondary explanatory factors that are insufficient to fully explain norm creation and evolution within the regional organization. It will empirically demonstrate how peace and security norms in Africa were created at the advent of the OAU and evolved over a four-decade span and continue to evolve today. AU norms cannot be explained without first understanding the OAU norms. There is a chain of events over time that tells one, coherent story. It is critical to theorize how norms are developed by regional organizations in order to understand norm creation within this level of the international system. Once we understand how regional organizations create norms, then this opens up space to determine how regional bodies contribute to norm creation and diffusion at other levels of the international system. Without looking at the regional level, we are missing an important piece of the puzzle and perhaps overlooking valuable ideas and norms that are being developed within regional contexts.

This book expands the literature on the capacity of marginalized regions to develop their own norms and subsequently adds to the scholarship on the role of marginalized regions to international affairs. As discussed in this chapter, there are concepts to explain how regions adapt norms to their own cultural and historical context as well as concepts to explain why regions choose to adopt certain international norms and not others. Much of the scholarship on Africa focuses on the post-Cold War era as the pivotal point for the evolution of norms at the regional level often focusing on geo-political events and pressure from western powers. However, this is a very small part of the story. Contestation over African peace and security norms did not begin in the post-Cold War context with the opening of international space but rather immediately upon independence.

There is a need to put forward an alternative theoretical approach to norm development that considers the agency of regional organizations in the Global South. Too often the agency of marginalized regions is over-looked, not only when it comes to their capacity to develop internal policies that suit their interests but also to contribute to international norms. This not only diminishes the agency of regions but also their capacity. In the case of Africa, several African institutions and leaders contributed in significant ways to the concepts of human security and sovereignty as responsibility that underpin the R2P norm, but their contributions are often overlooked.[56] By highlighting the agency and contributions of regional organizations, this book adds to an emerging literature and questions about why norms devel-oped in regional organizations are not seen as contributing to international norms and what ideas the international community may be missing by overlooking the regional level.

Book plan

The book proceeds chronologically from the OAU to the AU. The empirical chapters begin with a demonstration of what the peace and security shift from the OAU to the AU actually means. It is critical to show that the shift goes beyond just rhetoric. I show that evidence for the shift is seen not only in the constitutive documents but also in institutional frameworks and conflict man-agement practices of the regional organizations. From there, the book employs a chronological framework and relies on the methodology of process-tracing to examine the processes of norm and institutional creation and transforma-tion and the resulting policy and practice changes. This is done with empirical work that draws on extensive archival evidence collected during fieldwork from the AU Commission Archives in Addis Ababa, Ethiopia.

The period leading up to independence and the creation of the OAU are traced in Chapters 3 and 4. The eras of the OAU are traced in Chapters 5 through 9. Chapter 10 focuses on the progression of conflict management and intervention norms at the international level in order to demonstrate that Africa's evolution was distinct, and often *pre-dated* the evolution of international norms concerning interventionism. Finally, Chapter 11 discusses the creation of the AU leading into a final chapter outlining my conclusions.

Notes

1 Martha Finnemore and Kathryn Sikkink, "International Norm Dynamics and Political Change," *International Organizations* 52 (1998): 887–917; Thomas

Risse, "International Norms and Domestic Change: Arguing and Communicative Behavior in the Human Rights Area," *Politics and Society* 27, no. 4 (1999): 529–59; Christine Ingebritsen, "Norm Entrepreneurs: Scandinavia's Role in World Politics," *Cooperation and Conflict: Journal of Nordic International Studies Association* 37, no. 1 (2002): 11–23; Christopher J. Borgen, "Transnational Tribunals and the Transmission of Norms: The Hegemony of Process," *George Washington International Law Review* 39, no. 1 (2007): 685–764.

2 Peter J. Katzenstein, "Introduction: Alternative Perspectives on National Security," in *The Culture of National Security: Norms and Identity in World Politics*, ed. Peter J. Katzenstein (New York: Columbia University Press, 1996), 5.

3 Nico Krisch, "International Law in Times of Hegemony: Unequal Power and the Shaping of the International Legal Order," *The European Journal of International Law* 16, no. 3 (2005): 371.

4 Richard Price, "A Genealogy of the Chemical Weapons Taboo," *International Organization* 49, no. 1 (1995): 73–103.

5 Oliver Stuenkel, *Post-Western World: How Emerging Powers Are Remaking Global Order* (London: Polity Press, 2016); Deborah D. Avant, Martha Finnemore, and Susan K. Sell, "Who Governs the Globe?," in *Who Governs the Globe?*, ed. Deborah D. Avant, Martha Finnemore, and Susan K. Sell (Cambridge: Cambridge University Press, 2010), 1–32; Kathryn Sikkink, *Evidence for Hope: Making Human Rights Work in the 21st Century* (Princeton, NJ: Princeton University Press, 2017); Katharina P. Coleman and Thomas Kwasi Tieku, "African Actors in International Security: Four Pathways to Influence," in *African Actors in International Security: Shaping Contemporary Norms*, ed. Katharina P. Coleman and Thomas Kwasi Tieku (Boulder, CO: Lynne Rienner Publishers, 2018), 1–20.

6 Derek Beach and Rasmus Brun, *Process-Tracing Methods: Foundations and Guidelines* (Ann Arbor, MI: University of Michigan Press, 2013), 3.

7 Jeffrey T. Checkel, "Mechanisms, Processes, and the Study of International Institutions," in *Process Tracing: From Metaphor to Analytic Tool*, ed. Jeffrey T. Checkel and Andrew Bennett (New York: Cambridge University Press, 2015), 90.

8 Eric Helleiner, "Principles from the Periphery: The Neglected Southern Sources of Global Norms," *Global Governance* 20, no. 3 (2014): 359.

9 Finnemore and Sikkink, "International Norm Dynamics and Political Change," 895.

10 Finnemore and Sikkink, "International Norm Dynamics and Political Change," 906.

11 Risse, "International Norms and Domestic Change," 538.

12 Peter Howard and Reina Neufeldt, "Canada's Constructivist Foreign Policy: Building Norms for Peace," *Canadian Foreign Policy Journal* 8, no. 1 (2000): 11–12.

13 Howard and Neufeldt, "Canada's Constructivist Foreign Policy," 17–18.

14 Lloyd Axworthy, "RtoP and the Evolution of State Sovereignty," in *The Responsibility to Protect: The Promise of Stopping Mass Atrocities in Our Time*, ed. Jared Genser and Irwin Cotler (Oxford: Oxford University Press, 2012), 3.

15 Luis Eslava and Sundhya Pahuja, "Between Resistance and Reform: TWAIL and the Universality of International Law," *Trade Law and Development* 3, no. 103 (2011): 105.

16 Antony Anghie, *Imperialism, Sovereignty and the Making of International Law* (Cambridge: Cambridge University Press, 2005), 3.

17 Anghie, *Imperialism*, 198.

18 Anghie, *Imperialism*, 212–13.

19 Kathryn Sikkink, "Latin America's Protagonist Role in Human Rights," *International Journal on Human Rights* 12, no. 22 (2015): 208.

20 Sikkink, "Latin America's Protagonist Role in Human Rights," 214.

21 Coleman and Tieku, "African Actors in International Security."

22 Linda Darkwa, "Humanitarian Intervention," in *African Actors in International Security: Shaping Contemporary Norms*, ed. Thomas Kwasi Tieku and Katharina P. Coleman (Boulder, CO: Lynne Rienner Publishers, 2018), 25.

23 Coleman and Tieku, "African Actors in International Security," 6.

24 Coleman and Tieku, "African Actors in International Security," 7.

25 International Commission on Intervention and State Sovereignty, "The Responsibility to Protect," Ontario, Canada (December 2001), 2, http://respon sibilitytoprotect.org/ICISS%20Report.pdf (accessed 7 May 2020).

26 Alex J. Bellamy, *The Responsibility to Protect: A Defense* (Oxford: Oxford University Press, 2015), 3.

27 "Decision A/DEC.1/8/90 on the Ceasefire and Establishment of an ECOWAS Ceasefire Monitoring Group for Liberia (ECOWAS Peace Plan)," 7 August 1990, www.peaceagreements.org/view/1305 (accessed 7 May 2020).

28 Francis Deng, "Reconciling Sovereignty with Responsibility: A Basis for International Humanitarian Action," in *Africa in World Politics: Post Cold War Challenges*, ed. John W. Harbeson and Donald Rothchild (Boulder, CO: West View Press, 1995); Francis M. Deng et al., *Sovereignty as Responsibility: Conflict Management in Africa* (Washington DC: Brookings Institute Press, 1996).

29 Amitav Acharya, "The R2P and Norm Diffusion: Towards a Framework of Norm Circulation," *Global Responsibility to Protect* 5 (2013): 466–79; Darkwa, "Humanitarian Intervention."

30 Ramesh Thakur, "The Use of International Force to Prevent or Halt Atrocities: From Humanitarian Intervention to the Responsibility to Protect," in *The Oxford Handbook of International Human Rights Law*, ed. Dinah Shelton (Oxford: Oxford University Press, 2013) www.oxfordhandbooks.com/view/10.1093/law/9780199640133.001.0001/law-9780199640133-e-35 (accessed 7 May 2020); Charles Cater and David M. Malone, "The Origins and Evolution of Responsibility to Protect at the UN," *International Relations* 30, no. 3 (2016): 278–97; International Commission on Intervention and State Sovereignty, "The Responsibility to Protect," 1–2.

31 Amitav Acharya, *Whose Ideas Matter? Agency and Power in Asian Regionalism* (New York: Cornell University Press, 2009), 5–6.

32 Acharya, *Whose Ideas Matter?*, 22–23.

33 Amitav Acharya, "Norm Subsidiarity and Regional Orders: Sovereignty, Regionalism, and Rule-Making in the Third World," *International Studies Quarterly* 55, no. 1 (2011): 93.

34 Acharya, "Norm Subsidiarity and Regional Orders," 98.

35 Acharya, "Norm Subsidiarity and Regional Orders," 100.

36 "1963 Statements His Excellency Kwame N'Krumah, President of the Republic of Ghana," in *Celebrating Success: Africa's Voice over 50 Years (1963–2013)* (Addis Ababa: African Union Commission, 2013), 34–41.

37 "The Lusaka Manifesto on Southern Africa Proclaimed by the Fifth Summit Conference of East and Central African States" (Government of the United Republic of Tanzania, 14–16 April 1969), http://reference.sabinet.co.za/webx/access/journal_archive/00020117/33.pdf (accessed 7 May 2020).

38 "OAU Review 1963–1968: Special Issue – Fifth OAU Summit – Algiers Sept 1968" (Organization of African Unity, September 1968), 21–22. AU Commission Archives.

39 Ali A. Mazrui, *Towards a Pax Africana: A Study of Ideology and Ambition* (Chicago, IL: University of Chicago Press, 1967).

40 Paul D. Williams, "From Non-Intervention to Non-Indifference: The Origins and Development of the African Union's Security Culture," *African Affairs* 106, no. 423 (2007): 261–62.

41 Williams, "From Non-Intervention to Non-Indifference," 266.

42 Williams, "From Non-Intervention to Non-Indifference," 271.

43 Kei Koga, *Reinventing Regional Security Institutions in Asia and Africa: Power Shifts, Ideas, and Institutional Change* (London: Routledge, 2017), 2–3.

44 Koga, *Reinventing Regional Security Institutions*, 161–64.

45 Klaas van Walraven, "Heritage and Transformation: From the Organization of African Unity to the African Union," in *Africa's New Peace and Security Architecture: Promoting Norms and Institutionalizing Solutions*, ed. Ulf Engel and Joao Gomes Porto (Surrey: Ashgate Publishing Limited, 2010), 31.

46 Abou Jeng, *Peacebuilding in the African Union: Law, Philosophy, and Practice* (Cambridge: Cambridge University Press, 2012), 145–46.

47 Jeng, *Peacebuilding in the African Union*, 147–48.

48 Odd Arne Westad, *The Global Cold War* (Cambridge: Cambridge University Press, 2005).

49 Mark Blyth, *Great Transformations: Economic Ideas and Institutional Change in the Twentieth Century* (New York: Cambridge University Press, 2002), 7.

50 Blyth, *Great Transformations*, 37–41.

51 Blyth, *Great Transformations*, 8.

52 Nicholas J. Wheeler, *Saving Strangers: Humanitarian Intervention in International Society* (Oxford: Oxford University Press, 2000), 115.

53 "Lagos Plan of Action for Economic Development of Africa 1980–2000" (Organization of African Unity, 28–29 April 1980), www.resakss.org/node/6653 (accessed 7 May 2020).

54 Deng et al., *Sovereignty as Responsibility*.

55 Lt. Colonel Festus B. Aboagye, *ECOMOG: A Sub-Regional Experience in Conflict Resolution, Management, and Peacekeeping in Liberia* (Accra, Ghana: Seco Publishing Limited, 1999); see Francis M. Deng and I. William Zartman, *A Strategic Vision for Africa: The Kampala Movement* (Washington DC: Brookings Institute Press, 2002).

56 Acharya, "The R2P and Norm Diffusion"; Darkwa, "Humanitarian Intervention."

2

Peace and security from the Organization of African Unity to the African Union

One of the major critiques of the AU is that the shift in peace and security from non-interference under the OAU to non-indifference under the AU is purely cosmetic, and the results show no tangible difference in outcomes. This chapter spells out the extent of the change in norms, institutions, policies, and practices between the OAU and the AU to first show that there is a real difference between the two organizations. It sets a baseline of the OAU and AU norms, institutions, and policies and then explores how these played out in practice. I am not making an argument that AU peace and security policies and practices are perfect or that the norms that underpin non-indifference are fully internalized amongst member states or even fully developed within the AU. I am arguing that the change between the OAU and the AU is real with distinct legal, institutional, and policy implications that culminated in different practices emerging under each organization. Following this chapter, the remainder of the book will focus on the period surrounding the creation of the OAU in 1963 through to its formal replacement with the AU in 2002. AU norms, institutions, and policies have of course continued to evolve just as OAU norms did, but the focus of this volume is to explain the normative shift from the OAU to the AU and in doing so set out a theory of norm creation that illuminates how African regional organizations have shaped regional governance and influenced global governance.

OAU norms and institutions

The change from non-interference under the OAU to non-indifference under the AU is seen most clearly in the primary goals of these organizations as indicated by their respective charters and institutions as well as their practices around conflict prevention and management. Fundamentally the OAU was not primarily concerned with conflict management. While the OAU Charter mandated that states resolve their conflicts peacefully and authorized the creation of a Commission of Mediation, Conciliation and Arbitration, its primary goals concerned solidarity and the eradication of colonialism and racialism within Africa. The section of the OAU Charter setting out the purposes of the organization does not specify peace and security.[1] In contrast, the objectives of the AU set out in the Constitutive Act are far more encompassing and include specific points to "promote peace, security, and stability on the continent."[2]

Article III of the OAU Charter stipulates non-interference in internal affairs of member states, respect for sovereignty and territorial integrity, and the peaceful settlement of disputes through diplomatic means.[3] The primary institution established to manage conflict in Africa was the Commission of Mediation, Conciliation and Arbitration. However, the Protocol establishing this commission only gave it jurisdiction over disputes between states when both states willingly agreed to submit themselves to the jurisdiction of the commission, which effectively made it a hollow institution.[4] Instead of taking steps to improve the ability of the Commission of Mediation, Conciliation and Arbitration to function, African leaders chose again and again to appoint ad hoc committees comprised predominantly of heads of states to address conflicts as they arose.[5] The result was a system that only acted to address the most grievous conflicts, often after it was too late to prevent much of the suffering, with few effective efforts to find and implement lasting solutions.

The Protocol that outlined the structure and rules of operation of the Commission of Mediation, Conciliation and Arbitration was signed during the First Ordinary Session of OAU Council of Ministers on 21 July 1964, and from the start it was under-resourced and under-utilized. The 21 members of the Commission, as well as president and vice-presidents, were elected on 25 October 1965; the first funds arrived in September 1967; the president of the Commission did not have a physical office until April 1968; and the two vice-presidents of the Commission did not take up their posts until January 1969.[6] Efforts to reform the Commission were pushed either because of concern about the OAU budget or an uptick in conflicts in Africa, but no concrete reforms were implemented. In the first decade of the OAU, the ad hoc commissions that were established and used in lieu of the Commission of Mediation, Conciliation and Arbitration included the Algeria-Moroccan border dispute Ad hoc Commission, the Ad hoc Commission chaired by Kenyan President Kenyatta on the dispute between the Democratic Republic of Congo and its neighboring states, and the mission assigned to Congolese President Mobutu in respect to the dispute between Burundi and Rwanda among many others.[7]

As the Cold War drew to a close there was a renewed enthusiasm for enhancing the capacity of the OAU to manage conflict in Africa. The

July 1990 Report of the OAU Secretary General on the Fundamental Changes Taking Place in the World and Their Implications for Africa acknowledged the changing international landscape, the scourge of conflicts in Africa, and the inadequate response of the OAU in tackling conflict. The report states, "the political situation in Africa today is bedeviled by various conflicts that threaten not only human rights and social order but also prospects for survival, economic development, and even the sovereignty of some states."[8] The report then goes on to discuss potential reasons for the failure of the OAU in regard to conflict management. Specifically, it found that, "the settlement of conflicts requires perseverance and continuity, which the conflict resolution mechanisms of the OAU, operating on an ad hoc basis, have not been able to provide."[9] The report also highlights that the OAU had not until that point been involved in resolving internal conflicts because it lacked a legal mechanism that allowed for direct involvement.[10]

This marked the impetus for the creation of the Mechanism for Conflict Prevention, Management, and Resolution 1993. In establishing the Mechanism, African leaders sought to expand the scope of the work done by the OAU to manage conflict. In particular, the new approach needed to allow the regional body to address not only inter-state but also intra-state conflicts, and it needed to enable conflict prevention as well as conflict resolution.[11] However, member states stipulated to the OAU Secretary General that the work of the Mechanism should be predicated on the principles of the OAU Charter, namely non-interference in the internal affairs of member states, respect for sovereignty and territorial integrity, and peaceful settlement of disputes through negotiation or mediation.[12] The Mechanism was much more active than the defunct Commission of Mediation, Arbitration, and Conciliation, which in reality was never really operational. However, the fundamental principles on which it operated were the same, and the new body was unable to cope with the onslaught of conflicts in Africa during the 1990s. Shortly after the Mechanism became operational the Rwandan Genocide began on 6 April 1994. However, even when it met for its fifth ordinary session on 30 May 1994 the ongoing genocide was not on the agenda.[13] It was not until an extra-ordinary session on 13 July 1994 when the genocide was all but over when there was an agenda item on "the situations in Burundi and Rwanda."[14]

AU norms and institutions

The norms of the OAU are in contrast to the AU, which formally replaced the OAU in 2002 after a multi-year transition, and since the creation of the

AU there has been a legal and institutional transformation within Africa to better respond to crises and conflicts.[15] Article 4(h) of the AU Constitutive Act is the most dramatic indicator of the shift from the OAU to the AU, but there are additional indications of the shift in the foundational documents, institutions, and practices of the AU. Article 4(h) affirms, "the right of the Union to intervene in a Member state pursuant to a decision of the Assembly in respect of grave circumstances, namely: war crimes, genocide and crimes against humanity."[16] This is in stark contrast to the OAU Charter, which stipulated non-interference in the internal affairs of member states. Institutionally, the AU then created the African Peace and Security Architecture (APSA), which includes the AU Peace and Security Council (PSC), Panel of the Wise, Continental Early Warning System, and African Stand-by Force through the adoption of the 2002 Protocol Relating to the Establishment of the Peace and Security Council of the African Union (PSC Protocol). In 2004, the AU Assembly of Heads of State and Government passed the Common African Defense and Security Policy that added another core component to APSA.[17] The APSA is still very much being constructed and refined. Dr Solomon Dersso likens implementing the APSA to building a house while living in it. He states, "You are constantly finding things that need to be adjusted. Because of this the goal posts have been shifting, and there has been the double task of creating institutions while dealing with peace and security issues in Africa."[18]

The PSC is at the center of the APSA. It is meant to act as a collective security and early warning body with the capacity and mandate to coordinate efficient responses to conflict and crisis situations.[19] The Panel of the Wise is a five-member panel of highly respected African personalities charged with supporting the PSC with the task of maintaining peace and security by making pronouncements, undertaking fact-finding missions, and assisting with mediation efforts.[20] The Continental Early Warning System was established to anticipate and ultimately help to prevent conflicts. It gathers information on emerging threats or potential conflicts, and it receives information from open sources as well as AU field missions across the continent.[21] The African Stand-by Force was created as an institution to support the PSC through the deployment of peace operations, which could range from observer missions all the way through forcible military interventions to prevent or stop atrocities, but it has not yet reached full operational capacity.[22] In the interim, the AU Assembly of Heads of State and Government established the African Capacity for Immediate Responses to Crises. This mechanism draws on voluntary troop and equipment contributions from AU member states and is intended as a temporary arrangement pending the full operationalization of the African Stand-by Force.[23] To fund these initiatives, the AU set up the Peace Fund, which is made up of appropriations from the regular AU budget, voluntary contributions from member states, and contributions from international partners. Currently, the AU relies on significant international support and, as of 2015, member states have only been able to fund about 7 percent of the overall peace and security budget.[24]

The change in practice is seen by the increased activity of the AU institutions to address conflict and their willingness to deploy peace support operations. During its first year, the AU PSC held many more sessions at the highest level than the equivalent OAU body in its entire lifetime.[25] During the entire length of its existence, the PSC has held well over 500 meetings, issued communiqués on crises ongoing in numerous countries across the continent, authorized sanctions against the military junta in Guinea following a massacre of civilians, and authorized several peace operations. Eight AU-led Peace Support Operations have been deployed since 2003,[26] and between 2003 and 2015, the AU and African regional economic communities deployed approximately 100,000 personnel to address conflict in various countries through a number of different types of operations.[27] Recent or ongoing AU operations include the AU Mission in Somalia, the AU-UN Mission in Darfur, and the Regional Cooperation Initiative for the Elimination of the Lord's Resistance Army. Past missions that have either concluded or been taken over by the UN include the AU-led International Support Mission in the Central African Republic, AU-led International Support Mission in Mali, AU Electoral and Security Assistance Mission to the Comoros, AU Mission in Sudan (AMIS), and AU Mission in Burundi (AMIB).[28]

While efforts by African institutions to address conflict in Africa are imperfect and in many cases inadequate, there are significant changes between the norms and institutions of the OAU and AU. There are of course legitimate criticisms of AU responses to conflict and insufficient implementation of the non-indifference framework. For instance, Engel and Porto conclude that the AU is in the process of norm internalization because although the AU promotes the norms around non-indifference there are still member states opposed to their full implementation, indicating that a protracted process of internalization lies ahead, and they argue that the actors within the institution, particularly the most powerful states, will need to internalize the new norms of the AU in order to ensure its success.[29] Similarly, Karbo argues that while the AU has made progress in addressing violent conflicts, the AU must address other problems from poverty to marginalization to be effective, and member states must show greater commitment to implementing AU norms and programs through sustained financing and political will.[30] However, Murithi see the value in the AU Commission and argues that, "the AU has attempted to play a continental role as a norm entrepreneur, understood as a normative leader who encourages others to uphold a range of norms ... the AU has sought to advance norms related to peace and stability."[31]

My argument acknowledges that the AU has not fully implemented non-indifference. However, I argue it is important to acknowledge the shift even if norms and institutions are still evolving, and my focus is on understanding why the shift from non-interference to non-indifference happened in the first place. By premising the AU Constitutive Act on human security and including Article 4(h) African leaders codified an enhanced role for the AU in preventing and responding to conflicts and atrocities. This new legal framework was adopted despite ongoing concerns from African leaders about the protection of African sovereignty, despite ongoing territorial disputes between several African nations, and before the R2P doctrine was formally established. African leaders then authorized the creation of institutions within the AU with the mandates and resources to address conflicts in Africa. The AU has continually pushed the bounds of African peace and security policies by creating peace missions, engaging in conflict prevention and resolution, and pressuring member states to adhere to institutional principles. As such, there are real and profound differences between the OAU and the AU, and the case studies below outline how the legal and institutional changes have resulted in policy and practice changes.

Case studies

AU response to Darfur

When examining the willingness of the AU to implement the norms they have adopted, scholars and practitioners point to the genocide in Darfur, the NATO intervention in Libya, and recent atrocities in Burundi as examples of the failure of non-indifference. However, a closer examination of these cases reveals significant AU engagement to resolve the conflicts and mitigate civilian suffering, and with very few exceptions it is well beyond actions taken by the regional organization during the OAU period. These cases are again not meant to demonstrate that non-indifference has been fully realized, but they are meant to highlight the differences between the OAU and AU conflict management policies and demonstrate the extent of the normative, institutional, policy, and practice shifts between the two organizations.

Sudan has been a country embroiled in several violent conflicts for decades. In 2003, the Sudan Liberation Movement and Justice and Equality Movement launched attacks against Sudanese government targets in Darfur, and the government responded swiftly and brutally against not only the rebel groups but also civilians in Darfur. By 2004 thousands had been killed and hundreds of thousands displaced.[32] There was debate then about the nature of the atrocities taking place in Darfur and how not only the regional but the international community should respond.[33] Initially the government of Sudan tried to block discussion of the conflict and atrocities in Darfur claiming it was an internal matter, but the AU PSC did not accept this argument and persisted in discussing the issue and formulating a response, albeit one that was negotiated with the Sudanese government.[34] The AMIS was created after the signing of the N'Djamena Humanitarian Ceasefire on 8 April 2004 and the subsequent Addis Ababa agreement on 28 May 2004, which created a ceasefire monitoring commission.[35] Initially the AU deployed about 80 military observers, along with 300 Nigerian and Rwandan troops, to monitor the ceasefire.[36]

The ceasefire agreement fell apart despite the presence of observers. At which point the AU expanded their presence in Darfur and worked to negotiate a peace agreement. On 20 October 2004, the AU transformed the observer mission into a full peacekeeping mission and authorized 3,320 troops. The mission was mandated to:

> contribute to the improvement of general security in Sudan, provide a secure environment for the delivery of humanitarian relief and return of refugees, protect the civilian population in Darfur, monitor compliance of parties to the 2004 Humanitarian Ceasefire Agreement and the 2006 Darfur Peace Agreement, and provide assistance in the confidence-building to improve the political settlement processes in Darfur.[37]

From the beginning AMIS had difficulty fulfilling its lofty mandate. There were logistical issues with deploying the authorized troops and providing adequate equipment, and there was also confusion over the civilian protection clause of the mandate and its enforcement. All of this was happening at time when the APSA was still in its nascent stages and with ongoing fighting in Darfur. AMIS was deployed with little planning and with no peacekeeping structures on the ground. It was also underfunded and relied heavily on irregular donor support.[38] Strained by the enormity of the task the AU agreed to the AU-UN Mission in Darfur, which officially replaced AMIS on 31 December 2007.[39]

As seen above and explored in other literature, the AU was a key negotiator in processes to end violence in Darfur and deployed peace support missions early in the crisis.[40] Article 4(h) of the AU Constitutive Act was not explicitly invoked to force the Sudanese government to accept an intervention force, yet through negotiation the AU was able to convince Sudan to accept substantial intervention missions that the government in Khartoum was initially opposed to – first AMIS and then the AU-UN Mission. In this way, Article 4(h) was implicitly invoked during negotiations with the Sudanese government in Khartoum to allow for a more robust response to end the violence.[41] The legitimacy of non-consensual military intervention is still not fully internalized across all AU member states, and the AU PSC and AU bureaucracy has not always been able to respond as it would like. However, the threat of invoking Article 4(h) has been used as an important bargaining tool.

It is notable that international organizations also faced challenges in responding to atrocities in Darfur through the framework of R2P, and Darfur is widely regarded as a failure of the international norm of R2P. The norm of R2P was used to mobilize public opinion and push for action to end atrocities in Darfur, and the UN did respond by imposing sanctions, referring the situation to the ICC and, as described above, authorizing a hybrid AU-UN mission. Despite this the international response was not as immediate or forceful as was needed to halt violence against civilians.[42] The AU faced significant challenges of uneven political will amongst member states and resource constraints, but the regional organization engaged early after the start of the violence, employed coercive diplomacy with a member state, and deployed AU peace support missions that brought in other international actors.

The AU's response in Darfur would have been all but unthinkable under the OAU, and the Nigerian-Biafran civil war from 1967–1970 is a notable parallel. As will be detailed in Chapter 7, the Biafra region of Nigeria rebelled against the central government, and the government responded with overwhelming military force. Nigeria was hostile to outside interference even from within the African continent, and there was intense international interest and massive civilian casualties. In the case of the Nigerian-Biafran civil war the OAU was only able to respond with ad hoc bodies of African leaders who tried to persuade both sides to find a solution to the conflict. The case of Darfur is also an internal conflict with catastrophic humanitarian consequences, which has received significant international attention and a central government hostile to outside interference, yet the AU forced the government in Khartoum to the negotiating table and deployed multiple missions in an attempt to protect civilians. As the dire outcomes in Darfur continue to show, the AU has serious limitations, but the new policy of non-indifference is important and a fundamental leap from the OAU policy of non-interference.[43] Exploring the actions of the AU in Darfur while acknowledging the issues with the response is important to highlight how the AU used its innovative normative tools instead of relying on international norms.

AU response to Burundi

African-led action in Burundi has evolved significantly since the OAU's first engagement in the early 1970s. In the spring of 1972, an estimated 80,000 to 200,000 Hutus were systematically slaughtered by the Burundian government after a coup attempt.[44] The response of the OAU was complete support for the Burundian government. The Secretary General of the OAU along with the Prime Minister of Tanzania and President of Somalia visited Burundi on 22 May 1972. As a further show of support the OAU adopted a resolution in June stating in effect that, "the Council of Ministers was convinced that, thanks to (Burundian President) Micrombero's saving action, peace would be rapidly re-established, national unity consolidated, and territorial integrity preserved."[45] The visit and vocal support sent a message that the primary concern of the OAU was the security of states and territorial integrity and not the security of individuals or groups of people, even where atrocities were taking place on a massive scale.[46] This unquestioning show of support for national leaders in the wake of atrocities stands in contrast to the actions of the OAU in later decades and then the AU.

African leaders re-engaged in conflict and atrocity issues in Burundi in the early 1990s after the UN Security Council (UNSC) declined to muster an adequate response to an October 1993 coup and subsequent civil war. The African response during the 1990s OAU period was largely driven and financed by South Africa with Tanzanian President Julius Nyerere and South African President Nelson Mandela acting as mediators at various stages. The engagement in the 1990s shows the continuing evolution of peace and security practices within the African regional organization. In February 2003, the AMIB was authorized as the first armed peace mission of the newly created AU. The mandate authorized 3,500 troops from Ethiopia, Mozambique, and South Africa to oversee the implementation of ceasefire agreements, support disarmament of combatants, and create the conditions for the establishment of a UN peacekeeping mission. In June 2004, a UN mission did succeed the AU mission after AMIB had helped to stabilize the country.[47]

Since AMIB there have been repeated crises in Burundi, which both the AU and UN have been involved in managing with support to negotiations and multiple peace operations. In 2015, there were again concerns about the possibility of destabilizing violence and mass atrocities in Burundi. The AU PSC was actively involved in efforts to address this most recent resurgence of violence, and they called on all stakeholders to find a solution through mediation. The PSC also deployed AU human rights observers in Burundi and tasked the African Commission on Human and Peoples'

Rights to launch an investigation.[48] In April 2016, the AU had approximately 45 human rights observers in Burundi. The observers were there to document human rights abuses, investigate incidents, and proactively visit places where abuses could occur, such as detention centers. The observers sent information to the Human Rights Department at the AU Headquarters and then this information was passed to the AU PSC. AU Senior Human Rights Expert, Ambassador Salah Hammad, reported that, "the reports by human rights observers in Burundi of rape and other atrocities pushed the PSC to take more assertive action and deploy a small contingent of peace observers."[49]

In December 2015, the Burundian government continued to obstruct efforts to find a solution, and the AU PSC issued an ultimatum for the government to either cooperate or face additional sanctions and the possibility of a forceful intervention of 5,000 peacekeepers.[50] However, the Burundian government and President Pierre Nkurunziza were staunchly opposed to any AU plan to deploy a large peacekeeping force. In response to the AU ultimatum, Nkurunziza stated, "Everyone has to respect Burundi's borders. In case they violate those principles, they will have attacked the country and every Burundian will stand up and fight against them."[51] Ultimately, the AU decided against sending 5,000 peacekeepers to Burundi because it did not have the government's consent and instead chose to press for continued dialogue between the two sides to find a political solution.[52] However, the public rebuke of a member state and threat of a non-consensual peacekeeping mission is a significant step forward and represents an attempt at coercive diplomacy.

The AU has not been able to act as forcefully in Burundi as many policymakers within the organization would have liked, and despite having one of the strongest regional normative frameworks in the world there are still continuing issues around negotiating the balance between sovereignty and intervention. The line where it is appropriate for the AU to step in is not yet fully defined, but non-indifference has become an important and established tool.[53] The AU publicly challenged a member state and using Article 4(h) as a point of leverage deployed human rights and military observers to the country. As of April 2016, there were 45 human rights observers deployed across Burundi documenting and investigating human rights incidents and reporting back to the AU Commission; the reports by human rights observers pushed the PSC to take more assertive action and led to the deployment of military observers.[54] These actions stand in contrast to the OAU's actions in Burundi in the 1970s when only state security was recognized, and they also demonstrate how new AU tools, such as Article 4(h) and human rights observers, are being used to pressure member states.

AU response to Libya

Several years after the start of the conflict in Darfur, the AU faced responding to the crisis in Libya because of threats from the Gaddafi regime to commit crimes against humanity and possibly genocide. However, in this instance, the international community responded quickly through the UNSC in line with the R2P norm. On 17 March 2011, the UNSC passed Resolution 1973 authorizing member states to "take all necessary measures ... to protect civilians and civilian populated areas."[55] Then on 19 March 2011, France, Canada, the UK, and the US launched an attack on Gaddafi's regime. This military intervention prevented the fall of the rebel-strong hold Benghazi in order to protect civilians there, and in the months to come, the international coalition continued to attack Libyan targets. Eventually, the Libyan government fell after the rebels captured key cities, and Gaddafi was captured and executed in October 2011.[56]

Nigeria and South Africa were on the UNSC as rotating members at the time of the intervention and voted for Resolution 1973, which was used to authorize the use of force, but their initial support quickly disappeared after the resolution was used as grounds to intervene almost immediately instead of exhausting other options, including an ongoing peace process the AU was working to facilitate. Following the intervention, South African President Zuma stated, "We have spoken out against the misuse of the good intentions in Resolution 1973. We strongly believe that the resolution is being abused for regime change, political assassinations and foreign military occupation."[57]

On the surface, it may appear that African leaders were stepping back from Article 4(h) and their aspirations to better protect civilians in Africa from violence and mass atrocities. However, the AU PSC had been engaged in the situation in Libya since the initial protests in Benghazi. The PSC met and issued a number of communiqués expressing concern and condemning indiscriminate violence. After the situation deteriorated the PSC developed a roadmap to reach a political solution to the crisis that included an immediate cessation of hostilities, delivering humanitarian assistance to needy populations, and adoption of reforms to eliminate root causes of the conflict.[58] The AU strongly disagreed that all other options had been exhausted, and South Africa, in particular, had championed the peace plan as a viable solution to the crises. There were also concerns among African leaders about the use of Resolution 1973, specifically by outside powers, without explicit approval of the methods. Finally, despite the terrors of his regime, Gaddafi was a popular leader in some regions of Africa that had financially and ideologically supported African regional bodies.[59]

The AU preference for negotiated settlements and concerns about the use of force by outsiders should not strictly be interpreted as a sign of the lack of implementation of non-indifference. In the response to Libya, we see consistent themes in Africa's approach to conflict management and resolution: a preference for negotiation and mediation, primacy of African solutions, and trepidation about outside intervention. These themes existed during the OAU and continue with the AU, but the continuation of some themes does not negate far-reaching legal, institutional, and policy changes. As illustrated by the cases of the AU responses to conflict in Darfur and Burundi, the AU is more empowered and willing to challenge member states and act to manage and resolve conflict.

Summarizing the shift

The issues of capacity and unwillingness to act in certain cases do not negate the changes that have taken place at the regional level in Africa between the creation of the OAU and its replacement by the AU. These changes are briefly summarized in the table below and are evidenced by the differences in organizational goals as well as the legal instruments, institutions, and policies and practices of the OAU and AU.

On its own accord, the fact that African leaders codified the right of a regional body to intervene to stop atrocities in the AU Constitutive Act is striking. The AU then took concrete steps to develop its capacity to address violence, including the establishment of the APSA. The institutional mechanisms of the AU are far more robust than the institutional mechanisms of the OAU. The first conflict management body under the OAU was the Commission of Mediation, Conciliation and Arbitration. This body could only deal with cases of conflict between states and even then only when agreed by both parties. Given these constraints it was never fully funded, and it was never called upon to manage a dispute. The second OAU conflict management body was the Mechanism for Conflict Prevention, Management, and Resolution created in 1993. While it was a vast improvement on the previous body it focused on prevention because by its own admission it lacked capacity, expertise, and resources. Still far from perfect the AU conflict management structures have managed to steadily build up the capacity of the African regional body to prevent and respond to conflict.

The peace and security practices of the AU have also been drastically different from the early and even later practices of the OAU. Burundi offers one of the starkest examples of this change. In the 1970s, the response of the OAU to ongoing atrocities in Burundi was to offer support to the Burundian president and commend him for ensuring the territorial integrity of the state. The most recent threat of mass atrocities in Burundi

	Goals	Legal instruments	Institutions	Policies and practices
OAU	Promote unity Coordinate and intensify cooperation Defend sovereignty, territorial integrity, and independence Eradicate all forms of colonialism	OAU Charter (1963), Article III codifies noninterference Protocol on the Commission of Mediation, Conciliation, and Arbitration (1964) OAU Declaration on a Mechanism for Conflict Prevention, Management, and Resolution (1993)	Commission of Mediation, Conciliation and Arbitration Defense Commission Mechanism for Conflict Prevention, Management, and Resolution	Reluctance to publicly pressure member states Ad hoc commissions comprised of leaders using their good offices to resolve conflicts
AU	Achieve greater unity and solidarity Defend sovereignty, territorial integrity, and independence Accelerate political and economic integration Promote peace, security, and stability on the continent Promote democracy, good governance, human rights, sustainable development, and cooperation	AU Constitutive Act (adopted July 2000), Article 4(h) allows for intervention in certain grave circumstances Protocol Relating to the Establishment of the Peace and Security Council of the African Union (2002) Common African Defense and Security Policy (2004)	African Peace and Security Architecture, includes: Peace and Security Council Panel of the Wise Continental Early Warning System African Standby Force Peace Fund	Significant engagement from Peace and Security Council and other African Peace and Security Architecture bodies even in internal conflicts Public condemnation of member states and implicit use of Article 4(h) AU-led Peace Support Operations since 2003

Figure 2 Comparing the Organization of African Unity and the African Union

brought the deployment of AU human rights observers and peace observers, multiple high-level meetings on the issue, and a public condemnation of a member state with the threat of a military intervention. The AU has deployed multiple peace support missions in several countries and been actively engaged in numerous peace processes and negotiations to end violent conflict. The AU peace and security policies are still evolving, and the parameters of non-indifference are still being defined. However, the normative and institutional changes that have taken place thus far have allowed the AU to undertake sustained and robust, as opposed to ad hoc and weak, engagement in African conflict issues. The AU's work to solve conflict issues has not been perfect, but it is worlds apart from the OAU's approach. This book now turns to examining why the OAU adopted particular norms and how these manifested in institutions, policies, and practices. It then goes onto to examine how and why the shift from non-interference to non-indifference occurred. From this analysis I propose a theory of how African regional organizations developed norms to illuminate their regional governance role. This theory more broadly illuminates the importance of regional organizations in shaping their own spheres and their influence in global governance.

Notes

1 "Organization of African Unity Charter," 25 May 1963, https://au.int/en/treaties/oau-charter-addis-ababa-25-may-1963 (accessed 7 May 2020).
2 "Constitutive Act of the African Union," 26 May 2001, https://au.int/en/treaties/constitutive-act-african-union (accessed 7 May 2020).
3 "Organization of African Unity Charter," 4.
4 "Protocol of the Commission of Mediation, Conciliation and Arbitration," *International Legal Materials* 3, no. 6 (1964): 1116–24.
5 C.O.C. Amate, *Inside the OAU: Pan-Africanism in Practice* (New York: St. Martin's Press, 1986), 164.
6 "Amendments to the Charter and the Protocol of the Commission of Mediation, Conciliation and Arbitration," CM/334 (Addis Ababa, Ethiopia: Organization of African Unity, August 1970), 1. AU Commission Archives.
7 "Amendments to the Charter and the Protocol of the Commission of Mediation, Conciliation and Arbitration," 2.
8 "Report of the Secretary-General on the Fundamental Changes Taking Place in the World and Their Implications for Africa: Proposals for an African Response," AHG/169 (XXVI) (Organization of African Unity, July 1990), 5. AU Commission Archives.
9 "Report of the Secretary-General on the Fundamental Changes Taking Place in the World and Their Implications for Africa," 5.

10 "Report of the Secretary-General on the Fundamental Changes Taking Place in the World and Their Implications for Africa," 5.

11 "Report of the Secretary-General on the Establishment of a Mechanism for Conflict Prevention, Resolution, and Management," CM/1767 (LVII) (Cairo, Egypt: Organization of African Unity, 21–26 June 1993), 3. AU Commission Archives.

12 "Report of the Secretary-General on the Establishment of a Mechanism for Conflict Prevention, Resolution, and Management," 31.

13 "Provisional Agenda for the Fifth Ordinary Session of the Central Organ of the OAU Mechanism for Conflict Prevention, Management, and Resolution" Organization of African Unity, 30 May 1994). AU Commission Archives.

14 "Provisional Agenda for the Fourteenth Extra-Ordinary Session of the Central Organ of the OAU Mechanism for Conflict Prevention, Management, and Resolution" (Organization of African Unity, 13 July 1994). AU Commission Archives.

15 Jide Martyns Okeke, "United in Challenges? The African Standby Force and the African Capacity for the Immediate Response to Crises," in *Future of African Peace Operations: From the Janjaweed to Boko Haram*, ed. Cedric De Coning, Linnea Gelot, and John Karlsrud (London: Zed Books Ltd, 2016), 92.

16 "Constitutive Act of the African Union."

17 Ulf Engel and Joao Gomes Porto, "The African Union's New Peace and Security Architecture: Toward an Evolving Security Regime," in *Regional Organizations in African Security*, ed. Fredrik Soderbaum and Rodrigo Tavares (New York: Routledge, 2011), 16.

18 Solomon Dersso, Interview with Dr Solomon Dersso, Commissioner, African Commission on Human and Peoples' Rights. Interview by Kathryn Nash, 29 March 2016.

19 African Union Commission, *African Union Handbook 2015* (Addis Ababa: African Union Commission and New Zealand Ministry of Foreign Affairs, 2015), 46.

20 African Union Commission, *African Union Handbook 2015*, 50.

21 African Union Commission, *African Union Handbook 2015*, 49.

22 Okeke, "United in Challenges?," 93.

23 Okeke, "United in Challenges?," 98.

24 African Union Commission, *African Union Handbook 2015*, 59.

25 Musifiky Mwanasali, "From Non-Interference to Non-Indifference: The Emerging Doctrine of Conflict Prevention in Africa," in *The African Union and Its Institutions*, ed. John Akokpari, Angela Ndinga-Muvumba, and Tim Murithi (Auckland Park: Jacama Media Ltd, 2008), 44.

26 Tim Murithi, "The Role of the African Peace and Security Architecture in the Implementation of Article 4(h)," in *Africa and the Responsibility to Protect*, ed. Dan Kuwali and Frans Viljoen (New York: Routledge, 2014), 143.

27 Okeke, "United in Challenges?," 90.

28 African Union Commission, *African Union Handbook 2015*, 55–58.

29 Joao Gomes Porto and Ulf Engel, "The African Peace and Security Architecture: An Evolving Security Regime?," in *Africa's New Peace and Security Architecture: Promoting Norms, Institutionalizing Solutions*, ed. Ulf Engel and Joao Gomes Porto (Surrey: Ashgate Publishing Limited, 2010), 155–59.

30 Tony Karbo, "Conclusion," in *The Palgrave Handbook of Peacebuilding in Africa*, ed. Tony Karbo and Kudrat Virk (London: Palgrave Macmillan, 2018), 456–57.

31 Tim Murithi, "Briefing: The African Union at Ten: An Appraisal," *African Affairs* 111, no. 445 (2012): 663.

32 Paul D. Williams, "The African Union's Peace Operations: A Comparative Analysis," in *Regional Organizations in African Security*, ed. Fredrik Soderbaum and Rodrigo Tavares (New York: Routledge, 2011), 33.

33 Scott Straus, "Darfur and the Genocide Debate," *Foreign Affairs* 84, no. 1 (2005): 123–33.

34 Dawit Toga, Political Analyst, Peace and Security Department, Conflict Management Division, African Union Commission. Interview by Kathryn Nash, 1 April 2016.

35 "Humanitarian Ceasefire Agreement on the Conflict in Darfur," 8 April 2004, www.peaceagreements.org/view/647 (accessed 7 May 2020); "Agreement with the Sudanese Parties on the Modalities for the Establishment of the Ceasefire Commission and the Deployment of Observers in the Darfur," 28 May 2004, www.peaceagreements.org/view/92 (accessed 7 May 2020).

36 Williams, "The African Union's Peace Operations," 34.

37 African Union Commission, *African Union Handbook 2015*, 58.

38 Isiaka A. Badmus, *The African Union's Role in Peacekeeping: Building on Lessons from Security Operations* (New York: Palgrave Macmillan, 2015), 192–93.

39 Williams, "The African Union's Peace Operations," 35–37.

40 Jashobanta Pan, "African Union's Intervention in Sudan: Importance and Effectiveness," *Insight on African* 2, no. 2 (2010): 113–27.

41 Dersso, Interview with Dr Solomon Dersso, Commissioner, African Commission on Human and Peoples' Rights.

42 Bellamy, *The Responsibility to Protect*, 66.

43 Toga, Political Analyst, Peace and Security Department, Conflict Management Division, AU Commission Archives.

44 Leo Kuper, *Genocide: Its Political Use in the Twentieth Century* (New Haven, CT: Yale University Press, 1981), 164.

45 Kuper, *Genocide*, 164.

46 Caroline Thomas, *New States, Sovereignty, and Intervention* (Aldershot: Gower Publishing Company Limited, 1985), 72.

47 Paul D. Williams, "IPI Global Observatory," *Special Report: The African Union's Coercive Diplomacy in Burundi* blog, 18 December 2015, http://theglobalobservatory.org/2015/12/burundi-african-union-maprobu-arusha-accords/ (accessed 7 May 2020).

48 "Communique of the Peace and Security Council of the African Union (AU) at Its 557th Meeting Held on 13 November 2015, Adopted the Following Decision of

the Situation in Burundi." (African Union, 13 November 2015), www.peaceau.
org/uploads/psc-557-comm-burundi-12-11-2015.pdf (accessed 7 May 2020).

49 Salah Hammad, Interview with Ambassador Salah Hammad, Senior Human
Rights Expert, Department of Political Affairs, African Union Commission.
Interview by Kathryn Nash, 5 April 2016.

50 Williams, "IPI Global Observatory."

51 Anita Powell, "Burundian President Slammed Over AU Threats," *Voice of
America*, 31 December 2015, www.voanews.com/content/burunid-nkurunziza-
african-union-au-threats/3125705.html (accessed 7 May 2020).

52 "African Union Abandons Plans to Send Peacekeepers to Burundi," *BBC*, 31
December 2015, www.bbc.co.uk/news/world-africa-35454893 (accessed 7 May
2020).

53 Dersso, Interview with Dr Solomon Dersso, Commissioner, African Commission
on Human and Peoples' Rights.

54 Hammad, Interview with Ambassador Salah Hammad, Senior Human Rights
Expert, Department of Political Affairs, African Union Commission.

55 "Resolution 1973 (2011): Adopted by the Security Council at Its 6498th
Meeting, on 17 March 2011" (United Nations, 17 March 2011), 3, www.
undocs.org/S/RES/1973%20(2011) (accessed 7 May 2020).

56 Bellamy, *The Responsibility to Protect*, 187.

57 Nick Meo, "Libya: Jacob Zuma Accuses Nato of Not Sticking to UN
Resolution," *The Telegraph*, 14 June 2011, www.telegraph.co.uk/news/world
news/africaandindianocean/libya/8575984/Libya-Jacob-Zuma-accuses-Nato-
of-not-sticking-to-UN-resolution.html (accessed 7 May 2020).

58 Solomon Dersso, "The Quest for Pax Africana: The Case of the African Union's
Peace and Security Regime," *African Journal on Conflict Resolution* 12 (2012):
37–38.

59 "International Coalition for the Responsibility to Protect," *Accounting for the
African Union Response in Libya: A Missed Opportunity?* blog, 13 September
2011, http://icrtopblog.org/2011/09/13/accounting-for-the-african-union-au-res
ponse-to-libya-a-missed-opportunity/ (accessed 7 May 2020).

3

Pan-Africanism and the road to independence

The starting point for understanding norm creation within African regional institutions must be the norms created by the OAU in 1963. However, to analyze the decisions made by independence era leaders when choosing norms for the African regional organization, it is crucial to understand the impact of pan-Africanist ideas that developed throughout the twentieth century as well as the impact of key events that took place in the lead-up to independence. Pan-Africanism did not begin as an African-led movement. It began to emerge as a solidified concept in 1900, and throughout the first half of the twentieth century was largely shaped by members of the African diaspora. In 1945, the Manchester Conference brought together pan-Africanist theorists along with several African activists who would go on to lead African countries in the independence era. This conference transformed pan-Africanism from a theoretical concept based in the diaspora to a unifying yet still vague framework for African states to rally around in the independence era. Even if it was, and still is, a concept subject to evolution and contestation, it is a critical lens through which to view intra-Africa relations as well as regional diplomatic policies.[1]

The key events that led up to the independence era included the sacrifices Africa and Africans were called upon to make during World Wars I and II and the subsequent denial of basic rights by colonial powers, the reaction of the League of Nations to the Abyssinia crisis, and the contempt shown by colonial states to demands for independence. In Acharya's conception, subsidiarity emerged out of the post-World War II system where former colonial states were largely excluded from constructing the post-war order by major powers that dominated newly created economic and political institutions. Marginalized states reacted by rejecting norms that could lead to outside domination for their own regions and instead choosing norms that offered some protection from repression by major powers.[2] The concept of subsidiarity should be viewed as emerging not only in response to international power structures but in response to the treatment received by the colonies in the lead-up to and during World War II. Therefore, in order to understand OAU norms, one must understand how the major events in the immediate pre-independence era were perceived by African elites and how they shaped the perception and practice of pan-Africanism.

The perception of African elites is particularly important because independence era leaders had discretion to drive policy. The Heads of independent states exercised their agency as the decision-makers when it came to constructing the OAU and choosing its foundational principles. This is evidenced by the events of the OAU founding conference, which was held from 22–25 May 1963 in Addis Ababa, Ethiopia. State ministers met in the lead-up to the conference to draft a charter, but were unable to agree on regional priorities or which proposed charter to put forward as the basis for discussion and debate. The Heads of State and Government arrived at the conference and set the priorities and points of contention, and state ministers then took these directions as the basis for drafting the OAU Charter that was debated and adopted on the final day of the conference.[3] African leaders shared common experiences during the World Wars and in fighting for independence, and they also shared a common theoretical frame through pan-Africanism. As such, they shared a common belief in the need to ensure the total independence of the continent. However, they also had vastly different experiences in different colonial systems, and leaders differed on how to best achieve their goals. These commonalities and divergences shaped how individual leaders perceived the interests of the region and the most important tenets of pan-Africanism. Ultimately, they shaped the debates of the OAU founding conference and help to explain why certain norms were chosen over others.

The influence of pan-Africanism

The independence era leaders who created the OAU came from diverse backgrounds with varying educational and colonial experiences. However, there were common philosophical themes that emerged during the discussions that led to the OAU. Chief among these themes was pan-Africanism and what this concept meant in practice not just in theory for new African states. Pan-Africanism is complex idea that emerged over decades and continues to evolve today. In a very broad sense, pan-Africanism is about black race consciousness, self-determination of the black race, unity of the African people, economic development of Africa, and finding a dignified niche for Africans within the international system.[4] However, within this encompassing philosophy there are deliberate points of vagueness. Unity, in particular, is a fluid concept and the degree of desired cohesiveness and cooperation has been continually debated.[5] In a political sense, pan-Africanism manifested in African regional policies that valued coop-eration among states over integration, demanded self-government for all Africans, condemned colonial and racial regimes that continued in some parts of Africa even after the initial wave of independence, and facilitated initiatives to forge a new role for Africa in world affairs.[6]

In this chapter, I first trace the evolution of pan-Africanism and the events that influenced its evolution. From there, this book will demonstrate how the common experiences of the region and the diverging experiences of some independence African leaders shaped understandings of pan-Africanism. I will show the interaction between pan-Africanist ideas, the influence of key leaders and events, and regional interests that culminated in the OAU choosing non-intervention, state sovereignty, and territorial integrity norms. This conception of the creation of regional norms at the advent of the OAU will be shown to conform in many ways to Acharya's theory of subsidiarity. African states did not simply adopt the prevailing norms of the international system. They adopted norms the vast majority of leaders believed would best defend Africa against domination and interference. OAU norms drew on international norms but were altered in ways that shored up African inde-pendent states whilst diminishing the legitimacy of white-minority regimes and outside interference, showing that regional institutions can craft norms to protect their regional interests and further their values.

The development of pan-Africanism

The birth of pan-Africanism

Pan-Africanism first emerged at a conference in 1900 organized by H. Sylvester-Williams of Trinidad. The themes of the conference were freedom, a common African identity, and the equality of all men. However, the conference did not have deep roots in Africa itself and was attended by about 30 delegates.[7] The aim of the conference was to make connections between peoples of African descent living across the globe, discuss ways to encourage friendlier relations between Caucasian and African races, and begin a movement to secure full political and economic rights for African races.[8] Following the conference, a secretariat was established in London to carry on with the objectives dis-cussed by the delegates and to plan future conferences tentatively scheduled for 1902 and 1904. Unfortunately, the organization was short-lived, and no follow-on conferences came to fruition.[9]

Pan-Africanism as a movement disappeared until after World War I when it was resuscitated by W.E.B. Du Bois – a prominent African-American intellectual. The re-emergence came about in part as a means to promote recognition of the tremendous contributions of black Africans during World

War I. General Smuts estimated that by 1918, black Africa had provided France with 680,000 soldiers and 238,000 laborers.[10] Jomo Kenyatta – an independence era leader in Kenya – estimated that 300,000 Kenyans were conscripted to go to German East Africa in 1914 and of those, 60,000 did not return. For those who did return, Kenyan soldiers were subjected to the 1915 Crown Land Ordinance, which made lands formerly occupied by Africans crown land, and the 1919 Native Registration Ordinance, which required all natives over 16 to have their fingerprints taken.[11]

The first Pan-African Conference under the leadership of W.E.B. Du Bois was organized in 1919 to coincide with the ongoing peace talks at Versailles. As Dr Du Bois recalled, "I went [to Versailles] with the idea of calling a Pan-African Congress and trying to impress upon the members of the Peace Congress sitting at Versailles the importance of Africa in the future world. I was without credentials or influence, but the idea took on."[12] The 1919 pan-African Conference sought to remind western leaders of the sacrifices Africans had made on the battlefield during the fight for European freedom, and then propose a path for Africans to obtain more freedoms and rights. The delegates voted to request that the Allied Powers place all former German colonies under international supervision to be held in trust for the inhabitants until self-government could be established.[13] Additionally the pan-African Congress asked that the Allied Powers create a code for the protection of Africans and that the League of Nations establish a permanent office to monitor the implementation of these laws. Finally, the Congress demanded that Africans have a right to their land and natural resources, an education, and gradual extensions of self-government.[14] Following the 1919 Congress, W.E.B. Du Bois was able to hold three additional Congresses during the 1920s but ultimately struggled to keep the momentum going. When the Great Depression hit in 1929 there were no longer financial resources to continue pan-Africanist gatherings, and the movement died out until after World War II.

Inter-war period

Several events in the 1930s and during World War II had a profound impact on the evolution of pan-Africanism and its manifestation in the post-World War II era. The first event is the League of Nations inquiry into charges of forced labor and slavery against Liberia, one of the few African states to maintain its independence. The League of Nations commission found that although classic slavery did not exist there was a considerable amount of intra and inter-tribal domestic slavery.[15] The result was condemnations against Liberia and even some calls to have the country placed under the control of a foreign commission. Many African observers believed that the situation in Liberia was being exploited by those who did not believe Africans could govern themselves. The fact that the League of Nations did not bother to investigate colonial powers, many of which had abysmal human rights records in their treatment of colonial peoples, also exemplified the double standard faced by the few nations that were governed by Africans.[16] The treatment of Liberia showed that even independent African states must guard their autonomy against outside powers.

The second and far more important event was the Abyssinia crisis, the start of which was the Wal-Wal Incident on 5 December 1934. Wal-Wal is a region in the Ogedan that Abyssinia – now known as Ethiopia – considered part of its territory despite an occupation by Italian troops. An Anglo-Abyssinian Boundary Commission entered the territory, and Italian and Abyssinian forces exchanged fire with both sides suffering heavy losses. The Italian government demanded that Abyssinia make a series of humiliating and costly reparations, which the Abyssinian government declined, and the Italian government then used this as justification for escalation. It is clear that the Wal-Wal incident was used as a pretext for war with Abyssinia, as evidence has shown that Mussolini decided on war with Abyssinia well before the incident – at the latest in Autumn 1933.[17]

Following the Wal-Wal Incident and increasing Italian aggression, Abyssinia made repeated appeals to the League of Nations to address the situation. Eventually the Italo-Abyssinian Commission of Conciliation and Arbitration was established but did not achieve anything before the Italians launched an attack on 3 October 1935.[18] The League of Nations determined that the Italian government had resorted to war in disregard of its obligations under Article 12 of the Covenant of the League of Nations and subsequently voted to establish a committee to implement sanctions against Italy.[19] Ultimately the committee did nothing to truly implement the sanctions, and the sanctions were eventually ended on 15 July 1936 after Italy had driven the Abyssinian royal family into exile and occupied Abyssinia.[20]

The invasion of Abyssinia and the inept response from the international community convinced many Africans that they could not depend on the west to defend any African interests. As prominent pan-Africanist George Padmore recalled, "the brutal rape of Ethiopia combined with the cynical attitude of the Great Powers convinced Africans everywhere that black men had no rights which white men felt bound to respect if they stood in the way of their imperialist interests."[21] For many Africans the lesson to be learned was that Africa cannot depend on the Great Powers nor international institutions to defend the interests of Africa, and instead Africans must demand and then defend their rights and equal treatment in the global community.

World War II

Africans and people of African descent saw many setbacks in the 1920s and 1930s, from ongoing discrimination following their service during World War I, to often being the first to suffer economically during the Great Depression. The Liberia Scandal and Abyssinia crisis did nothing to dispel the dismal view many Africans held of the Great Powers. As the globe descended into World War II, many Africans were again asked to fight, and African lands provided precious resources towards the war effort. The British government drew extensively on the labor and raw materials of its colonies during World War II, including recruiting over half a million Africans for military service and labor. Britain relied on every colonial territory to contribute to the war effort, and the demands placed on the African colonies only increased after the loss of the colonies in Asia in 1942.[22]

Before the fall of France, the French government drew troops from the Armée d'Afrique from French North Africa and Troupes Coloniales from French West and Equatorial Africa. In spring 1940, the French government deployed 20 divisions of African troops – approximately 100,000 men – to western France to fight against the Germans. While records are incomplete, estimates are that the Germans killed approximately 17,500 African soldiers and took another 15,000 prisoner.[23] After the fall of France to Germany, the French resistance, led by General Charles de Gaulle, depended on French colonial territories for manpower, resources, and ultimately legitimacy. Free French Africa spanned Chad, Cameroon, Congo-Brazzaville, Gabon, and Oubangui-Chari.[24] Brazzaville became the capital of legitimate France for the resistance, and it was from this African city that the French resistance was able to continue their campaign to liberate the French motherland and maintain their credibility with other Allied Powers.[25] When France was eventually liberated, the contributions of Free French Africa and African troops were largely overlooked and even intentionally downplayed. Before the liberation of Paris in August 1944, de Gaulle ordered the blanchissement (whitening) of the Second Free French armored division by replacing African members with French resistance.[26]

The Allied Powers framed World War II as a war to protect freedom, and in this vein the Atlantic Charter was signed in August 1941 by President Roosevelt and British Prime Minister Winston Churchill, proclaiming in Clause 3, "the right of all peoples to choose the form of government under which they live; and they wish to see sovereign right and self-government restored to those who have been forcibly deprived of them."[27] Groups and individuals from across the British empire asked about the applicability of Clause 3 of the Atlantic Charter to British colonies. Churchill addressed this question by arguing that Clause 3 only applied to Europeans living under Nazi occupation. He stated:

> At the Atlantic meeting we had in mind, primarily, the restoration of the sovereignty, self-government, and the national life of the States and nations of Europe now under the Nazi yoke, and the principles governing any alterations in the territorial boundaries which may have been made. So this is quite a separate problem from the progressive evolution of self-governing institutions in the regions and peoples which owe allegiance to the British Crown. We have made declarations on these matters which are complete in themselves, free from ambiguity, and related to the conditions and circumstances of the territories and peoples affected.[28]

On the French side, de Gaulle convened a conference in Brazzaville in 1944 to begin to plan the future of French colonies. The participants were predominantly the governors of French colonies, and the only black man present was the governor of the Equatorial Federation. The starting point for the conference was that immediate independence after the end of World War II was unthinkable, but the conference did seek to find ways to ensure greater social and economic freedoms as well as increase indigenous participation in colonial governments.[29] In his speech opening the conference, de Gaulle said:

> At present the whole French empire is making an important contribution to the Allies' common effort. We do not believe that autocracy will be desirable or even possible in the world of tomorrow ... In French Africa, no progress will be possible if the men and women on their native soil do not benefit materially and spiritually and if they are not able to raise themselves to the point where they are capable of taking a hand in the running of their countries. It is France's duty to make sure this comes about. This is our aim. We know that it will be a long-term program.[30]

The suggestion that the colonies were not able to govern their own affairs after their resources and people rallied to the cause of the French resistance when the French homeland was captured was patronizing, and while de Gaulle's rhetoric may sound promising, in reality the French metropole made very few concessions to French colonies.

Pan-Africanism renewed

The competing visions of W.E.B. Du Bois and Marcus Garvey

These are the experiences with the major colonial powers that shaped the thinking of pan-Africanists going into the 1945 Congress – the hypocrisy of the League of Nations to condemn Liberia but not Portugal over slavery, the abandonment of Abyssinia, and the double standard of the Atlantic Charter while Africans sacrificed their lives and resources on the battle-field. It was held in Manchester, England and is the most notable gathering for the advent of pan-Africanism in Africa because participants included many men who would go on to lead countries in Africa after independence. George Padmore, Jomo Kenyatta of Kenya, Peter Abrahams of South Africa, and Kwame Nkrumah of the Gold Coast all helped to organize the conference and of course attended.[31] Other organizers included student and political organizations under the umbrella of the Pan-African Federation.

At Manchester the future leaders of independent African states discussed and debated the principles of an ever-evolving pan-Africanism and voted on resolutions clarifying their beliefs and demands. The competing visions of pan-Africanism from W.E.B. Du Bois and Marcus Garvey formed an important part of the debate about how pan-Africanism should be understood and practiced. This theoretical debate amongst pan-Africanist scholars illustrates the contestation and debate of a complex idea, a process that would happen again when pan-Africanism was carried back to Africa by independence era leaders. While both Du Bois and Garvey believed in self-determination and eventual unity of the African continent their priorities and methods differed significantly. Du Bois was born in Massachusetts, US, in 1868. He attended Fisk University on a scholarship and then went on to attend Harvard. He strongly believed that education would play a vital role in the African American struggle for equality. Du Bois helped to form the National Association for the Advancement of Colored People, which reflected his pacifist stance to racial problems and largely appealed to middle- and upper-class African Americans.[32] In the international sphere Du Bois worked to organize the pan-Africanist conferences held throughout the 1920s, and his aims were to secure the rights of Africans to participate in their governments or a mandatory trusteeship system leading to self-rule. His approach was steadfastly diplomatic and collaborative.[33]

Marcus Garvey was born in 1887 in St. Ann's Bay, Jamaica. In contrast to Du Bois, he began working as an apprentice at the age of fourteen. He travelled extensively in Central and South America in his early adulthood, and he formed an association to find practical ways to improve the conditions of people of African descent at home and abroad. Unlike the National Association for the Advancement of Colored People, Garvey's organization had broad appeal amongst many poor people of African descent.[34] It sought to unite people of African descent to demand their industrial, political, social, and religious emancipation and to achieve freedom for the continent of Africa.[35] His approach did not embrace collaboration or incrementalism, and he sought freedom for Africa in order to ensure people of

African descent from all over the world could return to their emancipated homeland. In these two distinct visions, it is clear that the background and experiences of individuals impacts the way they perceive ideas.

Du Bois and Garvey advocated for very different visions of pan-Africanism, and the result was debate amongst a wider swath of pan-Africanists about which vision to pursue and how to achieve that vision. On the one hand, Du Bois sought incremental change and valued collaboration, and on the other Garvey worked for immediate results and advocated for Africans to return to their homeland and rely on each other. The debates within the wider pan-African community would continue into the independence era when we see the competing visions of Nkrumah to form a strong African union and eschew contact with former colonial powers and more moderate and conservative leaders who saw value in continuing interaction and collaboration with major powers. While the competing visions of pan-Africanism fostered debate, the intellectual and organizational drive of George Padmore held the Congress together and ultimately helped to bridge the divide between the theory and practice of pan-Africanism. He is viewed as connecting the pan-African movement created by Du Bois and Garvey and the pan-African movement that continued to develop in Africa among independence era leaders.[36]

Manchester Conference outcomes

The predominant theme of the resolutions that came out of the conference was anti-imperialism. The delegates called for, "the principles of the Four Freedoms and the Atlantic Charter to be put into practice at once."[37] Other resolutions from the Congress stressed the economic as well as political exploitation of African peoples, the harmful impact of artificial territorial boundaries imposed by colonial powers, the unjustness of imperialism, and the need for increasing educational and job opportunities for Africans.[38] Additional discussions at the Congress focused on support to be given to the three countries in the world governed by black leaders – at the time these countries were Liberia, Haiti, and Ethiopia. The Congress resolution on these countries stated, "The Fifth pan-African Congress sends Fraternal greetings to the Governments and peoples of Ethiopia, Liberia, and Haiti and pledges its support in mobilizing world public opinion among Africans and peoples of African descent in defense of their Sovereign independence."[39] All of these issues can be captured in the challenge to colonial powers issued by the delegates, which read:

> The delegates of the fifth pan-African Congress believe in peace. How could it be otherwise when for centuries the African peoples have been victims of

violence and slavery. Yet, if the Western World is still determined to rule mankind by force, then Africa as a last resort, may have to appeal to force in effect to achieve freedom ... We are determined to be free. We want education. We want the right to earn a decent living; the right to express our thoughts and emotions, to adopt and create forms of beauty. We demand for Black Africa autonomy and independence ... Therefore we shall complain, appeal, and arraign. We will make the world listen to the facts of our condition. We will fight every way we can for freedom, democracy, and social betterment.[40]

As the Manchester Congress drew to a close there was a great deal of enthusiasm, not only to keep the pan-African movement alive but to forge ahead with a new phase and bring it back to Africa. At the Congress, pan-Africanism evolved from a protest movement by people of African descent into "an instrument of African nationalist movements fighting colonial rule."[41] Delegates forged enduring links amongst themselves, and many went on to create organizations to continue pan-Africanist work leading into the independence era. For example, Nkrumah and other West African delegates created the West African National Secretariat and eventually returned to West Africa to mobilize Africans within Africa. This organization, as well as others such as the Pan-African Federation, continued to publish pan-African material, advocate on behalf of Africans to the UN and European governments, and work with trade unions.[42] Moving into the post-war era, African nationalists carried this momentum forward to push for independence and then to create institutions to protect hard-won gains.

Notes

1 E.K. Dumor, *Ghana, OAU, and Southern Africa: An African Response to Apartheid* (Accra, Ghana: Ghana Universities Press, 1991), 26.

2 Amitav Acharya, "Norm Subsidiarity and Regional Orders: Sovereignty, Regionalism, and Rule-Making in the Third World," *International Studies Quarterly* 55, no. 1 (2011): 99.

3 C.O.C. Amate, *Inside the OAU: Pan-Africanism in Practice* (New York: St. Martin's Press, 1986), 56–59.

4 Sabelo J. Ndlovu-Gatsheni, "Pan-Africanism and the International System," in *Handbook of Africa's International Relations*, ed. Tim Murithi (New York: Routledge, 2014), 21.

5 S. Okechukwu Mezu, "Introduction: The Philosophy of Pan-Africanism," in *The Philosophy of Pan-Africanism: A Collection of Papers on the Theory and Practice of the African Unity Movement*, ed. S. Okechukwu Mezu (Washington DC: Georgetown University Press, 1965), 16–17.

6 Dumor, *Ghana, OAU, and Southern Africa*, 26–27.
7 George Padmore, *History of the Pan-African Congress* (London: The Hammersmith Bookshop Ltd, 1963), 8.
8 P. Olisanwuche Esedebe, *Pan-Africanism: The Idea and Movement, 1776–1991*, second edition. (Washington DC: Howard University Press, 1994), 41–42.
9 Esedebe, *Pan-Africanism*, 47–48.
10 George Padmore, *Pan-Africanism or Communism: The Coming Struggle for Africa* (London: Dobson Books Limited, 1956), 120.
11 Padmore, *History of the Pan-African Congress*, 41.
12 Padmore, *History of the Pan-African Congress*, 13.
13 Padmore, *Pan-Africanism or Communism*, 123.
14 Padmore, *Pan-Africanism or Communism*, 124.
15 Esedebe, *Pan-Africanism*, 95.
16 Esedebe, *Pan-Africanism*, 96.
17 Frank Hardie, *The Abyssinian Crisis* (London: B.T. Batsford Ltd, 1974), 23.
18 Hardie, *The Abyssianian Crisis*, 89.
19 Hardie, *The Abyssinian Crisis*, 101–2.
20 Hardie, *The Abyssinian Crisis*, 225.
21 Padmore, *Pan-Africanism or Communism*, 145.
22 David Killingray, "Labour Mobilisation in British Colonial Africa for the War Effort, 1939–46," in *Africa and the Second World War*, ed. David Killingray and Richard Rathbone (London: Palgrave Macmillan, 1986), 70–71.
23 Timothy Parsons, "The Military Experiences of Ordinary Africans in World War II," in *Africa and World War II*, ed. Judith A. Byfield et al. (New York: Cambridge University Press, 2015), 4.
24 Eric T. Jennings, *Free French Africa in World War II: The African Resistance* (New York: Cambridge University Press, 2015), 17.
25 Jennings, *Free French Africa in World War II*, 49.
26 Parsons, "The Military Experiences of Ordinary Africans in World War II," 9.
27 "The Atlantic Charter – Declaration of Principles Issues by the President of the United States and the Prime Minister of the United Kingdom," 14 August 1941, www.nato.int/cps/en/natolive/official_texts_16912.htm (accessed 7 May 2020).
28 Lord Hailey, Franklin D. Roosevelt, and Winston S. Churchill, "The Colonies and the Atlantic Charter," *Journal of The Royal Central Asian Society* 30, no. 3–4 (1943): 237.
29 I.C.B. Dear and M.R.D. Foot, eds., "Brazzaville Conference," in *The Oxford Companion to World War II* (Oxford: Oxford University Press, 2003).
30 Charles de Gaulle, "Speech Made by General de Gaulle at Opening of Brazzaville Conference" (30 January 1944), www.charles-de-gaulle.org/pages/stock-html/en/the-man/home/speeches/speech-made-by-general-de-gaulle-at-the-opening-of-the-brazzaville-conference-on-january-30th-1944.php.
31 Padmore, *History of the Pan-African Congress*, 74.
32 Tamba E. M'Bayo, "W.E.B. Du Bois, Marcus Garvey, and the Pan-Africanism in Liberia, 1919–1924," *Historian* 66, no. 1 (2004): 28–29.

33 Vincent Bakpetu Thompson, *Africa and Unity: The Evolution of Pan-Africanism* (London: Longman Group Ltd, 1969), 42.

34 M'Bayo, "W.E.B. Du Bois, Marcus Garvey, and the Pan-Africanism in Liberia, 1919–1924," 29–30.

35 Adekunle Ajala, *Pan-Africanism: Evolution, Progress, and Prospects* (New York: St. Martin's Press, 1973), 6.

36 George Padmore, *Africa and World Peace* (London: Frank Cass and Company Limited, 1972), ix.

37 Padmore, *History of the Pan-African Congress*, 57.

38 Padmore, *History of the Pan-African Congress*, 55–59.

39 Padmore, *History of the Pan-African Congress*, 63.

40 Padmore, *History of the Pan-African Congress*, 5.

41 Ajala, *Pan-Africanism*, 11.

42 Esedebe, *Pan-Africanism*, 147–48.

4

The creation of the Organization
of African Unity

The end of World War II heralded in a new international era. However, most states in Africa entered this era as colonies of the major powers without a voice or equal rights in the international system, and the next twenty years would be a struggle for independence. The independence of the Gold Coast in 1957 kicked off a wave of decolonization in sub-Saharan Africa, with most states achieving independence by the mid-1960s. The OAU was created in May 1963 soon after many African states gained independence. The choice to construct a regional organization was driven by elites, notably the leaders of independent states who had immense power in the immediate post-independence period. It is these leaders who were present at the summit that led to the creation of the OAU, and who defined the values of the OAU when they negotiated the Charter. There were many considerations taken into account when deciding the fundamental principles of the regional organization, including the very recent colonial era and continuing threats of domination from major powers, key events in the lead-up to the OAU founding conference, the collective understanding of pan-Africanist ideas, and African regional values and interests.

The process of construcing the OAU and choosing its defining norms demonstrates the importance of the idea of pan-Africanism as well as the interplay between ideas and other factors in norm creation and policy making. While an ambiguous idea can pose challenges, it can also be beneficial for uniting disparate groups.[1] In the case of pan-Africanism, groups of leaders were able to hold different interpretations about some aspects of pan-Africanism and how they should be applied. However, they were also able to unite under a few common positions, notably the necessity for total liberation of the continent, a place for Africa in the global community, and some degree of unity, without necessarily agreeing on the specifics of these points. This collective understanding of pan-Africanism was then used as a critical idea that would help to shape the parameters of the debate. The idea, combined with the influence of particular African leaders, the impact of key events, and the interests of the region explain why certain norms were selected and others were not. The norms that were chosen then shaped the conflict management policy of the region for decades to come.

At the creation of the OAU, independence era leaders chose norms that codified non-interference, absolute protection of state sovereignty and territorial integrity, and regional primacy while still allowing for collaboration with other states in the international system. Overall, independence era leaders adopted norms that in many ways conformed to existing international norms of state sovereignty and non-interference. They acknowledged the threat of interference from both within and outside Africa, maintained their links with the region as well as major powers, and agreed to regional cooperation with gradual progress towards unity. At first glance, it might appear that Africa went through a process of localization. African leaders constituted existing international norms but adapted them in ways that fit to the regional context by framing the norms in a way that promoted liberation and Africa's place in the world.

However, as this chapter will demonstrate, the norms adopted at the creation of the OAU conform in some ways to a process of subsidiarity, but it is not a perfect fit. The OAU was not only concerned about outside domination but also subversion from within the continent. African leaders had choices when it came to the norms they selected for their regional organization. It was not pre-ordained that they would adopt non-interference and state sovereignty norms, and there were other options on the table. Nkrumah put forward another option for a close regional union and coordinated defense, economic, and foreign policies, which was supported by Prime Minister Milton Obote of Uganda.[2] However, as speeches from African leaders will demonstrate, most leaders weighed their options and determined that the best way to secure their nascent states from regional and international threats of domination and interference was by codifying non-interference, protecting their sovereignty and territorial integrity, and participating in the international system while still promoting the primacy of the region to manage regional issues.

Independence leaders did not simply frame international norms in ways that were appropriate for the local context or graft them onto indigenous practices. They helped to develop new norms, incorporated new components to existing norms, and re-shaped the understanding of how international norms were applied. Independent African states, along with other former colonized states, promoted a norm of racial equality in the international system. Pan-Africanists had advocated for the interests of people of African descent since at least 1900, including promoting the inherent dignity and equality of races and advocating for self-rule.[3] Principles of racial equality were included in UN documents at its founding in 1945, but these principles were applied on a human rights basis to individuals. For instance, Article 55 of the UN Charter refers to respect for human rights and fundamental freedoms without distinction to race.[4] Furthermore, Article 2 of the 1948 UDHR asserts that all human beings are entitled to fundamental rights and freedoms that apply whether people live in an independent territory with international jurisdiction or a non-self-governing territory.[5] Human rights norms asserting racial equality were applied to individuals and not applied to states in the international system, as evidenced by Britain and France maintaining their empires and arguing that colonial people must undergo a progression towards self-rule. Pan-Africanist principles advocated for racial equality for individuals and also applied this norm to states. At the 1945 Manchester conference, delegates pushed to protect states governed by black leaders, which at the time were Haiti, Liberia, and Ethiopia, from outside domination and interference, and called for an immediate end to colonization and the application of the Four Freedoms of the Atlantic Charter to colonized peoples.[6]

When African leaders adopted norms protecting state sovereignty and advocating non-interference they linked the application of these norms to the conduct of states. States that did not respect racial equality and self-determination norms were outside of civilized international society and thus the norms of international society that respected the rights of states did not apply. This linking was implicit in the OAU policies that protected the sovereignty and territory of independent states while also creating and funding the Liberation Committee to financially and materially support movements that subverted white-minority and colonial regimes. This linking became explicit in the Lusaka Manifesto, which condemns the white-minority regimes in southern Africa by arguing that while implementation of equality may be flawed, all states need, at a minimum, to accept the principle of equality. When a state fails to accept this principle then the rest of the world has a right to assert, "that the arrangements within any state that wishes to be accepted into the community of nations must be based on an acceptance of the principles of human dignity and equality."[7]

In addition, as Acharya argues, the OAU adopted a norm on regional primacy that added to the existing norm of the role of regions in the international system as laid out by Chapter VIII of the UN Charter. Chapter VIII allows for the existence of regional arrangements and encourages such bodies to attempt to solve disputes peacefully within the local context before moving to the UNSC, but it still affirms the right of the UNSC to engage in any dispute that is brought to its attention.[8] African leaders went well beyond claiming a role for the African region and pushed for non-intervention by outside actors. They chose to assert that African should manage its own affairs and deal with any issues internally – what has essentially become African solutions for African problems.[9] Acharya attributes this norm to Nkrumah. However, as will be discussed in the coming chapters, archival evidence, notably speeches from independence era leaders and the record of the Africa Group at the UN, shows that many other leaders were also concerned with ensuring Africa managed its own affairs, and this is true even amongst leaders who valued cooperation with international actors.

African leaders chose norms that linked racial equality and self-determination with state sovereignty and non-inference as well as a norm of regional primacy. It was not a forgone conclusion that African leaders would choose to maintain colonial borders and conform to some existing norms of the international system, notably state sovereignty and territorial integrity. There were other options on the table, including regional integration. The speeches from the OAU founding conference demonstrate that African leaders were concerned about shoring up their new states and ensuring the final liberation of the continent. They crafted OAU norms that the vast majority of African leaders determined would best help protect African states and meet regional goals.

The creation of African states

Leading up to the creation of the OAU

Before African leaders could move to create the OAU, African states first had to become independent. After World War II ended, Britain and France were willing to make modest concessions to improve the conditions of Africans and give them a voice in their government, but there were no serious plans for near-term independence. Additionally, the wellbeing of colonial subjects was subjugated under the needs of the colonial powers, specifically domestic recovery and maintaining their international influence. When independence eventually did come it arrived in three broad phases. Countries in northern Africa came first with Libya gaining independence in 1951, Egypt in 1955, and Morocco, Tunisia, and Sudan in 1956. Then in the late 1950s and early 1960s a string of African states across the middle of the continent became independent with the Gold Coast leading the way in 1957. Finally, the remaining countries – largely Portuguese colonies or those with large settler populations concentrated in southern Africa – became independent much later.

Between the advent of the independence period in the 1950s and the creation of the OAU in 1963 there were several events in Africa that had momentous impact on inter-African relations, and despite the common thread of pan-Africanism and colonial domination there were gaping differences in interpretation amongst African leaders on key issues. Eventually the independent states of Africa split into blocs of radical, moderate, and conservative states. Those states in the conservative bloc, predominantly made up of former French colonies, advocated some degree of cooperation with major powers, were wary of both outside and African interference in internal affairs, and sought gradual integration amongst African states. On the other side of the spectrum, leaders from states in the radical bloc were very concerned about cooperation with major powers because of the possibility of neo-colonialism. They believed the greatest threat to Africa was outside interference, and advocated for a stronger union of African states as the best means to protect Africa and assert its influence. Finally, there was a middle cadre of states, led by Liberia and Ethiopia, that were deeply concerned by the ideological split and sought to unify Africa. The events of the Franco-Algerian war and the Congo crisis served to highlight these differences amongst African states and crystallize the divide between radical and conservative states in particular.

The Franco-Algerian war

The Franco-Algerian war for the independence of Algeria began on 1 November 1954 with the outbreak of an insurrection that was marked by a series of terrorist attacks followed by the announcement of the creation of the Front de Libération Nationale (FLN). The leaders of the movement proclaimed that their aims were: "the liquidation of the colonial system, the abandonment of all relics of reformism, and national independence through the restoration of the Algerian state."[10] The French government responded by claiming that they would defend their interests in Algeria at all costs, and the European population in Algeria responded with terrorist actions. In the mid-to-late 1950s, European extremists began leaving bombs in venues frequented by Muslims, and the FLN then took up urban terrorism in Algiers. French troops were dispatched to root out the terrorists in the capital. The battle of Algiers lasted from January to September 1957, and the French were eventually successful. However, it was a hollow victory after so much destruction.[11]

When General de Gaulle returned to power he sought a different approach to end the conflict and tried to win over the Algerian population with promises of a huge French investment in housing and jobs.[12] In September 1959, de Gaulle announced that once peace had been restored, Algerians would have the right to self-determination and a choice of three options – secession, total assimilation, or self-government in association with France. De Gaulle preferred the third option and campaigned for it. However, many Europeans in Algeria were skeptical of possible secession, and many Algerians were skeptical of the sincerity of the offer.[13]

The reaction from African states to the Franco-Algerian civil war was initially to support the FLN. When the second Conference of Independent African States took place in June 1960, the conference admitted representatives from the FLN as the provisional government of Algeria. The conference was strongly supported by Ghana and focused on liberation, supporting resistance movements, and combating neo-colonialism. However, the conference was mostly attended by leaders from radical states, and the aims of the conference and its position on the FNL did not indicate a uniform position amongst African states. The French held a referendum in 1958 in France and all overseas territories on a new constitution. Overseas territories were given the option to approve the constitution and become a part of the French Community or reject it and opt for immediate independence. Only Guinea rejected the constitution and thus became independent in October 1958. Most Francophone colonies accepted the constitution and became independent in the second half of 1960. Therefore, Francophone nations who maintained good relations with France were not represented at the June 1960 conference. By and large, Francophone countries were interested in maintaining functioning relationships with former colonial powers and the west, and this also influenced their stance on how to react to the Franco-Algerian war.[14]

Congo crisis

The second issue that caused fissures between African states was the Congo crisis which began shortly after the second Conference of Independent African States concluded. Belgium Congo gained formal independence at the end of June 1960 and immediately plunged into turmoil. The crisis served to deepen the disagreements between African states and led to the crystallization of these divisions after the creation of the radical Casablanca group of African states and the conservative Brazzaville group. The crisis began in early July 1960 with the mutiny of the Force Publique. After which, President Joseph Kasavubu and Prime Minister Patrice Lumumba requested technical assistance from the UN. However, it soon became very clear that much more than technical assistance was going to be needed to restore stability and security in the Congo. At this point other independent African states lobbied Kasavubu and Lumumba to appeal to the UN for more robust assistance. Once Congo made the request, the African contingent at the UN lobbied to ensure that the request was approved and then offered African troops.[15]

Unfortunately, the unity amongst African states did not last as the crisis progressed and disagreements emerged over the amount of trust to place in the UN and other African states, as well as worry over Belgium interference in the Congo. There was a dividing line between states that preferred a moderate approach and those that preferred a more aggressive approach to retake Katanga, a mineral-producing province that had threatened to secede. Belgium had dispatched troops following the mutiny to rescue citizens and claimed to be acting to protect their national interests. However, many African states viewed Belgium action as an aggressive move that contributed to the conflict.[16] While these disagreements were still festering several developments occurred that changed the playing field. First, Kasavubu dismissed Lumumba from the Congolese government. Second, Mobutu Sese Seko led a successful coup to overthrow Kasavubu, and finally, many former French colonies became independent and wanted to have a voice in the African debate about Congo.[17]

Following these developments, there was an attempt to foster reconciliation between Kasavubu and Lumumba. This ultimately failed, and dividing lines were drawn between African states that supported Kasavubu versus those who supported Lumumba. Additionally, there was disagreement amongst African states about whether to continue to rely on the UN or to pursue more robust action unilaterally. Guinea, Mali, Morocco, and to a certain extent Ghana, supported Lumumba and had lost confidence in the UN to find and implement a solution. This group of states was actively looking to work outside the UN and threatening to withdraw their troops from Congo. Tunisia, Sudan, Nigeria, and Ethiopia represented the moderate states that largely supported Kasavubu and were still willing to support the UN. Finally, the former French colonies largely supported Kasavubu, and denounced the interference by the UN and other African states, particularly Guinea and Ghana.[18]

Forming the blocs

The ongoing crises in Algeria and Congo and the split amongst African countries led to a series of conferences in the late 1950s and early 1960s where the division of African states along ideological lines became explicit. Ghana hosted the first gathering of leaders from independent African states in April 1958. At that time there were eight independent states in Africa (excluding South Africa) – Ghana, Liberia, Ethiopia, Egypt, Tunisia, Morocco, Sudan, and Libya. One of the most notable outcomes from this gathering was an agreement to coordinate activities amongst African ambassadors at the UN, but the leaders were not willing to go further to form any sort of formal union.[19]

Ghana's President Nkrumah was by far the leader most committed to a strong, political union of African states. Following the 1958 conference he began working with other willing states to make a union of African states a reality. Nkrumah held consultations with Sékou Touré of Guinea to form a Ghana-Guinea Union. Seeking to expand their union, Nkrumah and Touré met with Liberian President William V.S. Tubman in Sanniquellie, Liberia in July 1959. However, Tubman was deeply skeptical of anything that would require Liberia to cede part of its sovereignty and would only agree to join a loose association of states. The three leaders solidified their intention to form an association and hold a follow-up conference by signing the Sanniquellie Declaration.[20]

The second conference of independent African states was held in June 1960 in Addis Ababa, Ethiopia. Delegates from Ghana tried to get the Sanniquellie Declaration adopted as the basis for discussion about a potential political and economic union of states and promised that Ghana was willing to give up some or all of its sovereignty in the interest of a Union of African States. Delegates launched a withering attack on this proposal and Nkrumah's intentions. Their argument was that while pan-Africanism is key to resolving Africa's problems, a political union is premature, and Nkrumah was using this idea to become ruler of the continent.[21] Nigeria, in particular, was highly opposed to any sort of political union. Ultimately the conference revealed deep divisions between a group of states led by Ghana and Guinea, which wanted to form a union based on strong political integration, and other states led by Nigeria and Liberia, which only wanted a mechanism to facilitate coordination.[22]

At the same time, following the independence of French colonies, President Félix Houphouët-Boigny invited all the leaders of the former French territories to a gathering in Abidjan to discuss the Franco-Algerian war. At this meeting it was decided that these countries would meet again in Brazzaville in December 1960 to coordinate their policies on a range of issues.[23] The states represented at the conference became known as the conservative Brazzaville bloc and included Congo, Ivory Coast, Senegal, Mauritania, Burkina Faso, Benin, Niger, Chad, Central African Republic (CAR), Gabon, Cameroon, and Malagasy.[24] The communiqué issued by the Brazzaville conference called for self-determination to end the war in Algeria while also praising General de Gaulle for his efforts that led to the independence of all the states at the conference. Furthermore, the Brazzaville states denounced outside military intervention in Congo – including UN intervention – and called for a roundtable of Congolese stakeholders to facilitate a solution to the crisis. Finally, the conference communiqué spoke to the issue of Mauritania, which had recently been denied admittance to the UN because of a Soviet veto at the request of Morocco. Morocco claimed that Mauritania was part of its territory. The Brazzaville group expressed dismay at the veto and interference by outside powers.[25]

In response to the Brazzaville conference communiqué on the Mauritania issue, Morocco invited the leaders of Ghana, Guinea, Mali, Egypt, Libya, and the provisional Algerian government to a conference in Casablanca in January 1961. These countries became known as the radical Casablanca group. The conference communiqué condemned France's proposed referendum in Algeria and asked all countries to immediately recognize the provisional Algerian government. On Congo, the Casablanca countries supported Prime Minister Lumumba and called for more robust UN action to end the secession of Katanga. Finally, the communiqué described Mauritania as a puppet state taken by France that should ultimately be returned to Morocco.[26] Overall, Casablanca states were far more concerned by interference from major powers and the possibility of continuing domination; whereas, Brazzaville states were concerned about interference from both African states and other international actors, but also saw the value of cooperation with major powers.

Other leaders in Africa were alarmed by the emergence of two separate blocs of countries that they believed could be easily manipulated by the major powers. In order to reconcile the two groups, President Tubman of Liberia invited all independent Africa states to a conference in Liberia in May 1961, and in order to make the conference as inclusive as possible, he asked that countries from both the Brazzaville and Casablanca groups co-sponsor the invitation.[27] Unfortunately, despite these efforts, most of the Casablanca states refused to participate at the last minute, so the Monrovia conference ended up adopting many of the positions advocated by the Brazzaville countries. Additionally, it emphasized the equality of all African states and non-acceptance of any continental leadership, non-interference in the internal affairs of states, and cooperation based on tolerance, good neighborly relations, and exchange of views. There was a follow-up conference in Lagos in 1962 at which more Casablanca states participated. It was in Lagos that African leaders agreed that the next step would be a summit in Addis Ababa to finally create a framework for African unity. Ethiopia wisely waited until both the Congo and Algeria crises were resolved before beginning consultations for the Addis Ababa conference that would be held in May 1963.[28]

There were turning points in both Algeria and Congo in the early 1960s. Negotiations to end the Franco-Algerian conflict began on 18 May 1961. There were enormous questions over the conditions of the truce, including the position of Europeans living in Algeria and ownership of the Sahara (and its recently discovered oil and natural gas). Negotiations progressed slowly until a new wave of violence perpetrated by Europeans against Muslims that finally led to an agreement signed on 18 March 1962. France agreed to recognize the sovereignty of the Algerian state over 15 departments across Algeria and Sahara, and the Algerians agreed to a series of measures protecting French citizens and French interests in Algeria. This agreement cleared the way for a referendum on 1 July 1962, in which Algerians voted overwhelmingly for independence.[29]

In Congo, the game changed again with the murder of Lumumba in January 1961. This led to protests across Africa and the unification of the Casablanca group with the moderate counties on a way forward to resolve the Congo crisis. This coalition was strong enough to push through a robust resolution at the UN and keep up pressure on the UN and western powers to compel them to take action against Katanga. Additionally, the UN appointed several Africans to key positions, who were then able to act as mediators between the UN and Congolese factions, eventually leading to an agreement that re-instated Kasavubu and re-opened parliament.[30]

Re-uniting the continent

Of the thirty-two independent African states, thirty gathered in May 1963 in Addis Ababa to create a regional organization. The states that participated in the OAU founding conference were Algeria, Burundi, Cameroon, CAR, Chad, Congo, Zaire, Benin, Ethiopia, Gabon, Ghana, Guinea, Ivory Coast, Liberia, Libya, Malagasy, Mali, Mauritania, Niger, Nigeria, Rwanda, Senegal, Sierra Leone, Somalia, Sudan, Tanzania, Tunisia, Uganda, Egypt, and Burkina Faso. Morocco did not participate because of the inclusion of Mauritania, and Togo was prevented from participating because its representatives had toppled the previous government in a coup d'état in January 1963.[31] During the coup d'état Togolese President Sylvanus Olympio was assassinated, and this event, along with the others previously discussed in this chapter, would impact the discussions around OAU norms.

The conference was a momentous occasion both because of its potential to unite the continent and because it was a historic gathering of African leaders from independent African states.[32] The Foreign Ministers of the participating states met first. Their job was to draft the charter document the Heads of States would consider later in the week pertaining to the establishment of an organization of African states. There were four draft charters on the table for consideration by the Foreign Ministers – the Monrovia and Casablanca charters and those submitted by Ghana and Ethiopia. A subcommittee comprised of Algeria, Cameroon, Ethiopia, Ghana, Guinea, Madagascar, Nigeria, Tanzania, and Tunisia was formed to consider each of these charters and many other questions pertaining to the structure and aims of a continental organization.[33] The major questions were around how and to what extent Africa should unify and how to deal with the continuing existence of colonial and white-minority regimes.[34] These

issues manifested in debates around state sovereignty, territorial boundaries, regional and international cooperation, and approaches to liberation
struggles. Unfortunately, the disagreements proved insurmountable at the
ministerial level. The sub-committee was unable to reach an agreement on
which charter to use as a basis of discussion, and negotiations stalled until
the Heads of States arrived.[35]

When trying to understand the intentions and positions of the Heads
of States going into the conference, their opening speeches are illustrative.
Emperor Haile Selassie opened the conference as its host. Selassie was a
hugely respected leader within Africa because of Ethiopia's stand against
Italian invaders in the 1930s, and in line with Ethiopia's position within the
Monrovia bloc, he largely promoted moderate positions. In his remarks he
spoke of the recent colonial past and the responsibility of African leaders
to come together to mold the future of independent Africa while supporting those nations still struggling for independence.[36] Selassie clearly set the
expectation that the leaders could not leave Addis Ababa without an agreement in place for the formation of a regional organization. He stated:

> The commentators of 1963 speak, in discussing Africa, of the Monrovia State,
> the Brazzaville Groups, the Casablanca Powers, of these and many more. Let
> us put an end to these terms. What we require is a single African organization
> through which Africa's single voice may be heard, within which Africa's prob-
> lems may be studied and resolved. We need an organization which facilitates
> acceptable solutions to disputes among Africans and promotes the study and
> adoption of measures for common defense and programs for cooperation.[37]

He went on to strike a conciliatory tone between the radical and conservative groups, saying, "Unity is the accepted goal. We argue about
techniques and tactics. But when semantics are stripped away, there is little
argument among us. We are determined to create a union of Africans ... It
is our duty and our privilege to rouse the slumbering giant that is Africa."[38]
He stressed that the consequences of division amongst African states was
opening Africa's doors to foreign intervention. When speaking about the
specifics of a potential organization he argued for a well-articulated framework and permanent headquarters, economic cooperation to promote
development and trade amongst Africa nations, and permanent structures
to assist with the peaceful settlement of disputes to ensure quarrels between
states would be confined to the continent. Finally, he spoke of establishing
an African defense system to protect states that are threatened with outside
aggression and a university to train the future leaders of Africa.[39] However,
in all of this he offered few details and instead implored African leaders to
focus on starting the process of cooperation even if the exact parameters
of their continental organization would need to come together over time.

He was most concerned with bringing the continent together to deal with common challenges.

Leaders from the conservative bloc of former French colonies struck a different tone in their opening speeches. Drawing on a common theme of pan-Africanism, they agreed with the goal of eradicating colonialism and racialism. However, they also saw the value of cooperation with major powers, and they were wary of interference from other states within Africa. These leaders generally praised the idea of African unity, but they were interested in a progressive path towards unity and tended to emphasize economic unity before political unity. At the OAU founding conference, Léopold Senghor spoke about the aim of Africa unity. He stuck to his long-held positions on the importance of gradual unity, international and African collaboration, and economic development. He said, "The aim we must assign, which we do assign, to our action can only be the very aim which others nations and continents have set themselves: development through economic growth … By that I mean bringing each and every African to full worth."[40] Félix Houphouët-Boigny, President of Ivory Coast, argued that African leaders should not let themselves be carried away with enthusiasm and forget the very real challenges of unity, including differences among African countries of language, religion, ideology, and national cohesion.[41] He also stressed the responsibility of all African states to liberate the remaining African states still suffering under colonial or racial regimes. He believed that the leaders of free African states should lay the foundations of unity but wait for the complete liberation of Africa to finish the task.[42] Ultimately, he drew a distinction between unity and uniformity and stressed a unified position of Africa when dealing with other regional blocs while still allowing for differences among African states. He said:

> Every country has the imperative duty to respect the different paths that brother countries might take. This absolute tolerance constitutes a prerequisite for more highly-developed unification later on … Absolute tolerance, scrupulously and religiously observed by all in their dealings with one another, will bring about the disappearance of the grave threat which hangs over the future of our young states: the subversive intrigues originating in third African states, which are the accomplices of foreign states hostile to our unity, and therefore our real independence and happiness.[43]

As is evident, Houphouët-Boigny was concerned about forming a strong union in addition to interference from other African states. These concerns came on the heels of the Congo crisis in which the Francophone states were concerned about outside interference of any kind. In addition, the OAU conference was held immediately after the coup d'état in Togo and the assassination of President Olympio in which there were accusations of external African support for the coup. As such, there was deep skepticism of a strong union, not only to maintain state sovereignty but also to fend off subversion from within Africa. This concern was echoed by President Ahmadou Ahidjo of Cameron, who said, "We must accept the sovereignty of each and every one ... This implies absolute respect for one's neighbor; this implies abstaining from intervention in its internal affairs from encouraging or trying to maintain covert or overt subversion."[44]

Malian President Modibo Keita reiterated the concerns of many leaders about relations amongst African states, but he goes further in pushing for the inviolability of colonial borders. He argues that while the colonial system divided Africa it also allowed for nations to be born. He spoke of the colonial histories of each state and the deep imprints of each system and argued that these differences cannot be brushed away.[45] He stated, "If all of us here present are truly animated by the ardent desire to achieve African unity, we must take Africa as it is, and we must renounce any territorial claims, if we do not wish to introduce what we might call black imperialism in Africa."[46] President Keita proposed the rule that would preserve colonial frontiers. He argued that the colonial system allowed many African states to be born even while it divided the continent, and therefore, the colonial borders should be honored and preserved through a continental non-aggression pact.[47]

Regional powerhouse Nigeria largely ascribed to the same concerns outlined by many Francophone countries. Nigerian Prime Minister Alhaji Abuakar Tafawa Balewa drew a distinction between taking practical steps to increase economic, cultural, and educational collaboration and taking complex action to build a political union, and clearly stated that Nigeria stood for the "practical approach."[48] Finally, President Philibert Tsiranana of the Malagasy Republic stressed the hard-won independence of the states present at the conference, and rejected adjusting borders or forming a close union. In reference to re-drawing borders, he argued, "it is not conceivable that one of our individual states would readily consent to be among the victims, for the sake of unity."[49]

Nigerian Prime Minister Balewa also advocated that Africa had a role to play in the global community, stating, "Let us not forget that we in Africa are a part of the world. We have international obligations as well. Whatever we do we cannot isolate ourselves from the rest of the world."[50] He outlined the premise of an African Group at the United Nations that later came to fruition in an almost identical form to his vision.

May I suggest to the conference that it is time now that we find a permanent secretariat for such an African Committee in New York ... I think we have to do everything to get our proper position in the United Nations Organization.... It is absolutely essential that the African continent must have more appropriate representation in the Security Council and all the bodies of the United Nations, because we have more to gain thereby. That world organization, I have always maintained, is a sure guarantee of the independent sovereignty of African states.[51]

His statement shows evidence of the concern African leaders had for guarding the sovereignty of their states. Importantly he sees the UN as a protector of state sovereignty and advocates for Africa working within the global system and within the UN to shield itself from outside interference. African leaders did not simply conform to the international system but rather saw value in engaging with the system to protect African interests. As subsequent chapters will demonstrate, the African Group at the UN was effective in expanding the rotating membership of the UNSC to include more African states and in keeping African conflict issues off the UNSC agenda.

While most leaders called for prudence and progressive steps towards unity, Ghanaian President Kwame Nkrumah led the charge to push for a robust political union. Nkrumah viewed independence as just the first step in Africa's liberation struggle and was very wary of neo-colonialism. He argued, "Independence is only the prelude to a new and more involved struggle for the right to conduct our own economic and social affairs; to construct our society according to our aspirations, unhampered by crushing and humiliating neo-colonialist controls and interference."[52] Where Nkrumah differed from almost every other leader in Africa was his desire for a strong political union. He saw unity as being intimately linked to independence. Only a strong union of African states could rid Africa of the remaining vestiges of colonialism and protect itself against continued outside interference. He stated, "African unity is above all a political kingdom which can only be gained by political means. The social and economic development of Africa will come only within the political kingdom, not the other way around."[53] Nkrumah believed that unity was the only weapon Africa had against the Great Powers, which, he argued, continued to exploit Africa for military and economic benefits. Specifically, he advocated for a common African market and currency, an African Central Bank, a continental communications system, the creation of commissions to design common African diplomatic and defense policies, and proposals for common African citizenship.[54]

The union Nkrumah envisioned would clearly involve states giving up at least some degree of sovereignty, and the proposal received very limited support. One exception was Ugandan Prime Minister Milton Obote. He argued, "The time has come, and is indeed almost overdue for African independent states to surrender some of their sovereignty in favor of an African central legislative and executive body with specific powers."[55] However, even among those leaders aligned with Ghana in the Casablanca group, there was scant support for a proposal that would involve relinquishing any degree of state sovereignty. In his opening speech, President Nasser of the United Arab Republic – now Egypt – spoke about many of the same threats seen by Nkrumah, including military pacts with outside powers that threaten African security, the looting of raw materials, and global inequalities between the west and newly independent countries.[56] However, his proposal for the extent of African unity was far more modest. He said, "Let us fix a final date for the liquidation of colonialism, let us lay down projects for cultural and scientific cooperation, let us embark on the coordination of our economic cooperation towards an African common market."[57]

While there was plenty of disagreement amongst leaders there was also significant agreement on key issues, notably the necessity to rid the African continent of colonialism and racialism and secure Africa's place within a broader international community. Leader after leader affirmed these common beliefs. A firm moderate Emperor Selassie stated, "We name as our first great task the final liberating of those Africans still dominated by foreign exploitation and control."[58] A member of the Casablanca group, Algerian Prime Minister Ben Bella said, "So let us agree to die a little, or even completely, so that the peoples still under colonial domination may be freed and African unity may not be a word in vain."[59] Finally, Congo Brazzaville President Fulbert Youlou said, "above all, we must be free men and in Africa there should be only free men, which implies the complete liberation of the continent from all colonialism and its vestiges."[60] On the specifics of how to ensure liberation, Ugandan Prime Minister Milton Obote offered Uganda as a training ground for African troops who sought to overthrow colonial regimes, and Guinean President Sékou Touré proposed allocating 1 percent of national budgets for the liberation struggle in addition to fixing a date by which colonialism must be ended or other African states would forcibly expel colonial powers.[61]

On the issue of Africa's enhanced participation in the shaping of the world, President Touré asked, "Is not African unity the means for the African peoples to ensure their presence not at the base of a pyramid built up through arbitrary action and injustice, but on an equal footing with the other people of all the other continents in the conduct of world affairs?"[62] President of Francophone Chad François Tombalbaye argued, "There is no sense in building Africa in sovereign states, independent of each other for we know that it is from our union, and from it alone, that we draw sufficient strength to assert ourselves in the world."[63] Tombalbaye advocated for cooperation on the international scene and a unified African position, but he did not go so far as to support a political union of African states. While Emperor Selassie stressed that Africa must play a role in the world he also argued its affairs must be its own. He said, "The nations of Africa, as is true of every continent of the world from time to time dispute amongst themselves. These quarrels must be confined to this continent and quarantined from the contamination of non-African interference."[64]

In summary, the major points of disagreement amongst African leaders included diverse views on the most pressing threats facing African states, ranging from interference from major powers leading to neo-colonialism, to territorial disputes and subversion amongst African states. Additionally, African leaders differed on the degree to which they should cooperate with major powers, notably former colonial powers. There was general acceptance that African states should strive for unity, but there was profound disagreement on the speed and process through which unity should be achieved. Despite the areas of disagreement, there were areas of universal agreement. Drawing on common pan-Africanist themes that helped to define regional interests, African leaders agreed that the entire continent must be liberated from the scourge of colonial and racial regimes and that Africa needed to carve out a space for itself within the international sphere and advocate on its own behalf.

Following the opening speeches from Heads of States, the sub-committee comprised of Foreign Ministers who had previously considered draft charters returned to the negotiating table. This time they were given specific instructions to use the Charter draft submitted by Ethiopia as their working document. The sub-committee worked for two days on 23–24 May and then submitted their draft to the Heads of States on the last day of the conference, 25 May 1963.[65] The draft charter was presented, read, debated, and adopted by thirty Heads of States on the same day. While there was a significant amount of debate over the name of the organization, there was relatively little debate over the preamble other than to remove a clause that would have affirmed the belief, "that the aim of the government is the well-being of the governed."[66] The final text of the preamble touches on many of the themes that the leaders iterated in their opening speeches, including concern about outside interference, the need for cooperation, and protecting hard won sovereignty and territorial integrity. The charter states:

> Inspired by a common determination to promote understanding among our people and cooperation among our states in response to the aspirations of our people for brotherhood and solidarity, in a larger unity transcending ethnic and national differences,

Convinced that, in order to translate this determination into a dynamic force in the cause of human progress, conditions for peace and security must be established and maintained,

Determined to safeguard and consolidate the hard-won independence as well as sovereignty and territorial integrity of our states, and to fight against neo-colonialism in all its forms.[67]

Article I of the Charter covers the establishment of the OAU, while Article II speaks to the purposes of the Organization. As in several clauses of the preamble, we again see an emphasis on cooperation over a concrete union, non-interference, defeating the last vestiges of colonialism, and protection of sovereignty. The purposes of the OAU articulated in Article II, are:

(a) To coordinate and intensify their cooperation and efforts to achieve a better life for the peoples of Africa;
(b) To defend their sovereignty, their territorial integrity and independence;
(c) To eradicate all forms of colonialism from Africa.[68]

Finally, Article III outlines the principles of the OAU. All seven principles laid down in Article III significantly impacted peace and conflict policies and again echoed the statements in preceding articles. The OAU principles are:

1. The sovereign equality of all Member States.
2. Non-interference in the internal affairs of States.
3. Respect for the sovereignty and territorial integrity of each State and for its inalienable right to independent existence.
4. Peaceful settlement of disputes by negotiation, mediation, conciliation or arbitration.
5. Unreserved condemnation, in all its forms, of political assassination as well as of subversive activities on the part of neighboring States or any other States.
6. Absolute dedication to the total emancipation of the African territories which are still dependent.
7. Affirmation of a policy of non-alignment with regard to all blocs.[69]

The OAU principles were essentially the norms of the regional organization, and they reflect the experiences of the region and African leaders as well as the values and interests of the region. The values and interests of the region were underpinned by particular pan-Africanist ideas, which included a commitment to liberation and fighting against racialism, protecting African independence, and carving out a place for African influence in global society. There was of course dissent on this interpretation of pan-Africanism, but it was the interpretation that the vast majority of African leaders embraced. After decades of colonization and marginalization, the institution of the OAU sought to protect African states by promoting

the sovereignty and territoriality of independent African states and commit-
ting to the liberation of African states still suffering under colonial systems.
Furthermore, particularly after the Congo crisis and the assassination of
the Togolese President, there was concern about interference from major
powers and from other African states. Therefore, African leaders codified
norms of non-interference while condemning subversive activities within
Africa.

Understanding OAU norms

While individual African leaders were the actors debating and choosing
OAU norms, I stress the interplay of the agency of the leaders and the structure of the regional organization because it was the framework that allowed
for debate and multiple factors to come together to determine a regional
position. Ultimately, OAU norms aligned with regional priorities and were
based on a common understanding of pan-Africanist ideas. This shows
ideas and interests being mutually constitutive as the regional organization
sought to protect newly formed African states, enhance Africa's position in
the international system, and secure the African region from threats while
pursuing the final liberation of the continent and respect in the international
system.

OAU norms were largely in line with the prevailing norms of an
international system that also prioritized state sovereignty. However, that
does not mean there was no agency by African leaders when they chose
these norms for the OAU. There were several options that were proposed
by various African leaders, and the norms that were codified in the OAU
Charter were those that would best ensure the final liberation of the continent, secure Africa's place in the world, and protect independent African
states from interference. Furthermore, OAU norms went beyond simply
framing international norms in the local context or grafting the norm onto
local practices. Instead, the OAU Charter adapted international norms in
innovative ways to enhance the sovereignty and legitimacy of independent
African states while undermining colonial and white-minority regimes.
Understanding this process offers insights into processes of norm creation
within regions based on regional experiences, interests, and values. Instead
of simply creating regional norms based on international norms, the
regional body crafted innovative norms that then contributed to debates
about norms in international society.

There are of course critiques of the OAU and the vision of pan-Africanism
African leaders chose to embrace for their regional organization. Clapham
asserts:

The relations between African states were suffused with a rhetoric of solidarity which constantly emphasized their "unity", characteristically in opposition to external domination and especially colonialism. Like any political rhetoric, that of Pan-Africanism served in large part to conceal unpalatable truths ... The rhetoric of unity papered over the extreme reluctance of any but a very small minority of African rulers to sacrifice any of their power in the interests of any continental grouping.[70]

However, based on events from the decades leading up to independence, African leaders had good reason to adopt an interpretation of pan-Africanism that prioritized state security over a political union. The UN investigation into Liberia, the international response to the Italian invasion of Abyssinia, and the reluctance of colonial powers to grant independence showed African leaders that they should be concerned about state sovereignty. African leaders wanted to shore up their independence and use the rules of the international system to protect their status while undermining continuing white-minority and colonial regimes. In hindsight, absolute protection of state sovereignty had many consequences, which will be explored in subsequent chapters, and individual African states certainly turned to external powers when it suited their needs. But this volume is not about determining the utility of OAU or AU norms. It is about the processes by which these norms were created within the regional organization in order to understand why particular norms were chosen and the role of regional organizations in norm creation and diffusion.

As such, the norms chosen at the advent of the OAU can be viewed to a limited extent through subsidiarity described as a process in which, "local actors develop new rules, offer new understandings of global rules, or reaffirm rules in the regional context in order to preserve their autonomy from dominance, neglect, violation, or abuse by more powerful central actors."[71] The OAU offered new understandings and interpretations of global norms, and they also codified several norms with the explicit aim of protecting against outside dominance. However, subsidiarity is not a perfect fit through which to view this process because OAU norms were not simply to protect against outside domination. Instead the norms were meant to protect member states from outside domination, interference from both international and regional actors, and subversion from other African states. The extent of the innovation shown in OAU norms to simultaneously enhance the legitimacy of independent African states while diminishing regimes and behaviors that threaten independent Africa was profound. Therefore, while subsidiarity is a valuable framework for understanding norm creation in marginalized regions, there needs to be further theoretical frameworks that expound on the complexity of norm creation in regions that is not dependent on regions reacting to outside actors.

Protection from domination and interference

All of the leaders who attended the OAU founding conference were leaders of states that had been granted political independence. However, the experiences of the inter-war period and independence struggles taught many independence era leaders that African states must demand rights and continue to guard against outside political domination to protect existing rights. Despite being recognized states in the international system, the lack of action by the international community when Italy invaded Abyssinia indicated to some African leaders that African statehood was less respected than western statehood. There was also outrage amongst pan-Africanists when an international investigation into slavery in Liberia led to suggestions of a trusteeship with no mention of atrocities committed against Africans by colonial powers. Furthermore, the events within Africa in the immediate independence era showed other African leaders that they should be wary of interference from African states. Specifically, the Congo crisis led to stark disagreements amongst African leaders about the appropriateness of interventions by the UN, former colonial powers, and African troops, and the assassination of Togolese President Olympio just months before the creation of the OAU during a coup d'état created concerns about subversion from other African states.

As emphasized in speeches from African Heads of States and in the OAU Charter, the first great tasks of independence were to ensure the eradication of colonialism, build up Africa's legitimacy in the international system, and protect nascent African states against both internal and external threats. After a long history with colonialism and often bloody struggles to gain independence, African leaders were most concerned with maintaining their sovereignty and protecting against outside domination mostly from major powers but also from within the continent. This concern was expressed at the founding conference and throughout the early years of the OAU. At an OAU debate in 1964, the delegate from the Malagasy Republic emphasized:

> After having lost our liberty for years, having been under the yoke of colonialism, when we have now, with the granting of independence, just re-ordered this liberty, must we today lose it again to a supranational government with all the attribution [sic] which are comprised therein? How can internal sovereignty, or perhaps just the internal or external sovereignty of a country, be reconciled with the attributions of a supranational government?[72]

This demonstrates why African leaders were reluctant to push forward with a strong union government immediately after independence. African states had just been granted independence, and most African leaders were loath to give up any degree of sovereignty. The focus was on protecting their states, and despite arguments from Nkrumah about the benefits of a union government, other leaders were not convinced that such an arrangement would best protect African states and the African region more broadly.

The OAU adopted norms protecting sovereignty and territorial integrity because of continuing fears of domination and interference based on pan-Africanist ideas that helped to shape regional interests, advocacy by key leaders, and regional experiences. There were differences amongst the leaders about who they should fear – only outside powers or their fellow African states, but the majority of leaders came down on the side of adopting norms that protected states from both regional and international actors. This became the common regional position seen in OAU norms. In the immediate post-independence era, African leaders saw security as closely linked to the defense of sovereignty, and they constructed a normative framework where the African regional institution prioritized sovereignty as the best means to ensure member state security, enhance Africa's international legitimacy, and expel the last remnants of colonialism from the continent. As summarized by Amate:

> All of the African states that were represented in Addis Ababa were at the time relatively young, weak, and underdeveloped. They were all deeply concerned about the defense of their sovereignty and territorial integrity which they had achieved after much sweat and blood, the development of their human and natural resources, which had up to independence been exploited for the benefit of their colonial rulers, and the eradication of the remaining vestiges of colonialism in Africa, which had continued to remind them of the humiliating plight of their race.[73]

Innovative norms

The OAU took the norms of non-interference, protection of state sovereignty, and the role of regions in the global order and added to them in two important ways. First, the OAU linked adherence to non-interference to state legitimacy defined by the OAU as states agreeing in principle to international norms of racial equality and self-determination. Second, African leaders went beyond asserting a role for Africa in the global community and claimed regional primacy for regional affairs while advocating for internal solutions to African problems.

African leaders went beyond localizing international norms through framing or grafting, and instead they altered the international norms in fundamental ways that also served to guard against domination and interference. Pan-Africanists and other colonized people advocated for a norm of racial equality in the international system. Going back to 1900, pan-Africanist scholars and activists pushed for racial equality and self-determination through various means.[74] Principles of respect for racial equality were enshrined in Article I of the UN Charter and Article II of the UDHR.[75] However, these principles were applied to individuals as they are mentioned in the context of protection of human rights. They were not applied to state behavior as evidenced by members of the UNSC maintaining their colonies for decades after the signing of the UN Charter. In 1963 and throughout the tenure of the OAU, the organization advocated that the legitimacy of states depended on upholding norms of racial equality and self-determination. This is shown in the OAU's support for strict non-interference among independent African states while also authorizing and funding a Liberation Committee to support subversion in white-minority and colonial states. This argument is also made explicit in the Lusaka Manifesto that calls for all states who wish to be recognized in the community of nations to commit in principle to racial equality and self-determination.[76]

Acharya asserts that Nkrumah's efforts to stress non-intervention in African affairs and non-alignment of African states in superpower led alliances also constitutes subsidiarity. Through these principles, Nkrumah helped to develop a norm of regional autonomy.[77] Although the UN Charter gave regions a role to play in the global community, the OAU transcended the language in the UN Charter by claiming a regional right to autonomy for internal affairs. However, it was not just Nkrumah who advocated for this. While many African leaders were willing to cooperate with outside powers when it suited their interests, there was near universal consensus that outside powers should not interfere in internal affairs, particularly matters related to conflict between African states. This is best espoused in Selassie's speech at the OAU conference speech admitting that all regions from time to time have disputes amongst themselves, and Africa must be able to manage its own problems.[78] It was also implemented through the African Group at the UN that, as will be discussed in Chapter 5, largely kept African conflict issues off the UN agenda for decades while simultaneously pursuing UN action against apartheid South Africa.

In sum, the norms codified by the OAU that enshrine protection for state sovereignty, territorial integrity, non-interference, and regional primacy show innovation in norm creation at the regional level. As evidenced by the debates at the OAU founding conference, there were various paths the regional organization could have followed when selecting norms for its charter. OAU norms reflect a common understanding of the most important pan-Africanist principles of securing the final liberation of the continent and ensuring the protection of African states and their place in the world. These ideas and regional experiences helped to define Africa's fundamental interests and values, and advocacy by African leaders and regional experiences leading up to and after independence further influenced the selection of OAU norms. By prioritizing state sovereignty, territorial integrity, and non-interference, the OAU codified norms that African leaders believed would best protect member states against domination and interference, liberate the continent, and carve out a place for Africa in the global community.

The OAU transformed these norms in such a way that they shored up the legitimacy of independent African states while diminishing the legitimacy of outside interference and the remaining colonial and white-minority regimes. While subsidiarity offers valuable insights into the process of norm creation at the advent of the OAU, it does not fully encompass the process. OAU norms do not just reflect a fear of domination from powerful states and international actors but rather interference and subversion from within the continent. This shows the complexity of motivations. Furthermore, the scope of the innovation is profound and laid the foundation for a long-term, regional diplomatic strategy to pursue regional interests. As the next chapter will show, linking respect for state sovereignty with respect for the principles of racial equality and self-determination was the basis through which regional institutions sought to shame and exclude colonial and white-minority regimes based on their internal policies. Regional primacy while pursuing engagement in the international community was the basis of diplomatic efforts of the African region along with Global South allies to expand the UNSC and other UN organizations while simultaneously excluding African conflict issues from the UNSC agenda.

Notes

1 Peter A. Hall, "Conclusion: The Politics of Keynesian Ideas," in *The Political Power of Economic Ideas: Keynesianism Across Nations*, ed. Peter A. Hall (Princeton, NJ: Princeton University Press, 1989), 367.
2 C.O.C Amate, *Inside the OAU: Pan-Africanism in Practice* (New York: St Martin's Press, 1986), 57.
3 See history of pan-African movement in Chapter 3.
4 "Charter of the United Nations," 24 October 1945, www.un.org/en/charter-united-nations/index.html (accessed 30 September 2020).
5 "Universal Declaration of Human Rights," 10 December 1948, www.un.org/en/universal-declaration-human-rights/ (accessed 7 May 2020).
6 George Padmore, *History of the Pan-African Congress* (London: The Hammersmith Bookshop Ltd, 1963).
7 "The Lusaka Manifesto on Southern Africa Proclaimed by the Fifth Summit Conference of East and Central African States." Government of the United Republic of Tanzania, 14–16 April 1969, http://reference.sabinet.co.za/webx/access/journal_archive/00020117/33.pdf (accessed 7 May 2020), para. 9.

8 "Charter of the United Nations."
9 Amitav Acharya, "Norm Subsidiarity and Regional Orders: Sovereignty, Regionalism, and Rule-Making in the Third World," *International Studies Quarterly* 55, no. 1 (2022): 115.
10 Charles-Robert Ageron, *Modern Algeria: A History from 1830 to the Present* (London: C. Hurst & Co. Ltd, 1991), 108.
11 Ageron, *Modern Algeria*, 115.
12 Ageron, *Modern Algeria*, 119.
13 Ageron, *Modern Algeria*, 121–22.
14 Klaas Van Walraven, *Dreams of Power: The Role of the Organization of African Unity in the Politics of Africa 1963–1993* (Surrey: Ashgate Publishing Limited, 1999), 102–3.
15 Catherine Hoskyns, "The Part Played by the Independent African States in the Congo Crisis July 1960–December 1961" (Wiesneck: Gutenbergdruckerei Robert Oberkirch, 1963), 34.
16 Hoskyns, "The Part Played," 35.
17 Hoskyns, "The Part Played," 39–40.
18 Hoskyns, "The Part Played," 41–43.
19 Walraven, *Dreams of Power*, 93–95.
20 Amate, *Inside the OAU*, 40.
21 P. Olisanwuche Esedebe, *Pan-Africanism: The Idea and Movement, 1776–1991*, second edition (Washington, DC: Howard University Press, 1994), 175.
22 Amate, *Inside the OAU*, 44.
23 Amate, *Inside the OAU*, 44.
24 Amate, *Inside the OAU*, 46.
25 Amate, *Inside the OAU*, 44–45.
26 Amate, *Inside the OAU*, 47.
27 Amate, *Inside the OAU*, 49.
28 Amate, *Inside the OAU*, 49–50.
29 Ageron, 123–26.
30 Hoskyns, "The Part Played," 45–46.
31 Amate, *Inside the OAU*, 51.
32 Zdenek Cervenka, *The Unfinished Quest for Unity: Africa and the OAU* (London: Julian Friedmann Publishers Ltd, 1977), 4–5.
33 Amate, *Inside the OAU*, 52–53.
34 Cervenka, *The Unfinished Quest for Unity*, 6.
35 Amate, *Inside the OAU*, 56.
36 "1963 Statements His Imperial Majesty Haile Selassie I, Emperor of Ethiopia," in *Celebrating Success: Africa's Voice over 50 Years (1963–2013)* (Addis Ababa: African Union Commission, 2013), 1–6.
37 "1963 Statements His Imperial Majesty Haile Selassie I, Emperor of Ethiopia," 3.
38 "1963 Statements His Imperial Majesty Haile Selassie I," 2–3.
39 "1963 Statements His Imperial Majesty Haile Selassie I," 4.
40 "1963 Statements His Excellency Léopold Sédar Senghor," in *Celebrating*

Success: Africa's Voice over 50 Years (1963–2013) (Addis Ababa: African Union Commission, 1963), 86.

41 "1963 Statements His Excellency Félix Houphouët-Boigny, President of the Republic of Ivory Coast," in *Celebrating Success*, 51–52.

42 "1963 Statements His Excellency Félix Houphouët-Boigny," 50–51.

43 "1963 Statements His Excellency Félix Houphouët-Boigny," 52.

44 "1963 Statements His Excellency Ahmadou Ahidjo, President of the Federal Republic of Cameroon," in *Celebrating Success*, 13.

45 "1963 Statements His Excellency Modibo Keita, President of Mali," in *Celebrating Success*, 70.

46 "1963 Statements His Excellency Modibo Keita," 70.

47 Cervenka, *The Unfinished Quest for Unity*, 9.

48 "1963 Statements His Excellency Alhaji Abubakar Tafawa Balewa, Prime Minister of the Federation of Nigeria," in *Celebrating Success*, 79.

49 "1963 Statements His Excellency Philibert Tsiranana, President of the Malagasy Republic," in *Celebrating Success*, 62.

50 "1963 Statements His Excellency Alhaji Abubakar Tafawa Balewa," 81.

51 "1963 Statements His Excellency Alhaji Abubakar Tafawa Balewa," 82.

52 "1963 Statements His Excellency Kwame N'Krumah," 34.

53 "1963 Statements His Excellency Kwame N'Krumah," 35.

54 "1963 Statements His Excellency Kwame N'Krumah," 38–41.

55 Amate, *Inside the OAU*, 57.

56 "1963 Statements His Excellency Gamal Abdel Nasser, President of the United Arab Republic," in *Celebrating Success*, 111.

57 "1963 Statements His Excellency Gamal Abdel Nasser," 114–15.

58 "1963 Statements His Imperial Majesty Haile Selassie I," 2.

59 "1963 Statements His Excellency Ahmed Ben Bella, Prime Minister of Algeria," in *Celebrating Success*, 8.

60 "1963 Statements His Excellency Fulbert Youlou, President of Congo (Brazzaville)," in *Celebrating Success*, 21.

61 Cervenka, *The Unfinished Quest for Unity*, 8.

62 "1963 Statements His Excellency Sékou Touré, President of the Republic of Guinea," in *Celebrating Success*, 43.

63 "1963 Statements His Excellency François Tombalbaye President of the Republic of Chad," in *Celebrating Success*, 20.

64 "1963 Statements His Imperial Majesty Haile Selassie I," 4.

65 Amate, *Inside the OAU*, 58.

66 Amate, *Inside the OAU*, 59–60.

67 "Organization of African Unity Charter," 1.

68 "Organization of African Unity Charter," 3.

69 "Organization of African Unity Charter," 4.

70 Christopher Clapham, *Africa and the International System: The Politics of State Survival* (Cambridge: Cambridge University Press, 1996), 106–7.

71 Acharya, "Norm Subsidiarity and Regional Orders," 93.

72 "Verbatim Record: Council of Ministers First Committee (Political): Third

Session – Afternoon Session," CM (III) (1)/ SR.2 (Organization of African Unity, 14 July 1964), 12–13. AU Commission Archives.

73 Amate, *Inside the OAU*, 60–61.
74 Du Bois, "The Pan-African Movement."
75 "Charter of the United Nations"; "Universal Declaration of Human Rights."
76 "Lusaka Manifesto."
77 Acharya, "Norm Subsidiarity and Regional Orders," 115.
78 "1963 Statements His Imperial Majesty Haile Selassie I," 4.

5

The institutions and policies of the Organization of African Unity

Following the signing of the Charter, member states built up the OAU and created policies that reflected the organization's principles. The institutional priorities within the OAU reflected the norms chosen by the founding members, and the institutions that were most robust within the OAU were the Liberation Committee and the African Group at the United Nations. Other institutions, such as the Commission of Mediation, Conciliation and Arbitration and Defense Commission, were never fully functioning. Additionally, the policies, including the conflict management policy, which focused on peaceful resolution of disputes and non-interference, were also in line with OAU norms.

The African leaders who created the OAU recognized the danger of conflict on the continent and sought to create institutions to help African states address conflict. However, the danger of conflict within and between African states was viewed as a far lesser threat than encroachments on sovereignty and territorial integrity as well as the continued existence of colonization and white-minority regimes. These priorities were evident when the leaders of Africa met for the First Ordinary Session of the OAU in 1964. Of the resolutions adopted at the session, the leaders discussed the grave threats that border problems posed for Africa and affirmed that, "the borders of African states, on the day of their independence, constitute a tangible reality."[1] Other resolutions addressed the racial policies of South Africa, the matter of Southern Rhodesia, territories under Portuguese domination, as well as many others addressing current African disputes and the work of OAU institutions.[2] The institutions that were prioritized to receive funding and the issues that became the focus of discussions demonstrate the priorities of the OAU, and provide evidence that the OAU principles were not just enshrined in the Charter but in the organizational structure and policies.

Early OAU institutions and policies

Commission of Mediation, Conciliation and Arbitration

The Protocol of the Commission of Mediation, Conciliation and Arbitration was also signed during the First Ordinary Session on 21 July 1964. The peaceful settlement of disputes by negotiation, mediation, conciliation, or arbitration is enshrined as a principle of the OAU in Article III of the Charter. To support this principle the Commission of Mediation, Conciliation and Arbitration was created as one of the four main institutions of the OAU.[3] Part I of the Protocol stipulates the creation of a 21-member commission of people with recognized legal and professional qualifications. Part II lays down the general provisions of the Commission, including that it only has jurisdiction over disputes between states. A dispute may be referred to the Commission by the parties to the dispute, the Council of Ministers, or the Assembly of Heads of State and Government. However, if a state refuses to submit itself to the jurisdiction of the Commission there is little recourse to force the state to participate. The only recourse prescribed by the Protocol is that the matter can then be referred to the Council of Ministers for consideration.[4]

Given the importance that the OAU placed on the peaceful settlement of disputes, the Commission should have been given more prominence in the organization. However, despite the Commission being of interest to African leaders it was never fully resourced or utilized. This indicates that while African leaders paid lip service to conflict resolution, the priority was state security. During the first few years of the OAU, the Commission was included regularly on the agendas of OAU Heads of State and Government Summits. In 1966, the Heads of State and Government included a report on the progress of the Commission's work in the summit agenda along with several additional agenda items devoted to inter-state relations between African states in conflict with each other.[5] Unfortunately, the attention it was given in the early years of the OAU does not paint an accurate picture of the internal support for the Commission. In reality, it accomplished no tangible results, and its activities were hampered due to bureaucratic wrangling at almost every turn.

The 21 members of the Commission, as well as chair and vice-chair, were elected at the summit in Accra, Ghana in October 1965.[6] The background and expertise of the Commission's first members reflect the intent of African leaders to ensure the Commission had a judicial focus, thus limiting its ability to engage in political matters related to disputes. The first Chair, M.A. Odesanya, was Secretary General of the Bar Association of Nigeria. He had a long and distinguished law career in Nigeria where he headed a firm of lawyers in Lagos and was a legal advisor for notable organizations, including the Bank of Nigeria. While there were a few former ambassadors and parliamentarians elected to serve on the Commission the vast majority were attorneys, legal advisors, and judges.[7] Even after appointing staff to the Commission, it took several years for it to receive the funding and resources needed to be minimally operational. The first interim funds arrived in September 1967; the president of the Commission did not have a physical office until April 1968; and the two vice-presidents of the Commission did not take up their posts until January 1969.[8]

In 1968, in the midst of the Nigerian-Biafran civil war, the OAU Council of Ministers finally gave the Commission a very small budget for staff salaries and wages.[9] In his report to the OAU Council of Ministers in September 1967, the president of the Commission, Justice M.A. Odesanya, pleaded for the resources to enable the Commission to begin their work. He states:

> Funds ought to be provided now for the inaugural meeting of the Commission and for the interim remuneration of the members of the Bureau comprising the president and his two vice-presidents. I have so far had the opportunity of meeting only three members of my commission ... I have never met either of my two vice-presidents who according to the Protocol of my commission are to take important administrative and other decisions with me at the commission's Secretariat which has yet to be set up.[10]

The first formal meeting of the Commission did not take place until December 1967. It was attended by Haile Selassie and OAU Secretary General Diallo Telli, both of whom emphasized the important work of the Commission and the necessity to achieve peace and security before any other aspirations of the OAU could be achieved.[11] However, the supportive words were not backed-up by action to ensure that the Commission had the necessary resources and political support to fulfil its mandate. Justice Odesanya detailed the fundamental constraints of the Commission. He explained that, "under international law, no sovereign state could, without its consent, be compelled to submit to mediation, conciliation, or arbitration or to any other form of peaceful settlement. All the Council of Ministers could do would be to resort to diplomacy, persuasion, or refer the matter to the Assembly of Heads of States."[12] The mandate of the Commission extended only to inter-state disputes and excluded all internal state conflicts. The Commission also did not have any mandate to undertake conflict prevention work, so their only recourse was to address conflict issues in Africa after violence had broken out.

These were the constraints that the Commission operated under. Thus, its ineffectiveness was pre-ordained from the moment the member states chose to enshrine absolute non-interference and protection of state sovereignty and territorial integrity. Member states were very wary of supranational authority that might curtail any of their sovereign rights, and as a result the Commission was never given the mandate or resources to operate. Despite the lip service paid to the importance of conflict resolution and peaceful settlement of disputes, the actions of the OAU with regard to the Commission of Mediation, Conciliation and Arbitration paint a different picture. These actions show an allegiance to state security and the prioritization of sovereignty that manifested in a non-interference conflict management policy and weak institutional mechanisms to address conflict and atrocities.

The reality of the OAU approach to conflict management in the first decade was that it relied largely on important leaders on the continent to offer counsel and facilitate negotiation, and member states were encouraged to compromise and find an agreeable solution. In addition, it was mostly ad hoc except for coordinated efforts to prevent interference in internal affairs and promote regional primacy in managing conflicts in Africa.[13] Some OAU internal documents praise the work of ad hoc committees and their success at resolving conflicts, but in practice, they were often ineffective. Several of the resolutions reached through the good offices of ad hoc committees were simply temporary solutions that did not last. For example, the ad hoc body formed to manage the border dispute between Algeria and Morocco during the early days of the OAU had multiple meetings and few results over the several years of its existence. When it was first established, the Ad Hoc Commission on the Algeria-Moroccan Border Dispute was instructed by the Council of Ministers to investigate and designate blame for the outbreak of fighting between Algeria and Morocco in 1963 and put forward specific recommendations to settle the dispute. However, there was a debate about whether or not the Commission could hand down binding recommendations that was never settled by the Council of Ministers.[14] There were also ad hoc bodies formed to manage border disputes between Ethiopia and Somalia, Kenya and Somalia, and Rwanda and Burundi in the late 1960s.[15]

There were attempts by the Council of Ministers and Assembly of Heads of State and Government to reform the Commission in 1970 and 1977. In 1970, the push to reform the Commission came from concerns about its effectiveness and economy of spending. Liberia proposed that the Commission should function on an ad hoc basis because the permanent bureau comprised of the president, vice-president, and small office staff was not receiving enough work to justify a permanent space and full-time salaries.[16] The Commission was subsequently converted to a part-time body that would conduct its business when called upon, further weakening its ability to be effective. It was also decided that the member states involved in the dispute would have to meet all the expenses of the Commission members to decrease the OAU's costs.[17] Placing the expense burden for dispute resolution on states in the midst of violent conflict did nothing to encourage the use of the Commission, so it continued to lie dormant.

The catalyst for the 1977 attempt to re-energize the Commission of Mediation, Conciliation and Arbitration was the numerous disputes brought before the OAU that year, including disputes between Ethiopia and Sudan, Ethiopia and Somalia, Libya and Chad, and Tanzania and Uganda, among others.[18] At this juncture, the Assembly of Heads of State and Government tasked the OAU Administrative Secretary General with urgently considering the Protocol of the Commission of Mediation, Conciliation and Arbitration in order to submit recommendations to the Council of Ministers for how to make it a more effective body to respond to conflicts in Africa. The Administrative Secretary General recommended an amendment to the Protocol wherein member states instead of individuals would be elected to the Commission and then the member states would be bound to designate a judicially qualified person to serve on the Commission. In the Secretary General's view this would ensure disputes were settled through judicial processes while still accounting for political influence. However, instead of adopting the Secretary General's recommendations the Council of Ministers asked that the recommendations be studied further by legal experts. The Secretary General duly convened a meeting of legal experts and re-submitted the proposal only to have it deferred again and subsequently die.[19]

Instead of pushing the Council of Ministers to adopt amended procedures for the Commission, the Assembly of Heads of State chose again to appoint several ad hoc bodies in the interim period to address the most serious disputes, a practice that continued until the early 1990s.[20] This was in spite of the 1978 Report of the Administrative Secretary General, which pinpointed several issues with the ad hoc approach. The report said:

> The frequent appointment of Ad Hoc Commissions of Member States in the past to deal with disputes between Member States rather than resort to the Commission for Mediation, Arbitration, and Conciliation suggests that the Assembly of Heads of State and Government prefer political efforts for the settlement of disputes between its Members to a judicial enquiry by the Commission ... However, owing to political considerations, attempts are generally not made to probe the dispute in order to establish the case, and therefore find remedy. This would not be the case of the Commission of Mediation, Conciliation and Arbitration, which though taking notice of political considerations, will proceed into the dispute on purely judicial lines. Causes of disputes can thus be pinpointed and remedy recommended.[21]

The result of relying on ad hoc commissions and failing to provide the Commission of Mediation, Conciliation and Arbitration with an adequate framework and resources was a conflict prevention and management system that only acted to prevent the worst conflicts from breaking out and neglected coordinated efforts to find and implement lasting solutions. However, given the norms that were codified at the advent of the OAU, this conflict management policy is not surprising. The most cherished ideas held by African leaders were the necessity to fully liberate the continent and secure Africa's place in the world. This meant adhering to policies that protected African state security even in the event of internal conflict that had humanitarian consequences. African leaders defined their interests through adherence to their values and saw protecting African state sovereignty as their most important task. However, as the conflicts on the continent began to take their toll, there were attempts to make the conflict management policy more effective through institutional fixes. Unfortunately, none of these reforms were effective because the OAU was still operating within the same normative framework. This shows the importance of ideas in leading the way on institutional reform. It was not until new ideas of human security and sovereignty as responsibility emerged to act as a blueprint that meaningful institutional reform took place.

Defense Commission

Another specialized commission created by the OAU Charter was the Defense Commission. Article XX stipulated the creation of the Defense Commission. However, the Charter did not spell out the function of the Commission.[22] That debate was left to the First Ordinary Session of the Defense Commission held in Accra from 29 October to 2 November 1963. There were many proposals put forward, ranging from a continent-wide military high command supported by President Nkrumah, to less ambitious proposals centered around collaboration and training. The proposal that was accepted as the basis of discussion and ultimately adopted defined the functions of the Defense Commission as training military officers and specialists, facilitating joint exercises and periodic exchange of information, and establishing an emergency task force for the maintenance of peace and security.[23] However, as with the Commission on Mediation, Arbitration and Conciliation, little was done to implement the proposals or ensure the Defense Commission had sufficient resources to function. This may appear odd given that a strong Defense Commission could enhance the physical security and territorial integrity of African states. However, rather than being seen as only enhancing security, it was largely seen as a push towards greater unity, and a strong union government was viewed as a possible means to undercut state sovereignty.

The second meeting of the Commission took place from 2–4 February 1965, after which there was a gap of several years before the next meeting because the OAU Administrative Secretary General could not muster the necessary attendance to meet the quorum requirements. The Administrative Secretary General detailed the multiple attempts to convene a meeting of the Defense Commission without success and raised concerns about the indifference of member states to the collective defense and security of the African continent.[24] However, at the end of 1970, the Defense Commission met simultaneously with the Seventh Extra-Ordinary Session of the Council of Ministers because of an urgent situation of Portuguese aggression against the Republic of Guinea.[25] Aggression by a colonial power provided the impetus to once again commence discussion about establishing an adequate continental defense system for Africa. This example again demonstrates that Africa's regional priorities were eradicating colonialism and protecting African states. When a colonial power threatened the sovereignty and territorial integrity of African states there was a re-constituted effort to reform the Defense Commission.

In 1971, the Defense Commission recommended strengthening the technical defense expertise within the OAU General Secretariat and creating sub-regional defense units to be placed at the disposal of the OAU. In 1972, a 15-state committee was established to consider the recommendations of the Defense Commission as well as offer proposals on a common policy towards independent states and the standardization of military training. The committee met in 1973 and then presented its findings to the Council of Ministers. However, at this point the crisis with Portuguese aggression had faded into the distant past, so a decision on implementing any recommendations was deferred until all OAU member states were given an opportunity to study the committee's report and offer feedback.[26] Another incident of Portuguese aggression prompted both the OAU Council of Ministers and Liberation Committee to call upon the Defense Commission to urgently convene in early 1974. The Defense Commission then considered the recommendations from the 15-state committee but also decided to defer adopting them until after technical experts were set up as defense advisors in the OAU General Secretariat.[27] Thus the pattern of making recommendations and deferring important decisions continued in a way that gutted the capacity of the Defense Commission.

The difficulty in convening the Defense Commission was emblematic of the wariness that persisted throughout the OAU period and beyond about collective peace and security efforts; and the junctures at which there were renewed pushes for reforms indicates the primacy of Africa's goals to eradicate colonial regimes and protect independent African states. Through the Defense Commission we see a reinforcement of the norms that mattered to African leaders. The Defense Commission and, in general, a more unified defense policy were seen as part of an agenda to further unify the continent.

While the Defense Commission may have been valuable in protecting the territorial integrity of states it may have simultaneously diminished individual state sovereignty. The points at which there was interest in renewing the Defense Commission were when there was a more imminent threat from colonial powers. Thus, African leaders prioritized the Defense Commission when it served their primary goal of ensuring the total liberation of the continent.

African Group at the United Nations

While the Commission on Mediation, Conciliation and Arbitration and Defense Commission stagnated during the 1960s–1970s, the African Group at the UN and the Liberation Committee were perhaps the most active and effective bodies within the OAU. There had been collaboration amongst independent African states at the UN since the first conference of African states in 1958. However, there were splits in Africa between the Casablanca and Brazzaville groups that at times inhibited cooperation. With the founding of the OAU, independence era leaders passed a resolution calling African governments to constitute a more effective African Group at the UN. They stipulated that the reconstituted African Group should have a permanent secretariat to work towards achieving more equitable representation for Africa within the UN, particularly on the UNSC and Economic and Social Council.[28] There was initial confusion about how the African Group would operate, but it managed to adopt a workable operational framework and achieve results very early on. By December 1963, the African Group, in partnership with Latin American countries, convinced the UN to amend the Charter to increase the seats on the Security Council from 11 to 15, which raised the number of rotating seats from six to 10. The membership of the Economic and Social Council was also raised from 18 to 27 to allow for more participation by regions not represented at the founding conference of the UN.[29]

In 1965, the OAU Secretary General negotiated and signed an agreement of cooperation with the UN Secretary General and subsequently signed agreements with the heads of several UN agencies, including the UN Development Programme, Food and Agriculture Organization, UN High Commission for Refugees, and World Health Organization, among others. These agreements stipulated that UN agencies consult with the OAU when creating and implementing programs in Africa. They also provided ample opportunities for collaboration through training and conferences. In this regard, the OAU was a leader in institutionalizing a relationship between a regional organization and the UN.[30] The OAU was also institutionalizing its norm of regional primacy by working within the international system to construct agreements that mandated international organizations consult the OAU when operating in the African region. African states sought to embed themselves in the UN to enhance their influence and also craft the agenda where it suited their principles and regional interests. In practice this meant using the UN to condemn colonial and white-minority regimes to achieve total liberation while simultaneously keeping internal disputes within and amongst independent African states off the UNSC agenda.

The African Group played a critical role in keeping apartheid and decolonization issues on the agenda at the UN. Between 1967 and 1975, African states spoke about 42 different issues in front of the UN, including disarmament, economic development, and the Middle East. However, decolonization was by far the issue most persistently highlighted by African countries, with 94 percent of African states that spoke at the UN raising the issue at some point.[31] On the issue of apartheid, the African Group sought to discredit the government of South Africa within the UN system and pushed the Security Council to adopt more punitive measures in response to the government's racist policies. In 1974, the Africa Group succeeded in getting South Africa's credentials revoked for the General Assembly session, meaning that the country was not permitted to take a seat, speak, make proposals, or vote. The Tanzanian representative said:

> The Government of Tanzania is now convinced that the time has come for the UN to reconsider its relationship with South Africa because of the racist policies of that country ... We submit that every single day that apartheid South Africa continues to enjoy the rights and privileges of a member of this organization, while completely ignoring and violating the corresponding obligations of membership makes a mockery of the United Nations.[32]

This demonstrates the implementation of the OAU linking state legitimacy, and thus being afforded the privileges of sovereign states, with respect in principle for racial equality and self-determination.

Beyond expanding their influence in key UN institutions and pushing the UN on the issues that mattered most to Africa, the African Group also expertly patrolled the African issues that the UN took up, thus asserting the norm of regional primacy. After the debacle that was the UN peacekeeping mission in the Congo in the early 1960s, many African states were reluctant to allow UN involvement in solving conflicts in Africa, and the African Group was able to use its influence and sheer numbers to block UN discussion on African conflict issues unless there was unanimous agreement amongst African states to allow UN engagement. For example, the UN did not discuss the Nigerian-Biafran civil war despite strong interest at the international level due to the humanitarian costs of the conflict.[33] Instead, the African Group used it influence to focus UN attention on what it saw as causes of conflict, namely economic and social issues as well as racism and continuing colonization. The work of the African Group perfectly summarizes the priorities of wider OAU efforts – to protect African sovereignty, to expand the influence of Africa in the international community, and to eradicate colonial and white-minority regimes.

Liberation Committee

The end of colonial and white-minority regimes on the African continent were central missions of the OAU. The first two resolutions adopted by the founding leaders of the OAU in 1963 pertained to liberation issues and established a Liberation Committee to be initially comprised of Algeria, Ethiopia, Guinea, Congo, Nigeria, Senegal, Tanganyika, United Arab Republic, and Uganda. The resolutions went on to call all African countries to break diplomatic ties with Portugal and South Africa and also affirmed independent Africa's commitment to receive nationalists from liberation movements and give material aid to these movements.[34] Unlike other OAU commissions discussed at the founding conference, the Liberation Committee was created immediately and held its first meeting in June 1963. It is an early indication of the priority placed on supporting liberation because the continuation of colonial regimes represented an egregious affront to OAU values as well as the most pressing security threat faced by Africa.

The Liberation Committee was responsible for coordinating all assistance to liberation movements and managing a special fund set up to provide financial support. It was also responsible for promoting unity of action among liberation movements and when needed mediating between them to reconcile efforts.[35] Initially, the committee members decided to create three sub-committees to oversee political policy, defense policy, and finances. The role of the general policy committee was to consider political and publicity aspects of the liberation struggle. The role of the defense committee was to manage all requests for material aid and training assistance. The role of the finance committee was of course to manage the budget and advise the other committees on the resources available for their work.[36] The composition and activities of the Liberation Committee may have changed slightly over time and varied from providing material support to engaging diplomatically on behalf of liberation movements. However, the focus always remained on ensuring total liberation of the continent, and reform efforts often resulted in more resources. For instance, at the 1972 OAU Summit in Rabat, member states decided to increase contributions to the Liberation Committee's special fund by 50 percent, grant representatives of liberation movements the right to speak at OAU meetings, and expand the membership of the Liberation Committee.[37]

The OAU's decolonization strategies also evolved over time to become more ambitious and reflect the changing conditions on the continent. For instance, at the Fifth Summit Conference of East and Central African States in Lusaka from 14–16 April 1969, African leaders adopted the Lusaka Manifesto. The Manifesto articulates the position of the signatory states against the discriminatory regimes of Southern Africa and their reasoning for participating in the liberation movement through the auspices of the OAU. It was later endorsed through the OAU and used as a basis for liberation policy. The Manifesto states:

> The truth is, however, that in Mozambique, Angola, South-West Africa, and the Union of South Africa, there is an open and continued denial of the principles of human equality and self-determination. This is not a matter of failure in the implementation of accepted principles. The effective Administrations in all these territories are not struggling towards these difficult goals. They are fighting the principles.[38]
>
> While peaceful progress is blocked by actions of those at present in power in the States of Southern Africa, we have no choice but to give to the peoples of those territories all the support of which we are capable in their struggle against their oppressors. This is why the signatory states participate in the movement for the liberation of Africa under the aegis of the Organization of African Unity.[39]
>
> The Union of South Africa is itself an independent sovereign State and a Member of the United Nations. It is more highly developed and richer than any other nation in Africa. On every legal basis its internal affairs are a matter exclusively for the people of South Africa. Yet the purpose of law is people and we assert that the actions of the South African Government are such that the rest of the world has a responsibility to take some action in defense of humanity.[40]

In this manifesto we see the linkages between sub-regional liberation movements and the OAU. The OAU Assembly of Heads of State and Government endorsed the Lusaka Manifesto in 1969, and the OAU then took it to the UN where the General Assembly adopted a resolution welcoming the Manifesto on 20 November 1969.[41] It also demonstrates the explicit framing of state legitimacy as states that in principle accept self-determination and reject racialism.

The Lusaka Manifesto sought to discredit South Africa's claims that its policies were an internal matter that other states had no right to intervene in.[42] Here we see the OAU's non-interference norm in action. Non-interference was accorded to states that agreed in principle to racial equality and self-determination. When a state abrogates these principles, their policies become the concern of outside actors. Within Africa, this reasoning justified financial and material support to liberation movements that explicitly sought to interfere in the internal affairs of colonial and white-minority states. The Lusaka Manifesto solidified a unified African position on relations with South Africa, and African states worked together in the OAU and in the UN to try to isolate and impose sanctions on South Africa. The OAU non-interference norm enhanced the protections for independent African states and led to a conflict management policy of non-interference even in egregious cases in independent states. However, by linking adherence of non-interference to the acceptance of certain principles, namely racial equality and self-determination, independent African states were able to justify a regional policy that actively sought to undermine the internal policies of colonial and white-minority regimes.

In the first years of the OAU, the institutions and policies that were created within the OAU demonstrate adherence to the regional norms of non-interference, protection of state sovereignty and territoriality, and engagement with the international while insisting on regional primacy. They also show a commitment to the OAU goals of eradicating colonial and white-minority regimes and enhancing Africa's place in the world. This is not to say that these norms were fully internalized amongst member states, only that they were adopted and institutionalized within the OAU. The Committee of Mediation, Conciliation and Arbitration was given an unworkable mandate and scant funding. The Defense Committee was also never fully formed or funded, and interest in resuscitating it only emerged when there was a threat from an outside power. Meanwhile, the Africa Group at the UN and the Liberation Committee were given sufficient resources and political attention to work effectively. The Africa Group ensured outside powers did not interfere in African conflicts while also pushing international institutions to condemn states that did not endorse the principles of racial equality and self-determination. The Liberation Committee was devoted to the OAU's central mission of liberating the continent by aiding liberation movements and protecting the territorial integrity and state sovereignty of independent African states.

Notes

1 "Resolutions Adopted by the First Ordinary Session of the Assembly of Heads of State and Government in Cairo, UAR, From 17 to 21 July 1964" (Organization of African Unity, 1964), https://au.int/sites/default/files/decisions/9514-1964_ahg_res_1–24_i_e.pdf (accessed 7 May 2020), 17.
2 "Resolutions Adopted by the First Ordinary Session of the Assembly of Heads of State and Government in Cairo, UAR, From 17 to 21 July 1964."
3 "Organization of African Unity Charter," 25 May 1963, https://au.int/en/treaties/oau-charter-addis-ababa-25-may-1963 (accessed 7 May 2020).

4 "Protocol of the Commission of Mediation, Conciliation and Arbitration," *International Legal Materials* 3, no. 6 (1964): 1116–24.

5 "Provisional Agenda for the Third Ordinary Session of the Assembly of Heads of State and Government," AHG/13 (Organization of African Unity, November 1966). AU Commission Archives.

6 "Provisional Agenda for the Second Ordinary Session of the Assembly of Heads of State and Government," AHG/5 (Organization of African Unity, October 1965). AU Commission Archives.

7 "OAU Review 1963–1968: Special Issue – Fifth OAU Summit – Algiers Sept 1968" (Organization of African Unity, September 1968), 53–54. AU Commission Archives.

8 "Amendments to the Charter and the Protocol of the Commission of Mediation, Conciliation and Arbitration," CM/334 (Organization of African Unity, August 1970), 1. AU Commission Archives.

9 "Supplementary Budget of the Commission of Mediation, Conciliation and Arbitration of the Organization of African Unity," CM/219 (Organization of African Unity, September 1968). AU Commission Archives.

10 Justice M.A. Odesanya, "Report of the President of the Commission of Mediation, Conciliation and Arbitration," CM/172/Add. 2 (Organization of African Unity, September 1967), 2. AU Commission Archives.

11 C.O.C. Amate, *Inside the OAU: Pan-Africanism in Practice* (New York: St. Martin's Press, 1986) 157–58.

12 Amate, *Inside the OAU*, 158.

13 Zdenek Cervenka, *The Unfinished Quest for Unity: Africa and the OAU* (London: Julian Friedmann Publishers Ltd, 1977), 65.

14 "Resolving Conflicts in Africa: Implementation Options," 1993, 8. AU Commission Archives.

15 "Report of the Administrative Secretary-General of the OAU: A Review of the Years 1963–1968," CM/212 (Organization of African Unity, September 1968), 54–55. AU Commission Archives.

16 "Report of the Administrative Secretary-General on the Commission of Mediation, Conciliation and Arbitration," CM/315 (Organization of African Unity, February-March 1970), 2. AU Commission Archives.

17 "Resolving Conflicts in Africa: Implementation Options," 1993, 9. AU Commission Archives.

18 Amate, *Inside the OAU*, 162–63.

19 "Resolving Conflicts in Africa," 10–11.

20 Amate, *Inside the OAU*, 164.

21 "Report of the Administrative Secretary-General of the Commission of Mediation, Conciliation and Arbitration," CM/924 (XXXI) (Organization of African Unity, July 1978), 3. AU Commission Archives.

22 "Organization of African Unity Charter."

23 Amate, *Inside the OAU*, 170–71.

24 "Report of the Administrative Secretary-General on the Third Session of the Defence Commission," CM/340 (XV) (Organization of African Unity, August 1970), 1–2. AU Commission Archives.

25 "Report of the Administrative Secretary General on the Co-Ordination of Africa's Defence System," CM/655 (XXV) (Organization of African Unity, 18–27 July 1975), 1–2. AU Commission Archives.

26 "Report of the Administrative Secretary-General on the Co-Ordination of Africa's Defence System," 2–3.

27 "Report of the Administrative Secretary-General on the Co-Ordination of Africa's Defence System," 4.

28 "Resolutions Adopted by the First Conference of Independent African Heads of State and Government Held in Addis Ababa, Ethiopia, from 22 to 25 May 1963" (Organization of African Unity, 22–25 May 1963), https://au.int/sites/default/files/decisions/32247-1963_cias_plen_2–3_cias_res_1–2_e.pdf (accessed 7 May 2020).

29 Amate, *Inside the OAU*, 199.

30 Amate, *Inside the OAU*, 195.

31 Gregory L. Wilkins, *African Influence in the United Nations, 1967–1975: The Politics and Techniques of Gaining Compliance to UN Principles and Resolutions* (Washington DC: University Press of America, 1981), 26.

32 Wilkins, *African Influence in the United Nations*, 71.

33 Thomas Hovet, "Effect of the Africa Group of States on the Behaviour of the United Nations," in *Africa and International Organization*, ed. Yassin El-Ayouty and Hugh C. Brooks (The Hague: Martinus Njihoff, 1974), 12.

34 "Resolutions Adopted by the First Conference of Independent African Heads of State and Government Held in Addis Ababa, Ethiopia, from 22 to 25 May 1963."

35 Cervenka, *The Unfinished Quest for Unity*, 50.

36 Amate, *Inside the OAU*, 215–16.

37 Amate, *Inside the OAU*, 233–35.

38 "The Lusaka Manifesto on Southern Africa Proclaimed by the Fifth Summit Conference of East and Central African States," Government of the United Republic of Tanzania, 14–16 April 1969, para. 6, http://reference.sabinet.co.za/webx/access/journal_archive/00020117/33.pdf (accessed 7 May 2020).

39 "Lusaka Manifesto," para. 12.

40 "Lusaka Manifesto," para. 20.

41 Cervenka, *The Unfinished Quest for Unity*, 115–16.

42 Cervenka, *The Unfinished Quest for Unity*, 115–16.

6

The first decade of the Organization
of African Unity

The OAU's priorities were illustrated not only by the Charter but also by the institutions that were established and more importantly adequately funded and supported. Similarly, the OAU's response to conflicts was a further reflection of the norms chosen by the OAU and the priorities of the organization. The non-interference conflict management policy became firmly established, and the focus of the OAU's work to address conflict on the continent was appealing to the parties of the conflict to find a peaceful solution and to keep major powers out of African conflict issues. This chapter will demonstrate implementation of the non-interference conflict management policy and practice in the first decade of the OAU, and will also pinpoint the first indications of a shift. As conflicts began to take a toll and as the face of leadership in Africa changed there were pushes to move away from a strict non-interference policy, but the ideas were not yet there to guide a policy or institutional shift. The process of shifting away from OAU norms to AU norms was again premised on the experiences of region, advocacy by key leaders, and evolving pan-Africanist ideas that helped to shape regional interests and values.

Changes in African leadership

In the first decade of the OAU there were many changes to the membership of the organization and the representatives of member states. After the founding conference many more African states became independent. Additionally, the leadership of member states changed. Most notably Ghanaian President Kwame Nkrumah, who was Ghana's first president upon independence in 1957, was removed from office by a military coup in 1966.[1] Nkrumah was the fiercest and most consistent advocate for a strong political union among African states and, until he was deposed, he pushed the OAU at every opportunity to develop a stronger union. Emperor Haile Selassie, another giant of the cause of African unity, was deposed in 1974 after a revolt by the army in response to worsening conditions in Ethiopia. He died a year later in 1975.[2] Selassie was far more moderate than Nkrumah to be sure and generally favored a gradual approach to African union. However, the prestige of Ethiopia as one of the few African countries to resist colonialism and his leadership at the founding conference in 1963 were pivotal to African states reaching an agreement on the OAU Charter.

Several presidents who would have a profound impact on the OAU also came into power during this period or emerged as more prominent continental leaders. Colonel Muammar Al-Gaddafi came to power in Libya in 1970 after a 1969 uprising.[3] Gaddafi was staunchly opposed to the west and was active in both the pan-Arab and pan-African movements. Kenya became independent shortly after the 1963 OAU founding conference, and Jomo Kenyatta was named Prime Minister and then became President in 1964. Kenyatta had been a long-time pan-Africanist and was involved in planning the 1945 Manchester Conference.[4] Finally, Tanzanian President Julius Nyerere began to rise in prominence on the continental stage. Nyerere was also a committed pan-Africanist, and Tanzania was very supportive of OAU liberation activities while also challenging the OAU's stance on non-intervention.[5]

African conflicts and the reaction of the nascent OAU

The conflicts that emerged in Africa after the creation of the OAU were predominantly dealt with through ad hoc measures, namely commissions comprised of political leaders. In some instances, the ad hoc approach led to a resolution, though this was rare and even these were typically resolutions to end the immediate violence and not address the underlying issues. The OAU had no enforcement mechanisms, so outcomes were dependent on the willingness of the parties to find a solution and, to a certain degree, the mediating ability and prestige of the political leaders appointed to manage the conflict. The OAU focused almost exclusively on addressing issues between African states and largely did not get involved in conflicts that were internal or even gross human rights abuses. The exception to this rule was when an internal conflict reached such a magnitude that it was attracting international attention and thus potentially outside interference.

Border clashes between Morocco and Algeria

The first of many border issues to arise after the creation of the OAU was between Morocco and Algeria. The border between Algeria and Morocco had never been clearly defined. Prior to French colonization the areas that would become Algeria and Mauritania were under loose Moroccan control. When the French arrived, the Moroccan rulers led raids against French forces but were eventually defeated. Morocco was stripped of its provinces and made a protectorate, while Algeria became part of France. However, the 1844 Treaty of Tangiers ending the Franco-Moroccan war did not stipulate the boundary between Algeria and Morocco. The thinking at the time and for decades after was that the desert landscape unfit for human habitation, with its lack of water, made the delineation of an exact border unnecessary. Morocco gained independence in 1956 and sought to open negotiations with France to specify a border. Eventually this became a futile effort because of the Franco-Algerian civil war. Morocco then tried to open negotiations directly with the Algerian FLN, but the FLN was unwilling to partake in meaningful negotiations until after Algerian independence.[6] In the meantime, oil and other valuable minerals were discovered in the disputed border area. On 1 October 1963, mere months after the creation of the OAU in May 1963, Morocco sent troops to outposts in a disputed area. Algeria launched a counter-attack to re-take the outposts, and by mid-October the two countries were embroiled in war.[7]

When conflict broke out between Algeria and Morocco, the OAU first relied on the good offices of OAU Chairman Haile Selassie and then appointed an ad hoc commission. Selassie worked to get Morocco to accept OAU mediation and then arranged a meeting in Bamako, Mali on 29–30 October 1963 to negotiate the terms of a ceasefire. The ceasefire included an immediate end of hostilities, the establishment of a committee of military officers to define a demilitarized zone, and a request for an extraordinary meeting of the OAU Council of Ministers for the purpose of creating a com-mittee to find a definite solution to the border dispute. The OAU Council of Ministers met on 15–18 November 1963 to appoint the ad hoc committee. The resolution from the meeting stressed the importance of African states settling their disputes peacefully within an African framework and set up a seven-member committee under the chairmanship of Mali.[8] The Algeria-Morocco Ad Hoc Commission operated through 1967. During that time, it met about a dozen times and helped to facilitate negotiations between the two member states.[9]

The Commission first met in late 1963. Initial talks between the two states were deadlocked, but after several meetings and summits there was some degree of progress. When Algeria and Morocco were able to begin bilateral negotiations the work of the Commission turned to predominantly moni-toring the progress of the talks. By the end of May 1964, the two parties had agreed on a demilitarized zone and had created a framework to return nationals, resume free passage of people and property, and compensate and assist the victims of the violence. While these agreements stopped violent conflict along the border and helped to normalize relations it would take a further eight years of bilateral negotiations before an agreement on the border was reached in 1972.[10] While the OAU's intervention was timely and provided a useful catalyst to kick-start the negotiations, the talks were ultimately successful because of the willingness of the two parties to continue negotiations over a sustained period. This conflict highlights the positive role the OAU was able to play when there was still great enthusiasm within the regional organization for conflict management and critically when both parties were willing to come to the table. However, as subsequent conflicts will show, the ad hoc mechanisms used by the OAU were ill-suited to address conflicts and atrocities because of an interest in conflict management that ebbed and flowed and various degrees of interest from state parties to resolve conflict and allow OAU input.

Conflict in the Horn of Africa

Another border dispute amongst African states that came to the fore immediately after independence involved Somalia, Kenya, and Ethiopia. Somalis lived for many centuries across a large swath of East Africa. However, colonial administrations imposed borders that split the Somali people between Kenya, Ethiopia, and Somalia. Upon independence the Somali Republic sought to re-unify the Somali people and in fact Somalia included a clause in its constitution calling for re-unification. Somalia also rejected the OAU resolution that called for the inviolability of colonial borders and instead advocated for self-determination for all peoples.[11] Unsurprisingly, Somali ambitions to annex significant parts of Kenya and Ethiopia in order to be able to re-unify the Somali people led to tensions amongst the neighboring countries.

Somalia took its case to the OAU in May 1963 at the founding conference where it was met with sharp rebuke. In line with organizational norms, the OAU was primarily concerned with maintaining state sovereignty and territorial integrity and not in setting a precedent to re-draw state boundaries. When the OAU was not willing to do anything to settle the dispute, Somalia escalated its efforts to reclaim territory by appealing to foreign governments for military aid. This was of course in stark violation of the OAU Charter that sought to preserve the independence of Africa and eradicate foreign dominion and influence from the continent. With foreign aid from the Soviet Union, Somalia was able to expand its armed forces and began raids and propaganda campaigns against Ethiopia. In February 1964 full-scale fighting broke out.[12]

After violent conflict began, Somalia sought to resolve the issue through the UNSC while Ethiopia sought to keep the issue contained within Africa and addressed through the OAU. Somalia requested a special meeting of the UNSC in February 1964 to discuss what it considered to be acts of aggression by Ethiopia against the sovereignty of Somalia.[13] However, the African Group at the UN was successful in blocking the meeting and having the issue referred to the OAU for settlement by African leaders. The OAU Council of Ministers met in February 1964 in Dar es Salaam, Tanzania. They considered this issue and in what can be seen as a rebuke to Somalia resolved that disputes should first be settled in an African framework. They also urged both Somalia and Ethiopia to agree to an immediate ceasefire, refrain from further provocation, and enter into bilateral negotiations to resolve the border dispute.[14]

The countries agreed to a truce, and Somalia requested that observers monitor the ceasefire. However, Ethiopia rejected the proposal for observers, and the truce fell apart not long after it was agreed. The Council of Ministers met on subsequent occasions to discuss the conflict and also referred the issue to committees, but no effective steps were taken to find and enforce a resolution.[15] For example a good offices committee was established by the Assembly of Heads of State and Government in 1973 and comprised of eight members. Its task was simply to normalize relations between the two countries.[16] This effort failed too, and clashes and tension between the two countries continued for decades. The case of Somalia and Ethiopia demonstrates the limitations of the OAU when states involved were not amendable to mediation. The OAU had a strong interest in resolving the dispute, but the steps it was willing and legally able to take as outlined in its Charter were not enough to compel the parties to find a resolution. Furthermore, it placed a greater emphasis on keeping international actors out of the conflict than on compelling member states to find a solution.

The OAU and interventions from African leaders were more successful in resolving other border disputes in the Horn of Africa when the states involved were more willing to come to the table. Somalia and Kenya eventually reached an agreement to end their conflict and resumed diplomatic relations after an intercession by Zambian President Kenneth Kaunda.[17] The OAU also played a role in facilitating a solution to the clash over another small territory claimed by both Ethiopia and Somalia – French Somaliland. The matter was first brought to the attention of the OAU in 1963 through the Liberation Committee. The OAU visited the region and interviewed all concerned but, as in other conflicts, avoided taking sides. The conflict over the territory became much worse in 1966, at which point French President Charles de Gaulle promised a referendum. The matter was then discussed by the OAU Assembly of Heads of State and Government in November 1966. The body passed a resolution supporting a fair referendum, which took place in March 1967. Ultimately, with the support of the OAU, French Somaliland decided to become an independent country with loose ties to France. It became independent on 27 June 1977 as the Republic of Djibouti.[18]

Rwanda and Burundi

The crises in Rwanda and Burundi began with the Rwandan revolution in 1959. There were multiple crises through the late 1970s that show just how differently the OAU handled internal violence compared with conflicts between two African states. In both Rwanda and Burundi there are two dominant ethnic groups – the majority Hutu and the minority Tutsi. During the colonial period the Tutsi maintained power in both countries despite accounting for only about 15 percent of the population. In 1959, Hutus in Rwanda overthrew the Tutsi elite and established a Hutu-dominated government. However, when Burundi became independent it maintained a Tutsi-dominated constitutional monarchy.[19] The revolution in Rwanda, coupled with the maintenance of the status quo in Burundi, led to an influx of Tutsi refugees into Burundi. An estimated 50,000 Tutsi refugees arrived in Burundi between 1959 and 1965. They had been uprooted from their homes, persecuted, and many had lost relatives or friends to the violence in Rwanda. Their arrival contributed significantly to a deterioration of relations between Hutus and Tutsis in Burundi and created more fear among Burundian Tutsi elite about what would await Tutsis if Hutu majority-rule was also established in Burundi.[20]

The rising tensions led to violent conflict between the two states. The issue was raised in the OAU in February 1964 by the Ugandan government. The OAU Secretary General appealed to both countries to settle their differences and also address the refugee problem that could contribute to further inter-state conflict. The OAU then established a 10-member commission to examine the status of refugees in Africa.[21] The commission was set up as a fact-finding body with a mandate to study all aspects of the refugee crisis and make appropriate recommendations.[22] The concern of the OAU was clearly to address any issue that could contribute to inter-state conflict, so the main focus became finding a way to address the refugee problem, which the OAU viewed as the main cause of the tension between Rwanda and Burundi.

The appointed commission drafted the Convention Governing the Specific Aspects of Refugee Problems in Africa. It was presented to the OAU Council of Ministers in 1965 for comment and then submitted for signature to the Assembly of Heads of State and Government in September 1969. The preamble of the convention notes the need to adopt a humanitarian approach to managing refugee crises. However, interestingly it also recognizes that refugee problems are a source of friction among many member states and creates a distinction between refugees who seek a peaceful life and those who flee in order to create subversion in their home country from the outside.[23] The OAU norms again reflect a wariness of outside domination as well as interference from other African states and forms of subversion, so the convention sought to address the humanitarian plight of refugees while reinforcing OAU norms of non-interference. The convention is forward leaning in the protections is provides for refugees. It forbids member states from expelling a person who has a legitimate fear for their life, physical safety, or liberty. Article II mandates that granting asylum is a humanitarian act and cannot be viewed as an act of hostility by any other OAU member state.[24] Importantly the convention also takes pains to mitigate the possibility of inter-state tensions caused by refugees by stating that refugees should be settled as far away as possible from the border with the country of their origin. It also forbids member states from allowing refugees in their territories from attacking other OAU member states or participating in subversive activities.[25] The OAU was concerned with state security even when dealing with humanitarian issues, and the refugee policy was crafted in such a way that it gave protections to those fleeing but built in clauses to mitigate risks to states.

The actions of the OAU to mitigate tensions between Rwanda and Burundi stand in stark contrast to its actions in the face of internal atrocities. On 29 April 1972 a group of Hutus in Burundi attempted a coup and massacred Tutsis. The response of the Tutsi-led government in Burundi was swift and brutal. A UN team arrived on 22 June 1972 to assess the humanitarian situation. While the team could not verify an exact number, they estimated that between 80,000 and 200,000 Hutus had been systematically slaughtered.[26] The response of the OAU was complete support for the Burundian government. The Administrative Secretary General of the OAU, along with the Prime Minister of Tanzania and President of Somalia, visited Burundi on 22 May 1972. As a further show of support the OAU adopted a resolution in June stating in effect that, "the Council of Ministers was convinced that, thanks to (Burundian President) Micombero's saving action, peace would be rapidly re-established, national unity consolidated, and territorial integrity preserved."[27] The visit and vocal support sent a message that the primary concern of the OAU was the security of states and not the security of individuals or groups of people, even where atrocities were taking place on a massive scale.[28]

Nigerian-Biafran civil war

The Nigerian-Biafran civil war is another example of an internal conflict with profound human suffering and loss. However, in the context of the OAU response, it was exceptional because of the international community's interest, and the challenges it presented to OAU norms. In the year leading up to the outbreak of civil war in Nigeria there was significant instability, starting with a military coup and then a counter-coup in January 1966, followed by reprisal massacres of Igbo civilians and the resulting internal displacement in the same year. The civil war began on 30 May 1967 when the governor of the eastern region of Nigeria, C. Odumegwu Ojukwu, declared secession and the establishment of the Republic of Biafra. The war that followed was long, slow, and brutal. By the time the Biafra surrendered on 12 January 1970, an estimated 600,000 people, most of whom were civilians, had died.[29]

There was deep concern within Africa about the situation in Nigeria, but the official position of the OAU throughout the war was to press for an end to hostilities while strongly supporting Nigerian unity. The OAU annual meeting of the Assembly of Heads of States and Governments took place in Kinshasa, Zaire in September 1967. The civil war did not appear on the provisional agenda.[30] However, African leaders did set up a consultative committee of Heads of State from Cameroon, the Democratic Republic of the Congo, Ethiopia, Ghana, Liberia, and Niger under the chairmanship of Emperor Haile Selassie to try to facilitate a solution. The resolution stated that a six-person committee would assure the Federal Government of Nigeria of the OAU's desire for the territorial integrity of Nigeria while also exploring placing the services of the OAU at the disposal of the Federal Government to address the situation.[31]

The Federal Government of Nigeria in Lagos was not enthusiastic about the OAU discussion of the Biafra war, but they were placated by the clear language from them that the civil war was an internal situation and that Nigerians were primarily responsible for finding a solution. Even so, Biafra viewed the establishment of an OAU committee as a move to mediate between the two sides.[32] It is significant that the OAU formed a committee at all to address the Biafra war because it was a situation that was contained within Nigeria and thus fell into the category of interference in the internal affairs of a member state. However, it is also important to note that the threat of outside involvement from the Commonwealth, the UN, and even international charities influenced the OAU to become more involved. Throughout most of the conflict, the committee's main concerns were ending the hostilities, addressing the humanitarian situation, keeping the issues within the African context, and maintaining the territorial integrity of Nigeria.[33]

The OAU consultative committee towed a careful line. Committee members travelled to Lagos in November 1967 where they met with Nigerian leader Yakubu Gowon. Gowon stressed to the committee that they were not there to mediate, and the best contribution would be a call to rebel leaders to abandon any secessionist aims. The committee did just this and left the country without any consultations with the Biafrans.[34] Upon its departure the committee released a statement, saying, "the (consultative committee) mission reaffirmed the decision of the OAU Summit embodied in its resolution condemning all secessionist attempts in Nigeria. The mission also reaffirmed that any solution of the Nigerian crisis must be on the context of reserving the unity and territorial integrity of Nigeria."[35]

In the summer of 1968, the Nigerian-Biafran conflict gained more international attention when pictures showing the horrors of the war were featured in the western press. The UN had not commented on the matter because its member states, notably the Africa bloc, considered it an internal conflict. However, the international outcry over the humanitarian conditions and advocacy by UNICEF led the UN to reconsider its position. The UN called on the conflict parties to allow aid to reach civilians, and the UN sent an observer mission. However, the observer mission's access to the conflict zone was facilitated by the Federal Government of Nigeria. The observer mission was based in Lagos from 15 September 1968 to 17 January 1969, and during that time they spent no more than 20 days in eastern Nigeria, where the conflict was taking place, and they only had access to areas that had been stabilized by the Nigerian military. Ultimately, the UN observer mission made discreet recommendations to improve the conduct of the Nigerian military, but the overall effect was to improve the image of the Nigerian government.[36] In addition, the OAU re-engaged in the conflict during the summer of 1968. Emperor Selassie revived the committee and arranged for talks between Nigerian President Gowen and Biafran leader Ojukwu in Niamey from 15–19 July 1968. The Biafran leader demanded a ceasefire and withdrawal of troops, while the Nigerian President would not agree to either until Biafra renounced its secession claims. No progress was made at this meeting toward a lasting solution, but the two parties did agree to continue negotiations later in the year. Unfortunately, the talks held in August–September 1968 also failed when both parties refused to make any concessions.[37]

At the September 1968 OAU Assembly of Heads of State and Government, the delegates adopted another resolution on Nigeria, appealing, "to the secessionist leaders to cooperate with the Federal authorities in order to restore peace and unity to Nigeria … calling upon member states of the United Nations and the OAU to refrain from any action detrimental to the peace, unity, and territorial integrity of Nigeria."[38] The 1968 resolution also called on both parties for the cessation of hostilities, an improvement in the eyes of the Biafrans from the previous resolution, but the remainder of the resolution was very clear in its support for the Nigerian government. Additionally, the Algerians refused to issue visas for the Biafrans to attend the conference to plead their case. The OAU response clearly supported the regional norms of state sovereignty and territorial integrity, non-interference, and regional primacy. Upholding these norms had implications for the OAU's stance on self-determination. The OAU advocated for self-determination when there was foreign dominance but not in cases of internal secessionist movements. The OAU position was influenced by the Congolese civil war where the secessionist state of Katanga was backed by foreign powers, and many African leaders saw this as an attempt by former colonial states to weaken newly independent states and promote their economic interests.[39] Many of the leaders of OAU member states in the late 1960s saw a similar scenario in Nigeria and denounced the Biafra secession attempt as an international plot to weaken a great African state.[40] Even Nkrumah (by then deposed as the leader of Ghana) condemned self-determination on a small-scale and blamed it on neo-colonial influences.[41]

The official position of the OAU masked dissention within Africa, which was led by Tanzanian President Nyerere. Tanzania, along with Ivory Coast, Zambia, and Gabon recognized Biafra in opposition with the OAU position. Dissention on this issue was a profound threat to the African regional project and represented disagreement on the foundational principles of OAU – territorial integrity and sovereignty and a united African front to project to the world. Nyerere was the most vocal in his support for the cause of Biafra despite his reputation as a staunch pan-Africanist who advocated for unity across Africa. In the official statement that Nyerere released to justify Tanzania's recognition of Biafra he acknowledged that every state has the authority to defend its sovereignty and territorial integrity. However, he also argued that governments exist for the people that they govern, and citizens must be able to move freely and live safely within their country. In recognizing Biafra, Nyerere conceded that the Igbo lived in genuine fear because of past atrocities and the government's refusal to protect them or to allow them any kind of autonomy within Nigeria.[42] He reiterated, "the basis of statehood, and of unity can only be general acceptance by the participants ... You cannot kill thousands of people, and keep killing more, in the name of unity. There is no unity between the dead and those who killed them; and there is no unity in slavery or domination."[43] President Houphouët-Boigny of Côte d'Ivoire also publicly made the argument that unity cannot come at the cost of atrocities or inequality within a state. In his speech explaining the Ivoirian recognition of Biafra he said:

> Unity is the fruit of the common will to live together, it should not be imposed by force by one group upon another. If we are all in agreement in the OAU in recognizing the imperious necessity of unity, unity as the ideal framework for the full development of the African man, we also admit that it should not become his grave.[44]

Despite dissent from powerful member states, the OAU's official position remained unchanged. The consultative committee continued their work to negotiate a solution but were ultimately not successful. Their last meeting was held in Monrovia in April 1969, at which they divided into two groups to meet with both the Nigerians and the Biafrans separately, but the OAU continued to support the Nigerian government. The Assembly of Heads of State and Government also passed a resolution at its 1969 Summit stressing unanimous action by all African governments to enable a solution to the war and warning of the grave consequences for Nigeria and Africa if it continued. The resolution called for the war to be ended through peaceful means in accordance with the OAU Charter and asked all other international organizations and NGOs to desist from actions that would endanger an African solution to the crisis.[45]

As the OAU continued to support the government of Nigeria, Nyerere became ever more forceful is his advocacy on behalf of the people of Biafra. At the 1969 OAU Assembly, Nyerere met with Gowon, the head of the Nigerian government, to urge him to speak directly with the Biafran leaders. At first Nyerere appeared to be encouraged by Gowon's promises during the meeting and withdrew a pamphlet he had produced on the Nigerian-Biafran crisis. However, when the Nigerian government failed to deliver on the compromises discussed Nyerere circulated his pamphlet within the OAU and later published it on 4 September 1969.[46] The pamphlet argued that Biafra was different from other secessionist movements, including Katanga from Zaire and the American South from the US. It also argued that the secession of Biafra would not necessarily lead to other secessionist movements in Nigeria or more broadly across Africa. Nyerere stated, "it would be shameful if Africa, still groaning from the yoke of European Imperialism, was to make a cynical distinction between that and an internal African imperialism. Such an argument must be rejected by the whole of Africa."[47]

In the most enduring and repeated passage of the pamphlet Nyerere rages against the double standards of the OAU, stating:

> The OAU was established by the Heads of African States. But it is intended to serve the Peoples of Africa. The OAU is not a trade union of African Heads of State. Therefore, if it is to retain the respect and support of the People of Africa, it must be concerned about the lives of the People of Africa. We must not concern ourselves with our own survival as Heads of State; we must even be more concerned about peace and justice in Africa than we are about the sanctity of the boundaries we inherited. For the importance of these lies in the fact that their acceptance is the basis for peace and justice in our continent … The OAU must sometimes raise a voice against those regimes in Africa. In some countries in Africa it might be the only voice that can speak on behalf of

the people. If we dare not do that, even in private, we shall deserve the scorn of those who accuse us of double standards.[48]

Despite Nyerere's advocacy and the OAU's calls for a peaceful resolution, the Nigerian-Biafran war only ended when the Nigerian government completely overwhelmed Biafra with military force, killing hundreds of thousands of civilians in the process. Biafran commanders offered an unconditional surrender on 12 January 1970 and began settlement negotiations with the Nigerian government.

This conflict highlights the OAU's adherence to its own norms of territorial integrity and state sovereignty despite tremendous humanitarian costs, international attention, and fractures amongst OAU member states. The Nigerian-Biafran civil war is debated because of its implications for genocide studies and the role of external actors, such as British support for Nigeria or international non-governmental and religious advocacy for the civilian victims.[49] However, the internal disagreements within Africa about how to react to the conflict had profound implications for African norms. There was contestation of OAU norms by member states, but ultimately, the OAU took a position supporting Nigeria because of norms that prioritized state security and territorial integrity. The result of these norms was a non-interference conflict policy and support for self-determination only in cases of foreign domination.

This volume focuses on peace and security policies and examines how the creation and breakdown of OAU norms led to the creation of new norms and a new conflict management policy. However, it should also be noted that the breakdown in OAU norms also had other implications beyond conflict management. Eritrea and South Sudan were both secessionist territories that became independent after a long conflict and subsequent referenda, and both are now members of the AU. The Nigerian-Biafran civil war contributed to a body of international principles and practice that has slowly developed to manage self-determination claims.[50] For the purposes of this book, the conflict produced the first seeds of dissention against OAU norms that prioritized state security whatever the cost when leaders such as Nyerere argued that states could not be prioritized above people. As the next chapter will demonstrate, subsequent conflicts show further contestation of OAU norms.

Notes

1 Jacob Gordon, *African Leadership in the Twentieth Century: An Enduring Experiment in Democracy* (Lanham, MD: University Press of America, 2002), 138.

2 Gordon, *African Leadership in the Twentieth Century*, 78.

3 Gordon, *African Leadership in the Twentieth Century*, 82.

4 Gordon, *African Leadership in the Twentieth Century*, 122.

5 Gordon, *African Leadership in the Twentieth Century*, 143.

6 Etane Ebokely Benjamin Sakwe, "African States: Settlement of Political Disputes: The Role of the Organization of African Unity, 1963–1979, a Historical Review and Speculative Analysis" (1980). ETD Collection for AUC Robert W. Woodru Library. Paper 2187, 31–33.

7 Sakwe, "African States," 33.

8 Thomas Akhigbe Imobighe, *The OAU (AU) and OAS in Regional Conflict Management: A Comparative Assessment* (Spectrum Books Limited, 2003), 60–61.

9 "Resolving Conflicts in Africa: Implementation Options," 1993, 13. AU Commission Archives.

10 Imobighe, *The OAU (AU) and OAS in Regional Conflict Management*, 60–61.

11 Sakwe, "African States," 43.

12 Sakwe, "African States," 45.

13 Tunde Adeniran, "Pacific Settlement Among African States: The Role of the Organization of African Unity" (Kano, Nigeria: Nigerian Institute of International Affairs, 1980), 4.

14 Adeniran, "Pacific Settlement Among African States," 5.

15 Sakwe, "African States," 47–48.

16 "Resolving Conflicts in Africa," 14.

17 Sakwe, "African States," 51.

18 Sakwe, "African States," 53–54.

19 Imobighe, *The OAU (AU) and OAS in Regional Conflict Management*, 64.

20 René Lemarchand, *Burundi: Ethnic Conflict and Genocide* (New York: Woodrow Wilson Center Press, 1994), 60–61.

21 Imobighe, *The OAU (AU) and OAS in Regional Conflict Management*, 64.

22 "Resolving Conflicts in Africa," 15.

23 "Convention Governing the Specific Aspects of Refugee Problems in Africa" (Organization of African Unity, 20 June 1974), https://au.int/en/treaties/oau-convention-governing-specific-aspects-refugee-problems-africa (accessed 23 September 2020).

24 "Convention Governing the Specific Aspects of Refugee Problems in Africa," 7.

25 "Convention Governing the Specific Aspects of Refugee Problems in Africa," 7–9.

26 Leo Kuper, *Genocide: Its Political Use in the Twentieth Century* (New Haven, CT: Yale University Press, 1981), 164.

27 Kuper, *Genocide*, 164.

28 Caroline Thomas, *New States, Sovereignty, and Intervention* (Aldershot: Gower Publishing Company Limited, 1985), 72.

29 Michael Aaronson, "The Nigerian Civil War and Humanitarian Intervention," in *The History and Practice of Humanitarian Intervention and Aid in Africa*, ed. Bronwen Everill and Josiah Kaplan (New York: Palgrave Macmillan, 2013), 177.

30 "Provisional Agenda for the Fourth Ordinary Session of the Assembly of Heads of State and Government," AHG/27 (Organization of African Unity, September 1967). AU Commission Archives.
31 "Resolutions and Declarations Adopted by the Fourth Ordinary Session of the Assembly of Heads of State and Government Held in Kinshasa," (Organization of African Unity, 11–14 September 1967), 6, https://au.int/sites/default/files/decisions/9516–assembly_en_11_14_september_1967_assembly_heads_state_government_fourth_ordinary_session.pdf (accessed 7 May 2020).
32 Suzanne Cronje, *The World and Nigeria* (London: The Anchor Press Ltd, 1972), 292.
33 Adeniran, "Pacific Settlement Among African States," 6.
34 Cronje, *The World and Nigeria*, 293.
35 Sakwe, "African States," 73.
36 Marie-Luce Desgrandchamps, "Dealing with 'Genocide': The ICRC and the UN during the Nigeria-Biafra War, 1967–70," *Journal of Genocide Research* 16, no. 2–3 (2014): 287–90.
37 Sakwe, "African States," 76–79.
38 "Resolutions Adopted by the Fifth Ordinary Session of the Assembly of Heads of State and Government Held in Algiers," (Organization of African Unity, 13–16 September 1968), 3–4, https://au.int/sites/default/files/decisions/9517–assembly_en_13_16_september_1968_assembly_heads_state_government_fifth_ordinary_session.pdf (accessed 7 May 2020).
39 Brad Simpson, "The Biafran Secession and the Limits of Self-Determination," *Journal of Genocide Research* 16, no. 2–3 (2014): 339–40.
40 Simpson, "The Biafran Secession," 344.
41 Simpson, "The Biafran Secession," 347.
42 Godfrey Mwakikagile, *Nyerere and Africa: End of an Era* (Pretoria, South Africa: New Africa Press, 2009), 273–74.
43 Mwakikagile, *Nyerere and Africa*, 276.
44 Sakwe, "African States," 80.
45 "Resolutions Adopted by the Sixth Ordinary Session of the Assembly of Heads of State and Government Held in Addis Ababa" (Organization of African Unity, 6–10 September 1969), 6–7, https://au.int/sites/default/files/decisions/9518-assembly_en_6_10_september_1969_assembly_heads_state_government_sixth_ordinary_session.pdf (accessed 7 May 2020).
46 Cronje, *The World and Nigeria*, 310.
47 Mwakikagile, *Nyerere and Africa*, 302.
48 Mwakikagile, *Nyerere and Africa*, 306.
49 Lasse Heerten and A. Dirk Moses, "The Nigeria-Biafra War: Postcolonial Conflict and the Question of Genocide," *Journal of Genocide Research* 16, no. 2–3 (2014): 169–203.
50 Simpson, "The Biafran Secession," 350.

7

An era of change

The 1970s and 1980s were a period of turmoil and then change for the OAU. Several atrocities in the 1970s, notably the brutality of Jean-Bédel Bokassa and Idi Amin, would shock the continent and push the OAU to further re-evaluate its sole focus on state security. These events were coupled with continuing advocacy from African elites, who argued that the OAU's tolerance for internal conflict and atrocities in the name of strict non-interference were contrary to pan-Africanist ideals and damaging to the security and interests of the region. The events of the 1970s and the response of the OAU in the late 1970s and early 1980s show the process through which ideas that prioritized state security were discredited and the beginnings of evolving pan-Africanist ideas that led to a focus on human security. However, the process was not linear, and there were multiple failed attempts at reform before the ideas that would guide the shift from non-interference to non-indifference were fully formed.

It is also important to acknowledge that there were other atrocities during this period, such as those committed by the Derg in Ethiopia and by Francisco Macias Nguema in Equatorial Guinea, that are not covered. This chapter does not argue that regional responses to conflict and atrocities were consistently more proactive from the 1970s onward. It does demonstrate how particular conflicts and advocacy by particular leaders led to a contestation of the OAU norms and evolving responses from member states and the regional organization. There was contestation by some African leaders during the Nigerian-Biafran war, but it did not lead to a change in the OAU response, as the regional organization maintained a consistent policy of supporting the Nigerian government. However, events during the 1970s led to further contestation of the norms that prioritized state security, and the responses to these instances of contestation, along with the OAU reforms in the late 1970s and throughout the 1980s, indicate a gradual breakdown of OAU strict non-interference and state security norms.

The tumultuous second decade of the OAU

Despite inconsistency in responding to all atrocities, there were many events during the 1970s that had dire humanitarian consequences and stirred reactions from African leaders and the OAU. The resulting reforms and reform attempts during the 1980s indicate a gradual discrediting of OAU norms and multiple attempts at institutional transformation. In 1963, African leaders constructed the OAU around principles that sought to ensure African security through protecting independent African state sovereignty and territoriality, eradicating colonialism, and working within the international system to carve out a place for Africa in the global community while insisting on regional primacy. However, the idea that strict non-interference and protecting the sovereignty of African states was the best way to secure Africa was contested and, over four decades, slowly eroded showing a dynamic process of institutional transformation. The contestation and erosion were not consistent or linear. However, as this chapter will demonstrate, the events of the 1970s and advocacy by key leaders, notably Nyerere, were immediate pre-cursors for multiple reforms and attempted reforms. The timing of the conflict events and advocacy in the 1970s closely followed by reforms indicates that strict non-interference was challenged, and reforms were undertaken because of pressure from within the African regional organization. International pressure was not a determinant factor in spurring additional reforms during the 1990s. Instead, the reforms of the 1990s which ultimately led to the creation of the AU should be seen as continuation of a process that began in the 1970s.

A prerequisite of institutional change is de-legitimizing the ideas that underpin the existing institution.[1] The events of the 1970s represent stage two (See Figure 1) of the shift from non-interference to non-indifference wherein the ideas that formed the foundation of the OAU were delegitimized over time. The de-legitimization occurred through a combination of the repercussions of African conflicts and atrocities on the security and interests of the region, advocacy by respected leaders, and shifting interpretations of pan-Africanism. Stage three followed in the late 1970s and 1980s where there were attempts to reform the OAU by creating new institutions and through the adoption of policies and practices that embrace a more holistic vision of regional security. However, new ideas that articulated a complete vision of human security balanced against state sovereignty were not fully formed, so the ideas were not yet there to lead the way on a complete institutional and policy transformation.

Central African Republic under Jean-Bédel Bokassa

Jean-Bédel Bokassa came to power in the CAR after he led a 1965 New Year's Eve coup. In the first months of his rule, Bokassa made several decisions that directly benefited CAR's citizens, but in a short period of time he spiraled into a corrupt and brutal leader.[2] Over the next decade, Bokassa would torture and execute other government officials and hoard the national wealth of CAR in his personal accounts. On 4 December 1976 he proclaimed that the CAR would become the Central African Empire, and he would be emperor for life and establish a hereditary succession. He staged a coronation that cost CAR a third of its national revenue for the year.[3]

Bokassa's repression permeated every institution in CAR, including the schools and universities. Students went on strike in 1971 and 1972 to protest against poor conditions in their schools, and the military responded with force. In 1974, university students protested against the dismissal of professors for supposedly discussing political issues, and as a result several student leaders were detained. In 1975, university students again protested and demanded prompt payment of their bursaries. Bokassa's government responded by conscripting the student protestors into the army.[4] In February 1978 the Ministry of Education announced that all students would be required to buy uniforms made by a company controlled by Bokassa's family. The cost of the uniform, particularly during a time of economic hardship, was prohibitive for many families. On 15 January 1979, some schools began refusing entry to students not wearing the uniform. The students began to protest, and on 19 January the demonstrations came to a head with thousands of students demonstrating in the capital city of Bangui. The government sent heavily armed troops and tanks to suppress the protests. Eventually the government regained control of the capital and imposed a curfew, but the unrest signaled the beginning of the end for Bokassa.[5]

The French government propped up Bokassa for a few months with an injection of cash to pay government workers and student bursaries. However, it was always an uneasy calm, and protests resumed in March and April 1979. On 9 April, students began boycotting classes until the government released several prisoners who were arrested as a result of their involvement in protest activities. Bokassa responded by imprisoning students. On 18 April an unknown number of students of various ages were taken into custody at Ngaragba Prison, stripped, beaten, and crammed into tiny cells by the dozen. Many children died as a result.[6] Reports of the atrocities made their way to Amnesty International in early May. Joseph Perrin, a priest who was visiting CAR at the time of the killings, came forward with a wealth of information from interviews he conducted with victims and witnesses. His information indicated witnesses had seen the bodies of 62 dead children at the prison.[7] In mid-May 1979 Amnesty International issued a press release:

> On 18 April more than one hundred children are known to have been taken to Bangui's central Ngaragba prison where they were held in such crowded conditions that between twelve and twenty-eight of them are reported to have died from suffocation. Other children are reported to have been stoned by members of the Imperial Guard to punish them for throwing stones at the Emperor's car. Some have been bayoneted or beaten to death with sharpened sticks and whips.[8]

The information was picked up by international news outlets and met by widespread outrage and condemnation. The disclosure of the atrocities caused embarrassment for France and African countries that had supported Bokassa throughout his bloody reign. On 20 May Bokassa travelled to Kigali, Rwanda for the annual Franco-African Summit, and his peers from France and Francophone Africa, particularly President Houphouët-Boigny of Côte d'Ivoire, President Senghor of Senegal, and President Gnassingbé Eyadéma of Togo, insisted on an investigation.[9] A commission of inquiry comprised of African jurists from Côte d'Ivoire, Liberia, Rwanda, Senegal, and Togo was formed. It is true that there was tremendous pressure from France and international media following the Amnesty International report to investigate, but there was pressure to investigate atrocities in other instances, such as the Nigerian-Biafran civil war, that never resulted in public action by other African countries. This time African nations supported as well as participated in an investigation into the internal happenings of another independent African state. The commission of inquiry found information that went beyond what had been publicized by Amnesty International and developed a damning report.[10] The report found:

> In conclusion the Mission de constatation considers that in the month of January 1979, in Bangui, disturbances were repressed brutally by the security forces and that in the month of April 1979, the massacre of about 100 school children was carried out under the orders of Emperor Bokassa and almost certainly with his personal participation.[11]

The personal participation of an African leader in the murder of children was shocking to regional and international actors. The French withdrew their support, and Bokassa was overthrown in September 1979. Within the African context, it is notable that other African states pushed for an investigation and participated in one that published information beyond what was available in a report by an international human rights NGO. It is also notable that Bokassa was publicly condemned instead of dealt with quietly and within the African context.

Uganda under Idi Amin

Idi Amin came to power in Uganda after leading a military coup that ousted President Milton Obote in 1971. Immediately after the coup, Amin delivered an 18-point agenda of reform, which included improving rule of law and economic progress, among other things. Essentially he promised massive improvements to the lives of ordinary Ugandans who were largely disenchanted with the previous regime. As a result, most groups in Ugandan society supported the new regime.[12] The honeymoon period did not last long though, and soon Amin began implementing policies that elevated the military and played on populist sentiments.

It was essential that Amin controlled the armed forces with a mix of sticks and carrots, and he spent a huge portion of state resources placating members of the security services. Between 1972 and 1978, Uganda spent an average of 28.7 percent of its budget on security. Amin also used ethnic and religious divisions that were ripe within the armed forces to pit various groups against each other and prevent cohesion that could lead to a threat against his rule.[13] To appease broader swaths of Ugandan society, Amin sought the 'Africanization' of the economy through the expulsion of Asians in Uganda. He explained the policy by saying, "We are determined to make the ordinary Ugandan master of his own destiny, and above all to see that he enjoys the wealth of his country. Our deliberate policy is to transfer the economic capital of Uganda into the hands of Ugandans."[14] In practice this meant Amin enacted policies to expel Asians from Uganda and seize their property.

Amin led a notoriously violent regime. Within the first six months of his regime, thousands of members of the security forces who were suspected of loyalty to past regimes were tortured and killed to eliminate the threat they may have posed.[15] Throughout Amin's tenure thousands of prominent political opponents, including police commissioners, military officers, government ministers, teachers, doctors, business and union leaders, and the Chief Justice of Uganda, simply disappeared and were presumed killed.[16] The disappearance of prominent and valued members of society led to a situation where many Ugandans died not because of direct violence but structural violence due to a lack of doctors and medical supplies as well as the disrepair of critical infrastructure, such as boreholes.[17]

Despite open knowledge of Amin's atrocities, his regime survived and participated fully in the OAU. Kampala was even chosen as the venue for the 1975 OAU annual summit. However, Amin was not left completely unchallenged, and four African states boycotted the summit because of the chosen venue. President Nyerere of Tanzania was particularly forceful in his criticism of Amin, arguing:

> A strange tendency in Africa ... a tendency which, if we do not consider it carefully, will badly damage the respect for our continent ... Amin is a killer ... He has killed many more people than Vorster has done in South Africa. But there is a strange habit in Africa: an African leader, so long as he is African, can kill Africans as he please, and you cannot say anything.[18]

After years of terrible relations, Uganda invaded a small area of Tanzania in October 1978 claiming the territory belonged to Uganda. The area was quickly recaptured by Tanzanian forces. However, during the short-lived invasion approximately 1,500 civilians were killed, and the area was severely damaged due to pillaging.[19] President Nyerere believed that the area was not safe because of the lingering presence of Ugandan troops close to the border, and Tanzania launched a counter-attack, invading Uganda in January 1979.[20] Neighboring African states and the OAU became involved to try to mediate a solution to the crisis, but Nyerere would not agree to any mediation until the OAU condemned Uganda's aggression, Uganda renounced all territorial claims, and Uganda paid reparations for damages.[21] None of these conditions were met, and a viable mediation effort never materialized. Over several months, Tanzanian forces advanced further and further into Ugandan territory and continued to aid exiled Ugandan rebels seeking to overthrow Idi Amin. Ultimately, Amin was overthrown in April 1979, and it was Tanzanian and exiled Uganda troops who marched into the capital together.

Nyerere argued that Tanzania's invasion was a direct response to Uganda's aggression, and he steadfastly rejected the notion that the invasion was a humanitarian intervention in response to Idi Amin's brutal treatment of his own people. Nyerere claimed that there were two wars being fought in Uganda. One war was between Tanzanian and Ugandan forces as a result of Uganda's attempt to annex Tanzanian territory and as a punitive measure for Ugandan atrocities during the invasion. The second was between Amin and his supporters and the people of Uganda who sought to overthrow a brutal dictator. Of course, in practice this distinction was anything from clear-cut as Tanzania supported forces opposed to Amin and fought alongside them.[22]

Even though Uganda was the initial aggressor, the common perception among African leaders was that Tanzania's response was disproportionate, and Nyerere had always sought to overthrow Amin. In this sense, Tanzania's actions represented a grievous violation of non-interference, and the invasion was discussed at the OAU Summit in Monrovia in July 1979. Sudan and Nigeria explicitly criticized Tanzania for the invasion and accused Nyerere of obstructing all efforts to negotiate a peace. However, the response from the vast majority of African states was silence, which was seen as tacit approval.[23] In this way, the invasion was a milepost in the history of Africa, and from it and the subsequent (non) reaction of African leaders the first cracks in the doctrine of non-intervention began to form.[24] The fact that this case is often seen as an abuse of humanitarian intervention that resulted in a leader being deposed is immaterial to my argument. The response by outside actors to a violation of a norm is one indicator of the robustness of that norm,[25] and the critical aspect of the case is the non-response from the vast majority of African states to an egregious violation of non-interference.

The Tanzanian invasion of Uganda and the conflicts in Africa over the preceding decade, including atrocities in CAR and the Nigerian-Biafran war, highlighted the problems with OAU norms that prioritized strict non-interference and protection of state security in all circumstances. Nyerere had been arguing for changes to the OAU Charter for years, and the combination of the negative impact of the events of the 1970s, damage to African interests, and the advocacy of leaders led to reforms. Following the 1979 OAU Summit, the member states pushing for reform were strengthened, and the proposed reforms that were being considered at ministerial levels sped up.[26] Three examples of the reforms in the 1980s are the first multilateral peacekeeping force in Africa, the proposal to establish an OAU Political Security Council, and the adoption and ratification of the African Charter on Human and Peoples' Rights.

Reform in the 1980s

Africa's first multilateral peacekeeping force

Despite Nigeria's criticism of Tanzania's invasion of Uganda, Nigeria took a leading role in resolving an internal crisis in Chad with the eventual support of the OAU. Chad became embroiled in conflict soon after independence. The leader at independence, François Tombalbaye, was a southerner handpicked and educated by the French. His leadership was resented by many northerners who felt he did not represent their interests or identities. His move to establish a single-party state with a high tax burden and heavy government repression made matters worse and eventually threw the country into a civil war after several northern ethnic groups united to form the rebel group FROLINAT.[27] By 1975, Tombalbaye had been deposed through a coup led by Félix Malloum and a new government was formed with Malloum as the president and another rebel leader, Hissène Habré, acting as vice-president. Unfortunately, any peace was short-lived, and by February 1979 fighting erupted between forces loyal to Habré and those loyal to Malloum. It was at this point that Nigeria entered the Chadian reconciliation process.[28]

Nigeria's engagement in the Chadian crisis over several years was a result of several factors. The conflict in Chad not only caused internal strife but also drew in outside actors that Nigeria saw as a threat, notably Libya and France. Additionally, it caused thousands of refugees to stream across borders into Nigeria and Cameroon, and the Nigerian government saw the refugees as contributing to security concerns and rioting. At an OAU Summit, Nigerian President Shagari remarked that his country had "a legitimate interest and concern about the grave situation in Chad."[29] The first attempt by the Nigerian government to resolve the conflict in Chad was convening the Kano Conference in March 1979. The resulting agreement included a proposal to deploy a Nigerian peacekeeping mission to supplement the crisis management process.[30] Unfortunately, the 800-man mission was short-lived, ending in failure because of an unclear mandate and the unwillingness of the belligerents and local population to accept the legitimacy of the force.[31]

Undeterred, the Nigerian government convened Lagos II on 14 August 1979, which resulted in the Lagos Accord. This agreement also outlined the mission of a peacekeeping force as part of the crisis management process. However, there were several key differences because of the lessons learned during the Nigerian peacekeeping mission. Countries bordering Chad were barred from contributing troops to the mission, and there would be a neutral monitoring commission led by the OAU Secretary General to oversee the peacekeeping mission and ceasefire.[32] The countries that were supposed to provide troops for the neutral African force were Congo, Benin, and Guinea. However, only Congo sent a contingent of 500 troops, and even this force did not arrive until early January 1980. Like the initial Nigerian mission, the OAU-supervised mission had to be evacuated soon after it arrived due to renewed fighting and insufficient resources to protect the peacekeepers.[33]

After the failure of Lagos II, the Council of Ministers took up the issue at their June 1980 session.[34] The Assembly of Heads of State and Government then took up the issue at its July 1980 session in Sierra Leone. The Assembly adopted a resolution that called on member states to give finding an African solution one more attempt. It specifically asked member states that were able to provide peacekeeping forces and financial resources to do so through voluntary contributions. It then stipulated that if the OAU was unable to raise the necessary troops and funds then the issue should then be referred by the African Group to the UNSC to request additional assistance.[35] The internal situation in Chad was again discussed at the June 1981 Assembly of Heads of State and Government.[36] Senegal, Zaire, and Nigeria came forward as troop contributing countries. However, the OAU relied on both member states and outside powers for financial support, with France and the US contributing towards the costs. Even with this support, the peace-keeping mission came up against significant logistical and financial difficulties, so Kenyan President Daniel arap Moi appealed to the UNSC in his role as OAU Chairman for financial, material, and technical assistance.[37] The UNSC declined to commit itself to taking responsibility for a tremendously complex and expensive operation and instead responded only with a resolution asking for voluntary contributions to the peacekeeping force.[38]

This mission is notable because it was the OAU's first attempt at multi-lateral peacekeeping, and it was an African-led effort even if some outside funding was accepted. It supported the norm of regional primacy by establishing an "Africa First" practice wherein the OAU sought to manage the conflict within Africa before asking the African Group at the UN to raise the issue with the UNSC. It also represents a change within the OAU. The conflict in Chad was a civil war, but Nigeria partly justified its engagement to solve the crisis by citing the negative impact of refugee flows on regional security. This case highlights the evolving reasons that justified engagement in internal conflict issues as well as the development of a new tool – regional peacekeeping forces – to manage conflict in Africa.

In the Chadian case, there was a powerful regional state pushing for intervention, which certainly was an important factor. However, it is important that Nigeria framed its intervention as partly justified by regional security concerns. It is also important that the OAU supported the intervention and created a multilateral peacekeeping force to support the Nigerian-led peace processes because it demonstrates regional endorsement. Finally, the totality of the reforms in the 1980s must be taken into account. As will be shown, it was not just one instance. The 1980s saw multiple attempts at regional reforms and initiatives to promote issues that fall under conceptions of human security, such as economic development and human rights. The timing of these reforms immediately after several atrocities and advocacy by Nyerere and other African leaders indicates the importance of these events in pushing reform. Furthermore, the limited scope of these reforms and in some cases the failure of reform demonstrates that institutional change is dynamic and idea-driven. There is not one event or leader that can push through transformational change. The build-up to transformational change happens over time, and it must be underpinned by ideas, which may also take time to fully develop.

Proposed OAU Political Security Council

One of the first efforts to fundamentally change the institutions of the OAU was a proposal to create a Political Security Council, which would have the ability to proactively respond to conflict. The proposal for such a body was put forward by Sierra Leone in 1980. A formal report on the establishment of a Political Security Council was presented to the Council of Ministers in March 1981. The Council of Ministers decided to consider the proposal in part because of the weaknesses of other central organs, in particular the Commission of Mediation, Conciliation and Arbitration. The Commission, as well as the Secretary General, did not have the mandate or power to promptly and effectively respond to and manage conflicts.[39] However, there were also several states with reservations about the proposal, believing that such a body would mean an infringement on the principle of non-interference.[40]

The original proposal in 1981 closely resembles what would become the AU PSC. It called for a 15-member body with seats allocated by geographic sub-region.[41] The council would have been responsible for, "taking immediate and effective action to maintain peace and security, to prevent, as far as it lies in its power the escalation of political, military, and other conflict which threaten or is likely to threaten peace, security, and stability of the African continent."[42] The expectation was that this would be a permanent body that could meet at a moment's notice to address conflict as well as be at the disposal of the Assembly of Heads of State and Government, Council of Ministers, and Secretary General, among others.[43] While the proposal did not pass and never came to fruition during the tenure of the OAU, it was an early attempt to reframe African capacity to address conflicts that predates the end of the Cold War and international intervention efforts in the 1990s.

This failed reform attempt indicates that the ideas upon which the OAU was built, strict non-intervention and protection of state sovereignty and territoriality, were being challenged and discredited. It also represents efforts to better respond to conflict on the continent following the conflicts and atrocities of the 1970s. However, there was not a new set of ideas that could act as a blueprint to underpin lasting and transformative institutional change. It would take two more decades and the further development of human security and sovereignty as responsibility ideas before there was an institutional transformation and a normative shift. Nevertheless, failed reform attempts are an indication of the start of reform processes. In the African regional context, the process to reform began in the late 1970s after the conflicts and atrocities of that decade began to de-legitimize the ideas that underpinned the OAU's conflict management of policy of non-interference. It was not a linear reform process, and there are pushes to reform coupled with failure and inaction, but the indications of the start of the process in the late 1970s as a result of the events of that decade are clear.

Adoption of the African Charter on Human and Peoples' Rights

Another change within the OAU that actually came to fruition was the adoption of an African Charter on Human and Peoples' Rights and the subsequent creation of institutional infrastructure to support it. The African human rights system began to emerge in the late 1970s with discussions around a charter on human rights. It was a result of deliberate decisions by the OAU, and it signaled a departure from rigid adherence to the concept of state sovereignty as well as the growing importance of human rights as a regional issue.[44] As with the OAU multilateral peacekeeping force and attempts to establish a Political Security Council, the adoption of the African Charter and the gradual institutionalization of a regional human rights system should be seen as one step along the path of normative and institutional transformation following the impact of violent conflict and atrocities in the 1970s and advocacy by some leaders.

The African Charter on Human and Peoples' Rights, more commonly known as the Banjul Charter, was adopted in June 1981 in Nairobi, Kenya and entered into force on 21 October 1986. The preamble notes that human beings have basic, inherent rights while stressing the duties of individuals. It also stresses African traditions of rights and freedoms and the continuing struggle of African states to ensure freedom for Africans living under the last vestiges of colonialism.[45] Articles 1–18 of the Banjul Charter cover many of the same individual rights guaranteed by the UDHR. However, the Banjul Charter has a stronger provision for the right to seek and obtain asylum when persecuted. Articles 19–24 of the Banjul Charter cover collective rights, including self-determination, economic and cultural development, and national and international peace and security. Chapter II of the Banjul Charter stresses the duties of individuals to their family, community, society, state, and international community.[46]

A draft proposal for a Universal Declaration of Human Duties was presented by Mauritius at the 32nd Ordinary Council of Ministers in March 1979. The purpose of this declaration was to set out a list of fundamental human rights and the duties of citizens to protect those rights. After an initial consultation with member states, the OAU Secretariat circulated a short draft declaration at the July 1979 Council of Ministers summit.[47] The OAU Secretary General then organized meetings of experts to prepare a draft of the African Charter on Human and Peoples' Rights. The meeting of experts was convened in Dakar, Senegal from 28 November to 8 December 1979, and there was an OAU ministerial meeting from 9–15 June 1980 to discuss the draft charter.[48] The Banjul Charter was then adopted in June 1981 by the OAU Assembly of Heads of State.[49] Even though it did not enter into force until 1986, the process to draft it began much earlier, immediately after the conflicts and atrocities during the 1970s. The drafters of the Charter sought to capture an African conception of human rights, notably that it should give principle place to the right of non-discrimination and the duty of solidarity and cooperation in the struggle against foreign domination.[50] In this way, the Charter was still operating under a paradigm whose foundation was based in the protection of state sovereignty, but other rights and responsibilities entered the picture as being worthy of consideration and protection.

There are alternative arguments to explain why African leaders adopted the Charter and placed increased importance on human rights. Kufuor argues that African elites were trying to shore up their legitimacy. In the immediate post-independence period, African leaders were able to draw on the euphoria of independence to lead. However, as time progressed citizens expected their leaders to stimulate economic growth and development, build infrastructure, and enact policies to meet the basic needs of the people. When many of these expectations failed to materialize, African leaders encountered legitimacy crises leading to unrest and in some cases military coups. At which point, African leaders began to redefine legitimacy in terms of state respect for civil and political rights.[51] Thus Kufuor rejects the notion that the atrocities committed by some African leaders in the 1960s and 1970s were a motivation for the broader community of leaders to address human rights, arguing that the OAU did nothing to condemn leaders who committed the worst abuses.

However, this explanation does not take into account the disparities in attitudes and actions across Africa. Francophone Africa, along with France, compelled Bokassa to accept an inquiry by African jurists into his atrocities, and their report ultimately went further in condemning him than reports written by international human rights organizations. When the OAU decided to host its 1975 Summit in Kampala with Idi Amin as the chair, Botswana, Mozambique, Tanzania, and Zambia boycotted the Summit.[52] Furthermore, while a handful of OAU members condemned Tanzania for its invasion of Uganda, the OAU did not censure Tanzania despite a tacit understanding that a significant justification for the invasion was Amin's internal policies and abuses. These reactions suggest that while there were many leaders in Africa who were unconcerned with atrocities, there were other leaders who viewed these atrocities and conflicts with great concern.

From the outset of independence, norms in Africa have been contested within the regional organization with competing perspectives and multiple forces pushing backwards and forwards. This contestation is clearly evident from the speeches given at the founding conference of the OAU in 1963, and debates about regional norms continued to happen within the context of the regional organization throughout its tenure. After the 1970s, the momentum was on the side of those leaders within Africa who had been pushing for change, and the reforms of the 1980s are a result of that momentum as well as the damage continuing atrocities were doing to Africa's regional interests. Support for decolonization and racial equality were the issues where there was absolute consensus amongst African leaders in 1963 because there was a strong belief that the remnants of these systems on the continent were a fundamental threat to Africa's security and values. When Africa's inability to address human rights and conflict began to impact its ability to achieve the region's fundamental goal of eradicating colonial and racial regimes, a larger cadre of leaders began to take seriously the assertions of a much smaller collective of African leaders advocating for human rights and notions of human security instead of just focusing on state security.

Regional interests in the 1980s

Ending apartheid

By the mid-1970s, Portugal had relinquished control of its colonies, and the OAU turned its full attention to ending white-minority regimes, notably the apartheid regime in South Africa. White-minority regimes represented an affront to the pan-Africanist values of solidarity and racial equality, and the apartheid regime, in particular, was a threat to the security and economic interests of Africa because of its military capacity, support for other white-minority regimes, and economic clout. The importance of regional principles and pan-Africanist ideas in the formulation of OAU policies is equally as important as regional interests. Indeed, it should not be taken for granted that African states pursued policies that upheld a norm of racial equality as doing so came with the cost of potential military retaliation and forgoing significant benefits of economic cooperation with South Africa.[53] This shows again that ideas and interests can be mutually constitutive. It also shows the importance of ideas in institutional processes while acknowledging that interests can also be influential when they are underpinned by ideas.

From the beginning, South Africa was not considered for membership to the OAU because its policies were in clear violation of the OAU Charter. South Africa's racial policies were never considered a domestic issue, and it was not protected under the OAU's policies on protection of sovereignty and non-intervention.[54] This was reinforced in multiple documents, notably the Lusaka Manifesto, which categorized apartheid as a violation of the international principles of self-determination and racial equality.[55] It was also reinforced through the OAU Liberation Committee as well as policies and practices that mandated support for liberation movements seeking to dismantle colonial and white-minority regimes.

Upon its founding in 1963, the OAU passed a resolution condemning South Africa and agreeing to coordinated action to end apartheid.[56] It then adopted military, trade, and financial sanctions against South Africa.[57] Finally, the OAU also sought to influence the international policies towards South Africa, and its diplomatic offensive had two primary goals. Firstly, the OAU sought to convince the UN that South Africa constituted a threat to international peace and security and should be dealt with forcefully through Chapter VII of the UN Charter. Secondly, the OAU pushed to isolate South Africa in the international community and expel the country from multilateral organizations.[58] African states and their allies pushed the institutions of the UN for years to impose a wide range of consequences on South Africa, and progress came over many decades. The African Group had notable successes by putting apartheid on the agenda and excluding South Africa, particularly in UN institutions that functioned by majority-rule where they were able to bring business to a standstill until a particular issues of concern was resolved.[59] The African Group coordinated action to expel South Africa or severely restrict its participation in the Economic and Social Council, Economic Commission on Africa, International Labor Organization, World Health Organization, Food and Agriculture Organization, International Atomic Energy Agency, Universal Postal Union, and other specialized UN agencies.[60] South Africa's UN credentials were also rescinded in 1974 by Resolution 3207, which noted South Africa's continuing racial discrimination in violation of the UDHR and UN principles.[61]

In January 1976, the UN Centre Against Apartheid was established. This became one of the most important sources of information on apartheid for the international community and activists. Documents from the Centre's archive include data on the apartheid system, statements, reports, policy analysis, surveys of international support, and records of the activities of the anti-apartheid movement. This was a deliberate strategy by African states to expand the information available on the apartheid system and support symbolic and diplomatic isolation of South Africa.[62] The information on the brutality of the apartheid regime also helped to bestow legitimacy on liberation movements.

This advocacy, combined with Africa's consistent diplomatic, economic, and military support to liberation causes, was crucial in pushing the case for liberation forward. African states challenged South Africa regionally through OAU sanctions and isolation but also through the UN and other multilateral institutions. African pressure and multilateral cooperation ultimately led to sanctions from other international actors, as well as broad condemnation, thus demonstrating the importance of processes to de-legitimize and socially sanction state regimes.[63] The OAU pushed norms of racial equality and self-determination and linked the rights of sovereign states to acceptance of these principles. The African Group at the UN used non-adherence to these norms to shame racial regimes in international institutions with the ultimate goal of dismantling white-minority regimes. As such, Africa's diplomatic strategy to meet its primary regional goal and defend its core interests and principles was dependent upon upholding regional credibility.

The atrocities of Bokassa, Amin, and others had a negative impact on the ability of African leaders to credibly criticize the abuses of outside powers and white-minority regimes. Some African leaders recognized the damage this caused to the primary goal of the OAU to exert reputational pressure on the international community to condemn South Africa. Tanzanian President Nyerere, in particular, was vocal about the challenges African leaders faced when criticizing the human rights records of other states. He argued that Africans faced a double standard of having to answer for the atrocities of a handful of dictators and saw the impact it had on the legitimacy of African advocacy against apartheid. In a 1997 speech he said, "Idi Amin was in Uganda but of Africa. Jean Bokassa was in Central Africa but of Africa … They are all Africans, and perceived by the outside world as Africans … So I had to answer questions about the atrocities of the Amins and Bokassas of Africa."[64] While there may not have been unanimity amongst African leaders on the need to move away from strict non-interference and protection of state sovereignty, there was consensus amongst African leaders on the need to eradicate the last remnants of white-minority regimes from the continent. When the atrocities and conflicts of the 1970s began to damage the reputation of the continent and imperil efforts to shame and isolate South Africa, it became a more pressing concern for a greater number of leaders to address conflict. This is evident in the multitude of reforms that began to take place from the late 1970s onward.

Economic development

Even as the OAU was fighting the last remnants of racial regimes on the continent, new continental goals were emerging. In July 1979, the OAU Assembly of Heads of State and Government adopted the Monrovia

Declaration of Commitment with measures to enhance national and regional self-reliance and economic and social development.[65] Using the Monrovia Declaration as a guide, the leaders of African states developed a 20-year plan of action known as the Lagos Plan of Action for Economic Development in Africa: 1980–2000. The preamble of the plan stated:

> The independence of Zimbabwe marks the final turn in the total liberation of the continent. This has ushered in renewed and desperate attempts by the Pretoria regime to arrest the tide of history and to perpetuate the status quo in Namibia and South Africa itself ... We shall continue to pursue, with rigor, the liberation of the last remaining outposts of exploitation, racism, and apartheid ... The same determination that has virtually rid our continent of political domination is required for our economic domination. Our success in exploiting our political unity should encourage us to exploit the strength inherent in our economic unity.[66]

The Lagos Plan of Action committed African leaders to a plan to develop African economies and enhance development. It marked a shift away from only focusing on the political liberation of the continent, and it is another indication that the 1980s were the beginning of OAU reforms. The importance of economic development grew throughout the 1980s as multiple actors within Africa promoted it, and the increasing importance of economic development in and of itself is indicative of the expanding focus of the OAU in the 1980s.

Notes

1 Mark Blyth, *Great Transformations: Economic Ideas and Institutional Change in the Twentieth Century* (New York: Cambridge University Press, 2002), 39.
2 Thomas O'Toole, *The Central African Republic: The Continent's Hidden Heart* (Aldershot: Gower Publishing Company Limited, 1986), 49–51.
3 O'Toole, *The Central African Republic*, 53.
4 Brian Titley, *Dark Age: The Political Odyssey of Emperor Bokassa* (Liverpool University Press, 1997), 106.
5 Titley, *Dark Age*, 107–9.
6 Titley, *Dark Age*, 111–12.
7 Jonathan Power, *Like Water on Stone: The Story of Amnesty International* (Boston: Northeastern University Press, 2001), 82–83.
8 Power, *Like Water on Stone*, 82.
9 Titley, *Dark Age*, 115–16.
10 Power, *Like Water on Stone*, 85.
11 Titley, *Dark Age*, 124.

12 Mahmood Mamdani, *Imperialism and Fascism in Uganda* (London: Heinemann Educational Books Ltd, 1983), 37.

13 Jan Jelmert Jorgensen, *Uganda: A Modern History* (London: Croom Helm Ltd, 1981), 274.

14 Jorgensen, *Uganda*, 288.

15 Mamdani, *Imperialism and Fascism in Uganda*, 38.

16 Jorgensen, *Uganda*, 310–11.

17 Jorgensen, *Uganda*, 314.

18 Nicholas J. Wheeler, *Saving Strangers: Humanitarian Intervention in International Society* (Oxford: Oxford University Press, 2000), 115.

19 Oliver Furley and Roy May, "Tanzania's Military Intervention in Uganda," in *African Interventionist States*, ed. Oliver Furley and Roy May (Aldershot: Ashgate Publishing Limited, 2001), 74.

20 Furley and May, "Tanzania's Military Intervention in Uganda," 76.

21 Furley and May, "Tanzania's Military Intervention in Uganda," 78.

22 Caroline Thomas, *New States, Sovereignty, and Intervention* (Aldershot: Gower Publishing Company Limited, 1985), 102.

23 Thomas, *New States, Sovereignty, and Intervention*, 109.

24 Furley and May, "Tanzania's Military Intervention in Uganda," 90.

25 Richard Price, "Syria and the Chemical Weapons Taboo," *Journal of Global Security Studies* 4, no. 1 (2019): 39–40.

26 Thomas, *New States, Sovereignty, and Intervention*, 112.

27 Terry Mays, *Africa's First Peacekeeping Operation: The OAU in Chad 1981–1982* (Westport: Praeger Publishers, 2002), 20.

28 Mays, *Africa's First Peacekeeping Operation*, 30.

29 Mays, *Africa's First Peacekeeping Operation*, 23.

30 Mays, *Africa's First Peacekeeping Operation*, 35.

31 Mays, *Africa's First Peacekeeping Operation*, 40–41.

32 Mays, *Africa's First Peacekeeping Operation*, 47.

33 "Report of the Secretary-General on the Establishment of a Mechanism for Conflict Prevention, Resolution, and Management," CM/1767 (LVIII) (Organization of African Unity, 21–26 June 1993), 26. AU Commission Archives.

34 "Draft Agenda for the Thirty-Fifth Ordinary Sessions of the Council of Ministers," CM/1039 (XXXV) Rev. 1 (Organization of African Unity, 18–28 June 1980). AU Commission Archives.

35 "Resolution on Adopted by the Assembly of Heads of States and Government of the Organization of African Unity, Meeting in Its Seventeenth Ordinary Session in Freetown, Sierra Leone from 1–4 July 1980," AHG/ Res. 101 (XVII) (Organization of African Unity, 1–4 July 1980). AU Commission Archives.

36 "Draft Agenda for the Eighteenth Ordinary Session of the Assembly of Heads of State and Government," AHG/101 (XVIII) Rev. 1 (Organization of African Unity, 24–27 June 1981). AU Commission Archives.

37 "Report of the Secretary-General on the Establishment of a Mechanism for Conflict Prevention, Resolution, and Management," 27.

38 "Resolution 504 (1982) of 30 April 1982" (United Nations, 30 April 1982), https://undocs.org/S/RES/504(1982) (accessed 7 May 2020).

39 "Report of the Secretary General on the Proposal for the Establishment of a Political Security Council," CM/1118 (XXXVI) (Organization of African Unity, 23 February-1 March 1981), 1–2. AU Commission Archives.

40 "Report of the Secretary General on the Proposal for the Establishment of a Political Security Council," 2–3.

41 "Report of the Secretary General on the Proposal for the Establishment of a Political Security Council," 1, Annex 1.

42 "Report of the Secretary General on the Proposal for the Establishment of a Political Security Council," 2, Annex 1.

43 "Report of the Secretary General on the Proposal for the Establishment of a Political Security Council," 3, Annex 1.

44 Kofi Oteng Kufuor, *The African Human Rights System: Origin and Evolution* (New York: Palgrave Macmillan, 2010), 16.

45 "African Charter on Human and Peoples' Rights," 1986, www.achpr.org/legal instruments/detail?id=49 (accessed 7 May 2020).

46 Jennifer Moore, *Humanitarian Law and Action Within Africa* (Oxford: Oxford University Press, 2012), 104–5.

47 "Universal Declaration of Human Duties," CM/966 (XXXIII) Add. 1 (Organization of African Unity, July 1979). AU Commission Archives.

48 "Council of Ministers Thirty-Fifth Ordinary Session from 18–28 June 1980: African Charter of Human and Peoples' Rights," CM/1068 (XXXV) (Organization of African Unity, 18–28 June 1980), 1–3. AU Commission Archives.

49 "African Charter on Human and Peoples' Rights," 1.

50 "Council of Ministers Thirty-Fifth Ordinary Session from 18–28 June 1980," 1–2.

51 Kufuor, *The African Human Rights System*, 36.

52 Chris Maina Peter, *Human Rights in Africa: A Comparative Study of the African Human and People's Rights Charter and the New Tanzanian Bill of Rights* (London: Greenwood Press, 1990), 9.

53 Audie Klotz, *Norms in International Relations: The Struggle Against Apartheid* (London: Cornell University Press, 1995), 8.

54 Klotz, *Norms in International Relations*, 76.

55 "The Lusaka Manifesto on Southern Africa Proclaimed by the Fifth Summit Conference of East and Central African States." Government of the United Republic of Tanzania, 14–16 April 1969, http://reference.sabinet.co.za/webx/access/journal_archive/00020117/33.pdf (accessed 7 May 2020).

56 "Resolutions Adopted by the First Conference of Independent African Heads of State and Government Held in Addis Ababa, Ethiopia, from 22 to 25 May 1963," 5.

57 Klotz, *Norms in International Relations*, 5.

58 Zdenek Cervenka, *The Unfinished Quest for Unity: Africa and the OAU* (London: Julian Friedmann Publishers Ltd, 1977), 112.

59 Klotz, *Norms in International Relations*, 49.
60 Klotz, *Norms in International Relations*, 48.
61 "3207 (XXIX). Relationship between the United Nations and South Africa" (United Nations, 30 September 1974), https://digitallibrary.un.org/record/189829 (accessed 7 May 2020).
62 Klotz, *Norms in International Relations*, 50.
63 Klotz, *Norms in International Relations*, 152.
64 Julius Nyerere, "Without Unity There Is No Future for Africa," *New African*, May 2013, 159.
65 "Lagos Plan of Action for Economic Development of Africa 1980–2000," para. 2.
66 "Lagos Plan of Action for Economic Development of Africa 1980–2000," paras. 12–13.

8

Changing international and regional dynamics

The 1990s marked a time of tremendous turbulence and transition for Africa and the global community. The Cold War came to an abrupt and unexpected end, and African leaders knew that this would have ramifications for the continent. There were also events that unfolded in Africa, including the conflict in Somalia, the Rwandan Genocide, and the end of the last vestiges of white-minority regimes that contributed to the upheaval. All of these events pushed the OAU to re-evaluate its goals and approaches. While the immediate post-Cold War period is an important part of the story when examining the change from the OAU to the AU, it should not be seen as the whole story but rather the final chapter.

Africa in the early 1990s

The history of OAU conflict management and impetus for reform

Emerging into the new world order, African leaders knew the persistent challenges that Africa had faced for decades. The OAU had made significant progress in eradicating colonialism, but it still remained ineffectual when addressing conflicts in Africa, which hindered many other aspects of its work. OAU mediation tended to be much more effective when done between member states as the prevailing regional norms discouraged interference in internal conflicts and prioritized state security and territorial integrity. Internal OAU documents acknowledge the weaknesses of the organization in preventing and managing conflicts, particularly intra-state conflicts.[1] The OAU's capacity to effectively manage and resolve conflicts was hampered by the limitations of its mandate, stunted conflict management institutions, and lack of capacity and funding. The OAU Charter mandated non-interference and respect for sovereignty and territorial integrity, and this severely curtailed any legitimacy the OAU had to intercede in internal conflicts regardless of their regional implications. The Commission of Mediation, Conciliation and Arbitration, the one OAU institution that was established to deal with conflict, was never fully funded or utilized. Finally, the OAU had difficulty funding their work because many member states did not pay their dues.[2]

Efforts to address the weaknesses of Africa's capacity to manage conflict began well before the end of the Cold War, and the work done in the 1990s is simply a continuation. There were multiple attempts to reform the Commission of Mediation, Conciliation and Arbitration, but these efforts uniformly failed to attract enough support. In the 1980s, the OAU shifted its focus away from reforming the defunct Commission to alternative approaches to conflict management. This shift is illustrated in the OAU-supported peacekeeping missions in Chad and an effort to establish a Political Security Council within the OAU to oversee a regional response to conflicts. These efforts had limited success, but a new Secretary General with a renewed zeal for effective conflict management came to the helm of the organization at the end of the decade. In 1989, Salim Ahmed Salim became Secretary General of the OAU. Salim significantly expanded the scope of the Secretary General's role, and pushed member states to finally reform the OAU's approach to conflict management to address the already apparent weaknesses. Although the reforms coincide with the end of the Cold War, Salim was a driving force behind the institutional changes that had been underway for at least a decade.

As this chapter will show, the OAU Mechanism for Conflict Prevention, Management, and Resolution was established in 1993 and showed promise because it indicated an enhanced commitment from the regional body to address conflict. The Mechanism did facilitate regular OAU meetings on conflict issues and institutionalized offices and processes that could work to prevent and, if needed, resolve violent crises. However, it was still fundamentally hampered by the OAU Charter, which disallowed interference in the internal affairs of member states, and a lack of financial resources and personnel. Because of these constraints the Mechanism focused on conflict prevention and relied on the UN to intervene in the event of a large-scale conflict. The failure of the UN in Rwanda and the failure of the OAU Mechanism to prevent devastating conflicts in Burundi and the Democratic Republic of the Congo were vital in changing the calculation of the OAU about its primary focus on prevention and reliance on the UN.

Over the course of the OAU's existence, there was recognition of the importance of continental conflict management and many attempts to establish an effective system. In each instance, the previous ideas of what might be effective were broken down. Some ideas remained while others were discarded and replaced. In this way, we see an example of Blyth's theory of institutional change in action where the ideas of strict non-interference and

absolute protection of state sovereignty are discredited because of the repercussions of violent conflict and advocacy by key leaders. The experimenta-
tion of the OAU with institutional fixes and alternative conflict management
and resolution approaches contributed ideas and lessons learned that would
help with the development of new ideas of human security. These ideas, in
addition to the concept of sovereignty as responsibility, would in turn form
the basis of new intervention norms and peace and security practices that
would be adopted by the AU.

The OAU response to fundamental changes taking place in the world

Dr Salim Ahmed Salim served as OAU Secretary General from 1989 until
2001. Before serving in the OAU he served as Prime Minister, Deputy
Prime Minister, Minister of Defense, and Minister for Foreign Affairs in
the Tanzanian government. He was a part of the Tanzanian diplomatic
service for 27 years and held key positions prior to his ministerial positions. As a diplomat, he was Tanzania's Permanent Representative to the
UN and chaired several committees and conferences that sought to address
continuing colonialism in Africa and the apartheid regime.[3] While OAU
initiatives to better resolve conflicts and address development and human
rights had been building throughout the 1980s, the election of Salim
Ahmed Salim as the Secretary General aligned with more intensive efforts
to address the OAU's past failures. These efforts can be traced through the
Secretary General's reports to the Council of Ministers and Heads of State
and Government, the institutionalization of new conflict resolution mechanisms, and his public advocacy.

One of Salim's most pressing initiatives upon becoming Secretary
General was to build a more effective OAU that was responsive to changes
on the continent, including the end of many colonial regimes and evolving
regional interests, as well as responsive to changes in the global community
with the end of the Cold War. The OAU Secretary General's Report on the
Fundamental Changes Taking Place in the World and Their Implications
for Africa: Proposals for an African Response was presented at the Twenty-
Sixth Ordinary Session of the Assembly of Heads of State and Government
in July 1990. At this juncture, the OAU recognized the changing international landscape while also articulating the challenges that lay before the
African continent to develop economically, ensure the continuing independence of African states, and avoid further marginalization. This report is a
clear example of the OAU's acknowledgment of the need to reform and
adapt to changing regional and international dynamics and presents the
most coherent, albeit broad, outline of a policy response. It briefly outlines

the achievements of the OAU's first three decades but focuses on the work that still needed to be done.

The principle achievements of the OAU as perceived by the Secretary General were contributions to the decolonization of several countries and ongoing work to dismantle the apartheid system.[4] Colonial and white-minority regimes were coming to an end in Africa by 1990, but there were still concerns about outside domination and securing Africa's place in the world. OAU member states saw the increased challenges they were facing, particularly in the realm of development and economics and the threats to these initiatives posed by continuing conflict. The OAU was particularly active in its first decade around inter-state conflicts but often failed to address intra-state conflict, and the Secretary General posits that this failure is due to a lack of consistent effort and legal mechanisms to justify direct involvement in managing internal conflicts.[5] The report acknowledges that, "the political situation in Africa today is bedeviled by various conflicts that threaten not only human rights and social order but also prospects for the survival, economic development, and even the sovereignty of some states."[6] Salim linked damage to state sovereignty to persistent conflict while making a case for a more robust regional approach to conflict. This shows a prominent leader discrediting strict non-interference by arguing that this practice was actually damaging the very thing it was meant to protect – state sovereignty.

The report called for a re-emphasis on multi-stage planning through political and economic agenda frameworks. Under the political agenda, the most pressing matter was conflict resolution within Africa. It states, "The necessity to speedily bring to a halt all the fratricidal conflicts, to establish peace, and to harness available resources to build an enabling environment for development remains an inescapable duty of African governments."[7] A more robust conflict resolution framework to stem violent conflict became a prerequisite for continental development and, as demonstrated by the introduction of the Lagos Plan of Action in 1980, fostering economic development was an important goal in line with evolving regional interests. The Secretary General called for the OAU to play a more active role in conflict prevention, management, and resolution and for the establishment of permanent institutions to settle disputes and the reactivation of the Commission for Mediation, Conciliation, and Arbitration.[8] The Commission was not reactivated but rather replaced by the OAU Mechanism for Conflict Prevention, Management, and Resolution in 1993, which in theory was more empowered to address African conflicts. However, the Mechanism would prove to be just as constrained as the Commission because of the fundamental OAU norms of non-interference and protection of sovereignty.

The Report on the Fundamental Changes Taking Place in the World and Their Implications for Africa is not the first acknowledgment of the need for the OAU to evolve and to focus on issues beyond liberation. Many of the most pressing issues cited in the report, including persistent economic under-development and an inability of African states to manage violent conflict were issues that the OAU had recognized and tried to address throughout its history and in the 1980s in particular. The Lagos Plan of Action to enhance Africa's economic independence was developed in 1980 and implementation accelerated in 1986. With Nigeria leading the way, the OAU supported the first continental peacekeeping mission in Chad in the early 1980s, and throughout the late 1970s and 1980s the OAU gradually developed a continental human rights framework. The African Charter on Human and Peoples' Rights entered into force in 1986, and as of 1990, 40 OAU member states had ratified the Charter.[9] This demonstrates that while Secretary General Salim was able to use the changing geo-political landscape to reinvigorate action around these issues, they had been on the OAU agenda at the highest levels for at least a decade prior to the end of the Cold War.

The reform attempts of the 1990s were another effort at revising institutional mechanisms while still abiding by non-interference. Understanding the tension between upholding OAU norms and effectively responding to conflicts, Secretary General Salim addressed non-interference, arguing, "While the principle of non-interference in the internal affairs of Member States should continue to be observed, it should, however, not be construed to mean or used to justify indifference on the part of the OAU."[10] Here we see an allusion to a concept of non-indifference in a 1990 report. Non-indifference was certainly not used in the same way by Salim Ahmed Salim as it is used today to indicate an encompassing policy and architecture, but it is an early indication of efforts to balance non-interference with effective conflict prevention and resolution and a marker of evolving ideas. In Chapter 10, I will demonstrate that it was also before critical international precedents were set, including humanitarian interventions in Iraq, Somalia, and the former Yugoslavia. This will help to show that the shift from non-interference under the OAU to non-indifference under the AU was driven from within the African regional institution, and international pressure was not a determinant factor.

Influencing regional reform: civil society

The Kampala Forum

The contestation of non-interference ideas and the rise of alternative ideas happened largely within the African region. While African leaders working within the regional organization were hugely influential, the debate was also influenced by other actors. One of the most prominent examples of civil society engagement that influenced regional politics is the African Leadership Forum (ALF), which was founded in 1988 by former Nigerian President Olusegun Obasanjo. It was and continues to be influential because of the patronage of a powerful statesman, but it is also a body that brought together a wide swath of African society to engage in security and development issues. It has functioned as a body that seeks to improve African leadership through training while also providing a gathering point for engagement from civil society and business representatives to give input on pressing African issues. The most notable contribution of the ALF was the Kampala Document that emerged from the first Conference on Security, Stability, Development and Cooperation in Africa (CSSDCA), otherwise known as the Kampala Forum. Like the OAU, the ALF saw that Africa would be unable to develop economically or meet the challenges of a new era if it did not address conflict and security issues, and the Kampala Forum was an effort for a cross-section of influential Africans to tackle the inter-related problems of security, stability, development, and cooperation. The Kampala Forum also discussed fears of Africa's increasing marginalization in the new international order as the attention of the superpowers waned and Africa began to compete with the emerging eastern European bloc countries. Participants sought to design a holistic framework that engaged the international community but had Africans at the helm.[11]

The first step towards the Kampala Forum was convening prominent Africans from government, business, academia, and civil society to meet in Addis Ababa in November 1990. The ALF worked with the OAU Secretariat and the UN Economic Commission for Africa (UNECA) to host this meeting, so there was a direct injection of ideas into the African regional body. A further series of technical and consultative meetings led to the Kampala Forum in May 1991. The Forum was convened by the ALF, UNECA, and OAU and drew over 500 participants, from political and business leaders, to students and civil society activists. President Yoweri Museveni hosted the gathering, and it was attended by several other Heads of State, including Kenneth Kaunda of Zambia, Joaquim Chissano of Mozambique, former Tanzanian President Julius Nyerere, and Olusegun Obasanjo.[12] The fact that the ALF was founded by an African statesman and that the Kampala Forum was attended by many African Heads of States indicates that there was a direct line for the ideas developed at the Kampala Forum to enter into the discourse and impact the debates within the regional institution.

The Kampala Document is the outcome document from the 1991 conference, and it encompasses seven basic principles followed by policy recommendations. Principle II states, "The security, stability, and development of every African country are inseparably linked with those of other African countries. Consequently, instability in one African country impinges on the stability of all African countries."[13] Principle IV then goes on to assert that the interdependence of African states and the fundamental links between security, stability, and development demand a common approach and collective action.[14] Finally, the Kampala Document pushes for a more involved OAU on peace and security issues. While it acknowledges the primacy of the UNSC it advocates for the OAU in collaboration with the UN and African regional communities to have responsibility for security and development in Africa.[15] In all of this the Kampala Document is pushing forward the concepts of human security, sovereignty as responsibility, and interdependence:

> The Kampala Document rests on the premise that peace and security are necessary for the other three goals of stability, development, and cooperation. Lack of democracy, denial of personal liberty, and abuse of human rights are all causes of insecurity. The key to security, therefore, is the responsible exercise of sovereignty, in the absence of which cooperation among neighbors is required to deal with internal problems and conflicts.[16]

The original intention of the Kampala Forum was to create a document that would set down African principles on security, stability, development, and cooperation, which would then be adopted and enacted by states.[17] While there was significant participation from civil society and business sectors, this process was elite-led and headed by a former head of state with significant support from the OAU. Due to the significant buy-in from the OAU, the ALF expected that the OAU Assembly of Heads of State and Government would accept the proposals at their annual summit and begin to implement them. However, it was not adopted, and this was a setback for the Kampala Document proposals, showing that the path of institutional reform is not linear.

Institutional change is a dynamic process that happens over time and is predicated on ideas.[18] The strict adherence to non-intervention had been discredited by the atrocities committed by a handful of African leaders and the damage it was doing to OAU's missions of ridding the continent of racial regimes and advancing economic development. In the early 1990s credible ideas were beginning to emerge that could act as a blueprint for institutional change, and they were further developed throughout the course of the 1990s. However, it takes time and strong proponents to overcome resistance in a consensus organization. Two states primarily objected to the Kampala Document in 1991, but this was enough to send it back to the ministerial level where is languished. It returned to the forefront of African policy discussions after Olusegun Obasanjo was again elected president of

Nigeria, and was able to use his platform to raise it at the OAU Summits in Algiers and Sirte in the late 1990s.[19] At this point, Africa had also suffered further violent conflict and atrocities, from the wars in West Africa, to the Rwandan Genocide and the subsequent conflict in the Great Lakes region that had catastrophic human consequences and were damaging to Africa's interests.

Critical events, the advocacy of individual leaders, and evolving interests and values helped to discredit the OAU norms of strict non-interference and protection of state sovereignty at all costs. While the OAU attempted reforms in the 1980s, there was not transformative change because new ideas that could serve as a blueprint were not fully developed. Ideas that linked internal conflict with regional stability, endorsed a conception of human security, and promoted sovereignty as responsibility were developed by African leaders and institutions throughout the 1980s and 1990s, and African leaders drew on these ideas in the shift from the OAU to the AU. As described above, civil society organizations played a role in developing these ideas, and sub-regional organizations did as well. It is beyond the scope of this book to develop an in-depth explanation for how African sub-regional organizations developed their ideas and practices. However, they often did so prior to international actors, and sub-regional organizations are significant in the African context because they have been at the forefront of testing new ideas, policies, practices, and models that then influenced the regional body.

Influencing regional reform: sub-regional organizations

The legal and institutional structure of ECOWAS

Two sub-regional organizations are notable: ECOWAS and the Southern African Development Community (SADC). These were created with economic development and cooperation goals that were undermined by the proliferation of conflict, and each organization experimented with more robust responses to conflict situations, leading to a change in their constitutive documents to reflect their expanding peace and security work.[20] Both organizations implemented conflict resolution approaches that went well beyond what their constitutive acts and protocols allowed or envisioned, and their constitutive documents were revised after the fact to accommodate their new peace and security roles and practices. Ultimately, ECOWAS and SADC advanced the practice of conflict management in Africa by providing models of intervention, linking economic development with peace and stability, and setting precedents that contributed to evolving intervention practices at both the regional and international levels. This section will focus on exploring ECOWAS because of its early work in this area and its precedent-setting intervention in Liberia in 1990.

The West African sub-region is a particularly strong player in the peace and security realm although it did not start out that way. Throughout the 1960s and 1970s it became increasingly clear to many developing countries that bilateral trading relationships with major powers had costs and often hindered development. As a result, there were increased calls for cooperation and integration to strengthen self-reliance and bargaining power against powerful states, and West Africa was successful in creating a sub-regional economic bloc.[21] The basic principles of the organization were agreed at a ministerial meeting in December 1973, and the treaty creating ECOWAS was adopted at a Heads of State Summit on 28 May 1975 in Lagos, Nigeria.[22] The Lagos Treaty as it became known is the founding document and set out the ultimate objective of the organization as accelerating economic development of West African states through unity and the elimination of obstacles to free movement of goods, capital, and persons. It sought substantive cooperation in all economic fields, including industry, transport, telecommunications, agriculture, and natural resources, among others.[23] An Executive Secretary and Managing Director were both appointed in 1977, at which point ECOWAS began to function as a viable organization.[24]

The Lagos Treaty did not have provisions for political cooperation or regional efforts to address security threats. However, it soon became clear that this was a major weakness of the organization as it is impossible to foster economic development in the midst of violent conflict. The 1978 Protocol on Non-Aggression and 1981 Protocol Relating to Mutual Assistance on Defense sought to rectify this gap. The Protocol on Non-Aggression commits member states to refrain from aggression, use of force, or subversion against other member states. It also commits member states to settling any disputes that do arise peacefully or referring them to a central committee.[25] The Protocol on Mutual Assistance stipulates that any aggression towards one member state constitutes an attack on the entire West African community, and it commits all members to giving mutual assistance. It also allows for member states to take appropriate measures to address conflict in two additional circumstances. The first is in the event of armed conflict between two member states that cannot be settled peacefully, and the second is in the event of an internal conflict in a member state that is being engineered or supported by outside forces. Finally, the Protocol establishes a Defense Council and Defense Commission to deal with peace and security matters.[26] While the Protocol technically followed the prevailing norms prohibiting interference in the internal affairs it was vague enough to allow for interference in internal conflicts in a broad set of circumstances.

The focus of ECOWAS continued to expand, and the Community took on issues ranging from conflict resolution to democracy promotion. As such, the original 1975 treaty became not fit for purpose, and the ECOWAS treaty was revised in 1993, entering into force in 1995. The revised treaty affirms the aim of the Community to enhance economic cooperation and integration. However, the fundamental principles of ECOWAS were expanded to include the maintenance of peace and stability through good neighborliness, active cooperation between member states to maintain peace as a prerequisite for development, protection of human rights, and protection of democratic practices as agreed in the 1991 Declaration of Political Principles.[27] Article 22 establishes a technical commission on political, judicial and legal affairs, and regional security and immigration.[28] This differs from the original 1975 ECOWAS treaty, which focused on establishing technical commissions on economic issues with one ill-defined technical commission covering all social and cultural affairs.[29] Article 58 of the revised treaty deals with regional security whereas there was no such article in the original treaty. It stipulates that member states establish and strengthen, "appropriate mechanisms for the timely prevention of conflict prevention and resolution of intra-state and inter-state conflicts."[30]

It is important to note that the revised treaty stipulates cooperation to address internal conflicts as well as conflicts between states, and conflict prevention and management issues are included in the revised treaty whereas they were not included in the original. There was a gradual progression of peace and security practices in the West African sub-region. The additional protocols in 1978 and 1981 on security and defense issues were the first step. These protocols attempted to reform the existing sub-regional structure and provide a framework for a sub-regional response to conflict. However, the emergence of conflicts in Liberia and Sierra Leone that threatened not only the economic development of the sub-region but its very stability led to a robust response from ECOWAS that went well beyond what was permitted in the original 1975 treaty or additional protocols. The ECOWAS intervention in Liberia, in particular, provided a model that was used at both the sub-regional and regional levels.

Liberia was the first conflict that prompted a full-scale response from ECOWAS. The ECOWAS intervention and imposition of a ceasefire and interim constitution in Liberia in 1990 is particularly notable because it was the first attempt by an African sub-regional organization to undertake a military intervention and impose a peace process to halt an internal conflict. It was justified partly on humanitarian grounds, with the preamble to the ECOWAS decision stating:

Gravely concerned about the armed conflict existing in Liberia and the wanton destruction of human life and property ... Determined to find a peaceful and lasting solution to the conflict and to put an end to the situation which is seriously disrupting the normal life of innocent citizens in Liberia.[31]

ECOWAS actions laid the groundwork for subsequent sub-regional and regional efforts to address conflict. The intervention had many flaws, but that should not detract from its importance as a ground-breaking attempt by an African sub-regional organization to address conflict when other regional and international actors declined to do so.

The Liberian civil war began in 1989 when rebels launched an attack against Liberian security forces. It was brutal and characterized by mass violence against civilians as well as destruction of property and resources. All told, about 150,000 civilians were killed, representing 5 percent of the population and countless others were impacted by the brutality of the conflict.[32] ECOWAS took up the issue of conflict in the sub-region in May 1990 by establishing an ECOWAS Standing Mediation Committee (SMC) to investigate and promptly intervene in disputes between states that threaten the stability of the community. Member states were elected to serve on the mediation committee, including Gambia, Ghana, Togo, Mali, and Nigeria.[33] Building on the work of Liberian civil society, the SMC worked through the summer and proposed an ECOWAS peace plan at a summit in Banjul in August 1990, which included establishing an interim government, holding elections, and imposing a ceasefire. The most notable aspect of this plan was the establishment of a mechanism to monitor the ceasefire, which became known as ECOMOG (Economic Community of West African States Monitoring Group), and was mandated to restore law and order and monitor adherence to a ceasefire.[34] The most challenging part was getting the warring factions to accept it and abide by it, and Charles Taylor and his National Patriotic Front of Liberia rebel group were particularly reluctant to agree to a ceasefire, instead preferring an outright military victory.

ECOWAS proceeded with its peace plan and helped create an interim government and deployed ECOMOG. Its core mandate was to protect life and property and provide some semblance of law and order.[35] If ECOMOG was unable to persuade the armed factions to surrender and join the peace process then they were to enforce peace by any means possible. The initial force of about 2,500 troops from Gambia, Ghana, Guinea, Nigeria, and Sierra Leone was deployed in late August 1990.[36]

The military intervention was immediately challenged by the parties to the conflict, and in September 1990 ECOMOG adopted a stronger approach under a new field commander, Major General J.N. Dogonyaro, in order to compel parties to accept a ceasefire. ECOMOG delivered an ultimatum to rebels, blockaded strategic ports to prevent the delivery of arms and supplies to rebel groups, and carried out a bombardment of the rebel lines to create a buffer zone around Monrovia. With its strengthened approach, ECOMOG was able to evacuate 30,000 displaced people and secure the release of 5,000 prisoners.[37] Despite its show of strength, ECOMOG was not able to bring an end to the civil war and concerns amongst member states about ECOMOG's approach and viability began to emerge. The SMC had severely underestimated the logistical complications and financial burdens that such a mission would involve, and when ECOMOG was not able to easily control the Liberian territory or convince all the warring parties to agree to a ceasefire, fatigue and in-fighting amongst member states began to set in.[38]

Political negotiations and ECOMOG operations continued for years, and eventually the UN became more involved and took over the peace-keeping mission, although the UN often looked to ECOWAS for cues. On 19 November 1992, the UNSC adopted Resolution 788 supporting the October 1991 Yamoussoukro IV Accord as a viable framework for peace. The resolution recalled the decisions of the ECOWAS SMC as a framework for action. It also named the civil war in Liberia as a threat to international peace and security, particularly for the West African sub-region, and commended ECOWAS for its work to restore peace, security, and stability.[39] The resolution invoked Chapter VII of the UN Charter to call for a complete weapons embargo of Liberia and asked members states, "to respect the measures established by ECOWAS to bring about a peaceful solution to the conflict in Liberia."[40] Despite these efforts, the conflict continued, and the UNSC adopted Resolution 866 which created the UN Observer Force in Liberia on 22 September 1993. In July 1993 a new peace agreement had been signed – the Cotonou Agreement – which called on both ECOMOG and the UN to assist in its implementation. Resolution 866 recognized that the primary responsibility for implementing the agreement would fall to ECOWAS, while the UN mission would monitor implementation. It also notes that this is the first time that the UN would be cooperating with a peacekeeping mission already set up by a regional body.[41] Finally, there was regional support for ECOWAS efforts. OAU Secretary General Salim Ahmed Salim praised ECOWAS for its robust efforts to solve African problems and gain the respect of the international community while doing so.[42]

Precedents from the ECOWAS intervention in Liberia

ECOWAS justified its initial deployment in 1990 of a military force into a member state's territory to address an internal conflict on largely humanitarian and regional stability grounds. President Samuel Doe did appeal to several organizations, including ECOWAS, for assistance. However, it is unlikely that ECOWAS deployed ECOMOG in response to Doe's pleas. By August 1990, Doe was no longer in control of the country and held no real authority. Additionally, the mandate given to ECOMOG by the SMC focused on restoring law and order and creating conditions necessary for elections not on restoring Doe to the presidency.[43] The ECOWAS legal instruments that were in force in 1990 – including the ECOWAS Treaty, Protocol on Non-Aggression, and Protocol relating to Mutual Assistance on Defense – did not provide a legal justification for a military intervention, and the intervention was not approved by the UNSC before it was undertaken. Levitt therefore argues that ECOWAS justified its intervention with an emerging customary international law that allowed for humanitarian intervention.[44] It was clear that no regional or international body was prepared to intervene. The US declined to get involved despite close ties to Liberia, and the UN took cues from the UN African Group that discouraged outside involvement in African conflicts. As the humanitarian impacts of the conflict intensified, leading to refugee outflows and regional instability, ECOWAS assumed responsibility and in essence created a new type of interventionism.[45] The ECOWAS intervention was given retroactive approval by the UNSC through the resolutions discussed above, thus offering credibility to this approach and establishing it as a precedent in the international sphere.

Despite the supportive language in the UN resolutions, there is a great deal of debate about the extent to which the UN resolutions merely supported the ECOWAS initiative versus offering an endorsement of it. Between 1991 and 1996 the UN Security Council adopted fifteen resolutions on Liberia, and nearly all of them commended ECOWAS for its efforts or offered explicit support for ECOWAS initiatives to end the conflict.[46] However, some legal scholars argue that the ECOWAS intervention failed to meet the standards of a legitimate humanitarian intervention, and the UN was simply supporting the ECOWAS initiative because it had no choice. Ofodile contends that there is no right to humanitarian intervention if it is undertaken outside the auspices of the UN. Furthermore, the UNSC resolutions did not offer an endorsement of ECOWAS action but simply supported the only course of action on the table to end the conflict in Liberia.[47] As such, ECOWAS action in Liberia did not meet the standards for a humanitarian intervention that it claimed justified the military intervention. Based on previous UN debates, there are eight criteria to examine when assessing whether an intervention is truly humanitarian, including whether all peaceful means for solving the conflict had been exhausted, no immediate hope of relief, justifiable cost-benefit analysis, and limited duration and proportionality. On these criteria, Ofodile argues that the ECOMOG intervention did not meet the standards of humanitarian intervention because, among other things, all peaceful means had not been exhausted, the costs of the mission outweighed its benefits, and ECOWAS attempted to set up a government in Liberia.[48]

I argue that the legalities under international law are secondary to the practical outcomes for the purpose of understanding evolving intervention and peace and security norms. One of the stated purposes of the ECOWAS engagement in Liberia was to protect civilians. ECOWAS undertook action to halt the violence, including deploying military troops and facilitating the establishment of an interim government, of its own volition and without prior authorization from the UNSC. This was a first of its kind intervention by a sub-regional organization. Regardless of whether or not the UN intended to simply support an ongoing peace process or offer an explicit endorsement for a regional model of conflict management and response, the outcome was a perception of approval and a precedent for future efforts. The ECOWAS intervention provided a model that the OAU drew upon when trying to strengthen its capacity to respond to conflicts.[49] It was also pioneering in the international arena. ECOMOG troops entered Liberia in August 1990. This was just as the Cold War was ending and before international interventions in Iraq and Somalia in the early 1990s. The only other possible parallel is the Organization of Eastern Caribbean States intervention in Grenada in 1983. Although in the case of Grenada the international community and the UN condemned the intervention as setting a dangerous precedent, and there are sufficient differences, including the involvement of the US and a secondary motivation to prevent the spread of communism, that render the parallel inappropriate.[50]

Examining a broader spectrum of eight interventions by African states or sub-regional organizations between 1990 and 1998 Levitt concludes that, "African states are largely responsible for spurring new norms of international law relating to the use of force and the customary international law doctrine of humanitarian intervention."[51] Levitt's analysis sets out a timeline of African-led interventions that happened before or in tandem with other notable interventions by international bodies justified on humanitarian grounds. African states did not simply localize an emerging international norm of humanitarian intervention in the 1990s as there were intervention precedents from the African continent. The regional body did not draw inspiration from international norms but rather member states, civil society, and sub-regional institutions, and African leaders were active participants in its construction and implementation of new AU norms.

While other actors in the international community and the UN also pushed forward intervention norms in the early 1990s before a retrenchment in the mid-1990s, the precedents set by African sub-regional actors are often overlooked when delineating the key influences on the African region as a whole. In fact, the OAU states explicitly in internal documents that the regional body drew on sub-regional precedents. The 1993 Secretary General's response outlining the establishment of the OAU Mechanism for Conflict Prevention, Management, and Resolution states, "Member states argued that, the OAU had already witnessed the rudiments of such a mechanism as evolved by some of its own members within the framework of ECOWAS involvement in the Liberian conflict. That measure, they felt, should be extrapolated at the continental level."[52] Furthermore, Nigeria was heavily involved in supporting the concept of ECOMOG and then providing financial backing and troops. As will be described in Chapter 11, both Nigerian and South African leaders were pivotal voices in negotiations around the construction of the AU Constitutive Act.

Notes

1 "Introduction to the Report of the Secretary General to the 28th Ordinary Session of the OAU Assembly of Heads of State and Government," CM/1706 (LVI) Part 1 (Organization of African Unity, 22 June-1 July 1992), 17–19. AU Commission Archives.

2 Monde Muyangwa and Margaret A. Vogt, "An Assessment of the OAU Mechanism for Conflict Prevention, Management, and Resolution, 1993–2000" (New York: International Peace Academy, 2000), 6–7.

3 "Biography of Dr. Salim Ahmed Salim" (United Nations, April 2002), www.un.org/News/dh/hlpanel/salim-salim-bio.htm (accessed 7 May 2020).

4 "Report of the Secretary-General on the Fundamental Changes Taking Place in the World and Their Implications for Africa: Proposals for an African Response," AHG/169 (XXVI) (Organization of African Unity, July 1990), 4. AU Commission Archives.

5 "Report of the Secretary-General on the Fundamental Changes Taking Place in the World and Their Implications for Africa," 5.

6 "Report of the Secretary-General on the Fundamental Changes Taking Place in the World and Their Implications for Africa," 5.

7 "Report of the Secretary-General on the Fundamental Changes Taking Place in the World and Their Implications for Africa," 23.

8 "Report of the Secretary-General on the Fundamental Changes Taking Place in the World and Their Implications for Africa," 24.

9 "Report of the Secretary-General on the Fundamental Changes Taking Place in the World and Their Implications for Africa," 7.

10 "Report of the Secretary-General on the Fundamental Changes Taking Place in the World and Their Implications for Africa," 23.

11 Ayodele Aderinwale, "The Conference on Security, Stability, Development and Cooperation in Framework and the Role of Regional Institutions," in *Peace, Human Security and Conflict Prevention in Africa*, ed. Moufida Goucha and Jakkie Cilliers (Pretoria, South Africa: Institute for Security Studies, 2001), 62.

12 Aderinwale, "The Conference on Security," 62.

13 Francis M. Deng and I. William Zartman, *A Strategic Vision for Africa: The Kampala Movement* (Washington DC: Brookings Institute Press, 2002), 6–7.

14 Deng and Zartman, *A Strategic Vision for Africa*, 7.

15 Aderinwale, "The Conference on Security," 64.

16 Deng and Zartman, *A Strategic Vision for Africa*, 7–8.

17 Deng and Zartman, *A Strategic Vision for Africa*, 5.

18 Mark Blyth, *Great Transformations: Economic Ideas and Institutional Change in the Twentieth Century* (New York: Cambridge University Press, 2002), 35–37.

19 Aderinwale, "The Conference on Security," 63.

20 Erika de Wet, "The Evolving Role of ECOWAS and the SADC in Peace Operations: A Challenge to the Primacy of the United Nations Security Council in Matters of Peace and Security?," *Leiden Journal of International Law* 27 (2014): 353.

21 "ECOWAS: Achievements, Challenges, and Future Prospects" (Lagos, Nigeria, n.d.), 4–5.

22 "Development of the Community – The First Five Years" (Lagos, Nigeria, 1981), 9.

23 "The 1975 Treaty of the Economic Community of West African States," (Economic Community of West African States, 28 May 1975). Archiving and Documentation Division, Communications Directorate, ECOWAS Commission.

24 "Development of the Community," 9.

25 "Economic Community of West African States Protocol on Non-Aggression" (Economic Community of West African States, 20 April 1978), http://docum entation.ecowas.int/download/en/legal_documents/protocols/Protocol%20 on%20Non-aggression.pdf (accessed 7 May 2020).

26 "Protocol A/SP. 3/5/81 Relating to Mutual Assistance on Defence" (Economic Community of West African States, 29 May 1981). Archiving and Documentation Division, Communications Directorate, ECOWAS Commission.

27 "Economic Community of West African States (ECOWAS): Revised Treaty," (Economic Community of West African States, 24 July 1993), 6–7. Archiving and Documentation Division, Communications Directorate, ECOWAS Commission.

28 "Economic Community of West African States (ECOWAS): Revised Treaty," 15.

29 "The 1975 Treaty of the Economic Community of West African States," 23.

30 "Economic Community of West African States (ECOWAS): Revised Treaty," 36.

31 "Decision A/DEC.1/8/90 on the Ceasefire and Establishment of an ECOWAS Ceasefire Monitoring Group for Liberia (ECOWAS Peace Plan)," 1.

32 "OAU Conflict Management Review: Echoes from Liberia" (Organization of African Unity, n.d.), 3. AU Commission Archives.

33 Earl Conteh-Morgan, "The Politics and Diplomacy of the Liberian Peace Process," in *Peacekeeping in Africa*, ed. Karl P. Magyar and Earl Conteh-Morgan (London: Macmillan Press Ltd, 1998), 46.

34 "ECOWAS: Achievements, Challenges, and Future Prospects," 29.

35 Lt. Colonel Festus B. Aboagye, *ECOMOG: A Sub-Regional Experience in Conflict Resolution, Management, and Peacekeeping in Liberia* (Accra, Ghana: Seco Publishing Limited, 1999), 62.

36 Aboagye, *ECOMOG*, 81.

37 Aboagye, *ECOMOG*, 89–90.

38 Michelle Pitts, "Sub-Regional Solutions for African Conflict: The ECOMOG Experiment," *Journal of Conflict Studies* 19, no. 1 (1999), https://journals.lib. unb.ca/index.php/JCS/article/view/4379/5057 (accessed 7 May 2020).

39 "Resolution 788 (1992): Adopted by the Security Council at Its 3138th Meeting" (United Nations, 19 November 1992), http://unscr.com/en/resolu tions/788 (accessed 7 May 2020).

40 "Resolution 788 (1992)."

41 "Resolution 866 (1993): Adopted by the Security Council at Its 3281st Meeting" (United Nations, September 22, 1993), http://unscr.com/en/resolutions/866 (accessed 7 May 2020).

42 "ECOWAS: Achievements, Challenges, and Future Prospects," 29.

43 Jeremy Levitt, "African Interventionist States and International Law," in *African Interventionist States*, ed. Oliver Furley and Roy May (Aldershot: Ashgate Publishing Limited, 2001), 19–20.

44 Levitt, "African Interventionist States and International Law," 21.

45 Pitts, "Sub-Regional Solutions for African Conflict."

46 Levitt, "African Interventionist States and International Law," 20–21.

47 Anthony Chukwuka Ofodile, "The Legality of ECOWAS Intervention in Liberia," *Columbia Journal of Transnational Law* 32 (1994–1995): 414–15.

48 Ofodile, "The Legality of ECOWAS Intervention in Liberia," 396.

49 "Report of the Secretary-General on the Establishment of a Mechanism for Conflict Prevention, Resolution, and Management," CM/1767 (LVIII) (Organization of African Unity, June 1993), 32. AU Commission Archives.

50 Ofodile, "The Legality of ECOWAS Intervention in Liberia," 382.

51 Levitt, "African Interventionist States and International Law," 15.

52 "Report of the Secretary-General on the Establishment of a Mechanism for Conflict Prevention, Resolution, and Management," 32.

9

The final decade of the Organization of African Unity

The OAU Report on the Fundamental Changes Taking Place in the World along with the influence of leaders within the OAU and the impact of events over time set the stage for another reform of the body's approach to conflict. However, again the OAU chose to pursue an institutional fix by creating a new mechanism but still working within the normative confines of the existing organization. Although there was a stronger push for institutional reform, which resulted in the creation of a new, permanent body within the OAU, there was not the consensus needed to transform the institution. As mentioned above, two states opposed the ideas put forth in the Kampala Document, and this was enough to stop its adoption by the OAU Assembly of Heads of State and Government. The Mechanism for Conflict Prevention, Management, and Resolution was established in 1993, but it was ineffective in stemming the flow of conflicts and atrocities that plagued the continent. As this chapter will demonstrate, the failures of the Mechanism to prevent numerous conflicts, and the Rwandan Genocide in particular, would have a profound impact on African leaders. It would be the experiences of the 1990s, and the full development of human security and sovereignty as responsibility ideas, that would provide the final push for the normative and institutional transformation of the OAU into the AU.

The Mechanism for Conflict Prevention, Management, and Resolution

Creating the Mechanism

In February 1992, the OAU Council of Ministers endorsed a proposal to establish a permanent Mechanism for Conflict Prevention, Management, and Resolution. The OAU recognized that two of the fundamental weaknesses of the previous conflict resolution mechanism – the Commission of Mediation, Conciliation and Arbitration – were its sole focus on inter-state conflicts and the lack of any kind of conflict prevention mandate.[1] The Secretary General's July 1992 report to the Assembly of Heads of State and Government reiterated the gravity of several conflict situations in Africa and their humanitarian and economic repercussions, and it detailed the efforts made to resolve outstanding conflicts and the institutional processes to establish a permanent and empowered conflict resolution body.[2] The Mechanism for Conflict Prevention, Management, and Resolution was formally established in 1993 after much debate about how to rectify the weaknesses of previous approaches.

When examining the Commission of Mediation, Conciliation and Arbitration as well as numerous ad hoc commissions, the OAU clearly struggled with the appropriate balance between approaches that might best be described as either judicial or political. The Commission of Mediation, Conciliation and Arbitration approached conflict resolution through judicial processes. Conflicting parties had to request assistance from the Commission. They would then enter into legal process to try to find a solution. While negotiations on political issues could feasibly take place within the confines of these processes, there was no way to compel parties to address thorny issues, and the operational assumption was that states would want to resolve conflicts between them. The ad hoc commissions went to the opposite extreme. There were no processes or institutions in place to prevent or manage conflict. They were formed only when the OAU deemed it necessary or politically expedient, which typically meant when a conflict began to garner international attention or impact regional goals. Finally, ad hoc commissions depended on the good offices of prominent and respected leaders to be able to push conflicting parties to agree to a ceasefire and address the issues causing the conflict.

The conflict resolution approaches taken by the OAU for the first three decades of its existence can be best described as fire extinguishers that acted to contain conflicts and prevent them from spreading or drawing international attention. Despite going to the trouble of creating the Commission of Mediation, Conciliation and Arbitration, the OAU almost always offered an ad hoc response wherein statesmen offered guidance and support without the deliberative judicial processes that may have prescribed more effective remedies for the conflict but would have been problematic for leaders and relationships.[3] Over time the OAU became ever more reluctant to get actively involved in conflicts for fear of damaging African solidarity, and preferred to encourage bilateral negotiations.[4] The establishment of the Mechanism for Conflict Prevention, Resolution, and Management in 1993 was the first successful effort to overhaul the OAU's conflict management framework, although it was done within the existing normative constraints.

The Assembly of Heads of State and Government adopted the OAU Declaration on a Mechanism for Conflict Prevention, Management, and Resolution, otherwise known as the Cairo Declaration, in June 1993. The Declaration affirmed that the Mechanism will operate within the confines of the OAU Charter, and it specifically mentioned the importance of sovereign equality amongst member states, non-interference, respect for sovereignty and territorial integrity, inviolability of colonial borders, peaceful settlement of disputes, and the consent and cooperation of parties to a conflict.[5] The primary objective of the Mechanism is the anticipation and prevention of conflicts. Where those efforts fail, the Mechanism was then empowered to undertake peacemaking and peace-building functions. The Declaration does explicitly allow for civilian and military observation and monitoring missions provided they are of limited scope and duration. The OAU chose to focus on preventative measures and peacemaking work and to avoid creating an institutional mechanism that could manage large-scale conflict simply because the OAU could not afford to finance large-scale peace-enforcement and re-building operations. However, the Declaration does mandate that if such a response is needed then the regional body should call upon the services of the UN while working with international bodies to find meaningful ways to contribute.[6]

While the Declaration does not mention exceptions to non-interference, the Secretary General's 1993 report on the establishment of the Mechanism does highlight the debate that took place amongst the member states on this issue. In these discussions, the OAU Charter takes precedence, but it was recognized that there are exceptional circumstances that may require an exceptional response. Somalia and Liberia were recognized as examples of exceptional circumstances where extreme suffering and a complete breakdown of law and order necessitated OAU involvement. The report states, "In such cases, the OAU did not only have the right but also the obligation to get involved even before appealing to the international community."[7] However, OAU member states decided that such cases where outside interference is warranted must be decided on an individual basis, so there was no considered approach of when exceptional intervention is justified, only an acknowledgment that it was justified in two past cases. That these discussions occurred, though, is evidence of a debate about the nature and appropriateness of intervention within the regional organization in the early 1990s.

Functionally, the Mechanism was made up of two bodies – the Central Organ and the Conflict Management Division. The Central Organ was comprised of 16 member states elected annually, and served as the decision-making body of the Mechanism. The Central Organ was mandated to meet once a year at the Heads of State and Government level, twice a year at the ministerial level, and monthly at the Ambassadorial level. The Central Organ could also be convened by the Chairman or at the request of a member state or the OAU Secretary General.[8] These procedures indicate the OAU's attempt to regularize engagement on conflict issues instead of only engaging with a conflict after it reached a crisis point, and reflects the prevention mandate of the Mechanism. The Conflict Management Division was meant to be the operational arm of the Central Organ. It operated under the leadership of the Secretary General, and was responsible for collecting and disseminating information on conflict in Africa, undertaking research into the causes of conflict and providing expert analysis, preparing policy options to address conflict, supporting observer missions, and coordinating support to peace missions. The OAU also created an Early Warning System to monitor impending conflict situations and a Peace Fund to finance the Mechanism's activities.[9]

The goals and structure of the OAU Mechanism were reactions to past failures, while also being inspired by models and practices that came from sub-regional organizations. In this we see the direct impact of sub-regional organizations on the formation of ideas and practices at the regional level. ECOWAS provided a particularly important model through its intervention in Liberia, which began in 1990. While there were many flaws with the ECOWAS intervention that was still ongoing at the time, it also provided a model of an African regional organization engaging in an internal conflict situation. Even if an exact copy of the ECOWAS model was not adopted, the approach provided the OAU, "with a sense of confidence, a road map, as well as critical lessons on which to build for the future."[10]

There was also a palpable sense of a renewed threat of outside intervention if Africa did not rise to the challenge to address its own conflicts. This is again an instance when a primary goal of the OAU was threatened, and it was part of the impetus to seek to reform the organization's approach to conflict. The Secretary General's report on the establishment of the Mechanism stated:

> It is imperative for the Organization to take a decision to establish the Mechanism as soon as possible, otherwise others outside the continent would intervene fill the vacuum thus created; and mention was made of Somalia as a case in point. Africa, it was stressed, was fortunate that the intervention in Somalia had not occurred on a unilateral basis but under the multilateral auspices of the UN. One could not, however, be certain that unilateral interventions would not occur in the future. In that regard, it was better for Africa to intervene to put its own stamp on conflict situations rather than stand the risk of being completely marginalized.[11]

Successes of the Mechanism

The Mechanism was a significant improvement over the defunct Commission of Mediation, Conciliation and Arbitration and inconsistent ad hoc measures. However, its effectiveness was hampered by resource constraints, an over-reliance on the UN to solve the most serious conflicts, and an inability to overcome the principle of non-interference. The work of the Mechanism was institutionalized within the OAU. Meetings at all levels occurred regularly with discussions on the current conflicts in Africa and progress on addressing them. For example, the first ministerial-level meeting of the Central Organ took place in November 1993 just a few months after the creation of the Mechanism in July. The Ministers discussed the Peace Fund, strengthening the General Secretariat in the field of conflict management, and received updates on the conflicts taking place in Africa.[12] Simply institutionalizing the practice of regular high-level engagement on conflict issues is significant considering the previous completely ad hoc approach. Despite this modest progress, the Mechanism still encountered great difficulties in effectively preventing and responding to conflicts. There were some small successes but also massive failures, which pushed the OAU ever closer to a complete revision of its Charter and peace and security structures.

The OAU was actively involved in Burundi in the 1990s. After the carnage of the Rwandan Genocide, there was particular concern about Burundi because it suffered from the same tensions between Hutus and Tutsis. The OAU deployed a very small observer mission in Burundi in the mid-1990s. At any given time it was comprised of only a few dozen observers. While it was too small to have any real impact, it may have been an important signal that helped to reduce tensions for a short period. The OAU also supported bilateral efforts by Tanzania and then South Africa to find a negotiated settlement to the conflict, and it endorsed the decision of states in the sub-region to impose sanctions on Burundi to pressure the government to end the violence. Finally, it continued to participate in consultations and issued statements condemning the violence that had killed approximately 200,000 people since 1993.[13] However, despite OAU and sub-regional engagement the effort to prevent violence largely failed.

The OAU also became engaged in an internal conflict in Comoros in the late 1990s. Despite being an internal conflict, it was at the request of the elected government, so it was clearly supported by international law and OAU norms. The trouble began in August 1997 when separatists took over two of the four islands that make up Comoros. The government of Comoros responded by sending troops to regain control of the islands and appealing to the OAU and other organizations for assistance. The OAU took up the appeal by sending a special envoy and ministerial mission to convince the separatists and the government to come to the negotiating table. The OAU ministerial mission monitored the progress of the talks and reported that efforts to find a negotiated settlement had stalled. In line with the Mechanism's primary function of conflict prevention, the Central Organ responded by sending a 24-person Observer Mission in the Comoros (OMIC) to build confidence and show support for a diplomatic solution.[14]

OMIC had moderate success and was able to work with one island, but separatists from the island of Anjouan refused to work with them. They moved forward with their plans for secession by arranging a referendum and drafting a constitution, at which point the OAU increased their pressure. The OAU argued that Anjouan separatists were threatening the territorial integrity of a member state. Violence once again broke out in late 1998, and the President of Comoros requested military assistance from the OAU. The OAU was not able to send military assistance, but they did launch a new peace initiative by calling for a conference involving all parties to the conflict. The conference took place in Madagascar in early 1999 and led to the signing of the Antananarivo Agreement by some separatists, but again the delegation from Anjouan remained unwilling to accept anything short of independence. Violence once again broke out, and OMIC was largely withdrawn, with only a small team remaining to try to re-establish dialogue. The OAU Central Organ reiterated its commitment to supporting a peaceful resolution and continued to work in Comoros, which included launching two subsequent observer missions.[15] However, it was very difficult for the OAU to prevent conflict when engaging in a scenario where one party was unwilling to find a negotiated solution and with no credible threat of military force to compel a compromise.

Failures of the Mechanism

While the OAU may have made very limited contributions in some conflict scenarios, there were also numerous catastrophic failures. The 1994 Rwandan Genocide and wars in the Democratic Republic of the Congo are the most notable failures of the OAU Mechanism, either because of complete inaction or ineffectiveness, and both of these events had tremendous ramifications for Africa and the global community. The OAU achieved rare success with assistance to negotiate of an end to the war between the Tutsi Rwandan Patriotic Front (RPF) and the Hutu Rwandan government. Between 1990 and 1992, the OAU supported mediation efforts.[16] Then in 1992, Tanzania hosted peace talks in Arusha that culminated in the Arusha Accord signed in August 1993. An OAU Military Observer Group in Rwanda arrived there in 1991 and stayed throughout the early 1990s. It was integrated into the UN Assistance Mission for Rwanda (UNAMIR), which arrived in the country in October 1993.[17] This was how the Mechanism was supposed to work. The OAU had undertaken a peace-building effort through the deployment of a small, financially feasible observer force and facilitated negotiations leading to a peace agreement. The UN then came in with additional resources and funding when a larger peacekeeping mission was needed to implement the agreement. However, the assumption that the UN would be reliable in responding to large-scale conflicts or atrocities in Africa when needed was soon completely dispelled.

On the evening of 6 April 1994, a plane carrying Rwandan President Juvénal Habyarimana was shot down as it was landing in Kigali. This was taken as a signal by Hutu extremists, who had long been planning genocide against the Tutsi population, to begin to implement their plan. Moderate leaders who could oppose the slaughter were targeted first in this meticulously planned atrocity, and then the violence emanated out across the country. Between April and July 1994, when the RPF finally succeeded in regaining control of the country and stopping the killing, 800,000 Tutsis and moderate Hutus were killed.[18] There were indications that a catastrophe was on the horizon. On 11 January 1994, UNAMIR Force Commander Roméo Dallaire sent a cable to the UN Department of Peacekeeping Operations (UNDPKO) with information from an informant about secret weapons caches and a plan to exterminate the Tutsis. The informant told UNAMIR in chilling detail that he was paid to train militias to kill, and he estimated his personnel could kill 1,000 Tutsis in 20 minutes. He also detailed a plot to draw Belgium soldiers into a fight where they would be killed thus prompting a withdrawal of the Belgium contingent from UNAMIR.[19] UNDPKO responded by advising Dallaire to not take any action that could feasibly lead to a use of force and instead to inform the President of Rwanda on the assumption that he would not be aware of any of the plots being undertaken by members of his government to kill civilians.[20]

Both the international and the regional responses to the Rwandan Genocide were abysmal. Despite the efforts of the UNAMIR Force Commander, the UN did nothing to prevent the impending tragedy, and after the genocide began the UN focused on protecting expatriates and then disengaging as much as possible. On 7 April 1994, UNAMIR troops were ordered not to intervene as Hutu militias set up roadblocks and began to hunt down Tutsis and moderate Hutus, including the Rwandan Prime Minister. On the same day, 10 Belgium peacekeepers were kidnapped, tortured, and murdered just as the informant had described. Days later, France and the US sent in troops to evacuate their nationals, and no assistance was given to Rwandans. On 14 April, Belgium withdrew its troops from UNAMIR, and the following week the UNSC voted unanimously to cut the number of troops in UNAMIR from 2,500 to 270. By this time tens of thousands of Rwandans had been killed, and the genocide would continue until mid-July when the RPF regained control of the country. To avoid the necessity of action, the genocide was characterized as tribal, and despite rivers being clogged with bodies and refugee flows into the millions, major powers did not muster the political will to respond. The UN would eventually vote to restore UNAMIR strength, but no additional troops would arrive until several months after the end of the genocide.[21]

Despite having good intentions to end the violence in Rwanda, the OAU made disastrous miscalculations during the Arusha peace process and failed to act in much the same way that the UN did after the genocide began. The Arusha peace process to end the civil war was a sincere, African-led initiative to stop a conflict before it escalated further. The premise of the diplomatic effort was that if a negotiated settlement to the civil war between the Rwandan government and the RPF could be reached then that would help to address the underlying tensions between Hutus and Tutsis. This was a miscalculation, and ultimately the intransigence of the Hutu extremists and the polarization of the country undermined the peace process.[22] Like UNDPKO, African diplomats were aware of at least the possibility of large-scale atrocities. On 17 January 1994, the UN Secretary General's Special Representative for Rwanda told African diplomats in Kigali that there were training camps presumably for training those who would take part in killing Tutsis.[23] Once the genocide began, the OAU was just as feckless as the international community. Throughout the entirety of the genocide, the OAU refused to call it genocide or take sides. The OAU chose to remain neutral, and it urged both parties to declare a ceasefire and return to the negotiating table, which of course failed to acknowledge the one-sided nature of the slaughter. In the meantime, the OAU welcomed the interim Rwandan government that was carrying out the genocide as the official representatives of Rwanda at the June 1994 OAU Summit. While some African states did condemn the genocide and advocate for a more robust response there was no such push from the African regional body.[24]

Rwanda had a profound impact on how Africa and the global community dealt with conflict and atrocities, but these changes were not immediately apparent. It took several years for the lessons to be drawn out and for changes to be made. The OAU Assembly of Heads of State and Government created an International Panel of Eminent Personalities in 1998. It was completely independent and asked not only to investigate the causes of and response to the genocide but also to give recommendations to prevent future catastrophes. The Panel of Eminent Personalities condemned both the international community and the region for their actions leading up to the genocide and after the killing began. In particular, they denounced neutrality when dealing with the two sides. Their report concluded:

Until the day the genocide ended with the RPF's military victory in the civil war, the UN, the governments of the US, France, and Belgium, African governments, and the OAU, all failed to define the massacres as full-blown genocide. All continued to recognize members of the génocidaire government as legitimate official representatives of Rwanda. All except the French government retained a neutral public stance between a government practicing genocide and that government's sole adversary, the RPF. In practice, however, neutrality allowed the genocide to happen.[25]

The Panel also made strong judgments against miscalculations about the willingness of extremists to honor an agreement and the capacity of the OAU to undertake peacemaking with no enforcement mechanisms. On the OAU's role of facilitating a peaceful resolution to the conflict in Rwanda leading up to the genocide, the Panel found:

> Much of the history of the 1990s is the story of well-meant initiatives, endless consultations, incessant meetings, commitments made, and commitments broken. These frenetic activities reflected the real world of the OAU Secretariat, which has no capacity to make decisions independent of its members, to force any parties to do its bidding, or to punish anyone for ignoring its wishes. What the OAU can do is call meetings, hope the invited attend, facilitate agreements, and hope the participants abide by their word.[26]

Finally, the Panel also condemned the international community for their action to protect expatriates in Rwanda but for their apathy towards Rwandan civilians. They argued that this was reflective of a wider attitude toward Africa, and this had profound ramifications for Africa's trust in international bodies to address conflicts on the continent. The Panel summarized the view of the region by saying, "The consequence, as OAU officials point out, is that the international community is only willing to intervene when it is not needed, a reflection of Africa's marginalized status within the international community."[27]

The Rwandan Genocide was a tragedy that had ramifications well beyond a singular event. Millions of refugees flowed from Rwanda into neighboring countries. Among those refugees were people who had participated in the genocide who continued to pose a security threat to Rwanda and the region. In May 1997, Laurent Kabila ousted Mobutu Sese Seko from power with the support of Rwanda and Uganda. When Kabila was unable to deal with the security threat of génocidaires hiding amongst refugee populations in eastern Congo, Rwanda and Uganda withdrew their support. In August 1998, a rebellion broke out in Eastern Congo, and the anti-Kabila rebels were supported by Rwanda and Uganda. The conflict would soon draw in most of Congo's neighbors. The OAU once again tried to address the problem by organizing negotiations, and in July 1999 a ceasefire was agreed through the Lusaka peace process.[28] Unfortunately the ceasefire did not hold, and the violence continued.[29]

The lessons the Panel of Eminent Personalities spelled out manifested in changes that were made in the transition from non-interference under the OAU to non-indifference under the AU. The first lesson from the Panel was the danger of neutrality. Even today, the AU is an organization that abides by the values of sovereign equality of member states and consensus diplomacy. Disagreements are debated behind closed doors. However, as discussed in Chapter 2, in recent years the AU has publicly condemned some member states and implicitly invoked Article 4(h) in negotiations with member states. The second lesson was the difficulty of undertaking effective peace-building with no capacity to coerce actors into meaningful negotiations or enforce peace. When the APSA was created, the PSC was given greater capacity to impose sanctions and compel actors to end conflict, and the inclusion of Article 4(h) also meant a mechanism that could be used implicitly or explicitly to coerce a state or group to end violence or face the deployment of a non-consensual peacekeeping force. Finally, the Panel's findings also highlighted the inadequacy of depending on the UN to respond to major conflicts or atrocities in Africa. Contrary to the declaration establishing the OAU Mechanism for Conflict Prevention, Management, and Resolution, the African regional body needed to build up its capacity and resources to respond to a major crisis. Jean Ping, former Chair of the AU Commission, reflected on the impact of the Rwandan Genocide in a 2008 speech at the Round-Table High-Level Meeting of Experts on the Responsibility to Protect in Africa. He emphasized the findings of OAU Panel of Eminent Personalities on the failure of the UN and OAU to respond to the Rwandan Genocide, and argued that the Genocide traumatized Africa and pushed the regional organization to change its position on peace and security. He stated, "there is no doubt that the provision in Article 4(h) of the AU Constitutive Act was informed not only by the shame generated by the Rwandan Genocide but also by the realization that one cannot be indifferent to a fire engulfing a neighbor's house because it could very well end up razing his house as well."[30]

Impact of the events of the 1990s in Africa

The 1990s were a time of transition for both Africa and the world. The end of the Cold War signaled a shift in global power structures and alliances, and African leaders were concerned about the impact of this monumental event on Africa and changing dynamics on the continent. Notably, the OAU was concerned about economic aid being funneled away from Africa and economic competition with Eastern Europe.[31] The regional body also had long-standing concerns, including the stagnant African economy, the impact of conflict on the continent, completing the work to eradicate the apartheid regime, and further marginalization in the international community.[32] There was an uptick in regional reforms in the 1990s with the creation of the Mechanism for Conflict Prevention, Management, and Resolution and increased work to address and prevent conflicts in a sustained and consistent way. However, an uptick in reforms that coincided with the end of the Cold War is not necessarily an indication of a major geo-political event being a determinant factor in those reforms.

The OAU had been an active regional organization since its inception in 1963, but its focus was on protecting nascent African states and eradicating all forms of colonialism. To do this it codified norms that ensured non-interference, protection of state sovereignty and territorial integrity, and regional primacy. The conflicts and atrocities of the 1970s began the process to discredit these ideas because of the dire humanitarian repercussions and negative impact on regional interests. This led to attempts to reform the regional organization throughout the 1980s and 1990s. The period of reform began in the late 1970s and early 1980s, and there was an uptick in reforms when Salim Ahmed Salim came to the fore as OAU Secretary General in 1989. Salim was certainly able to use the end of the Cold War and concerns about the new world order to galvanize reform efforts. However, the work to make the OAU a more effective and responsive organization to regional needs did not begin with the end of the Cold War but rather was a continuation of earlier efforts. Additionally, the challenges the OAU sought to address – economic development, conflict management, and Africa's place in the world – were also long-standing issues of concern for the region.

The OAU conflict management reforms of the 1990s were another round of largely ineffective reforms because they were still underpinned by OAU norms of non-interference. Events during the 1990s, notably the Rwandan Genocide and the wars in West and Central Africa, were critical events during this time period that acted as the final push to discredit OAU norms. These events were in tandem with the further development of the concepts of sovereignty as responsibility, interdependence of African security and development, and human security. These ideas provided the blueprint for institutional transformation in the late 1990s. As the next chapter will demonstrate, there were international efforts to push forward ideas around intervention and conflict resolution throughout the 1990s that culminated in the R2P report, but these developments were often in tandem or lagging behind similar developments in Africa.

Notes

1 "Report of the Secretary-General on the Establishment of a Mechanism for Conflict Prevention, Resolution, and Management," CM/1767 (LVIII) (Organization of African Unity, 21–26 June 1993), 3. AU Commission Archives.
2 "Introduction to the Report of the Secretary General to the 28th Ordinary Session of the OAU Assembly of Heads of State and Government," CM/1706 (LVI) Part 1 (Organization of African Unity, 22 June–1 July 1992), 6–19. AU Commission Archives.
3 "Report of the Secretary-General on the Establishment of a Mechanism for Conflict Prevention, Resolution, and Management," 6.
4 "Report of the Secretary-General on the Establishment of a Mechanism for Conflict Prevention, Resolution, and Management," 14.
5 "OAU Declaration on a Mechanism for Conflict Prevention, Management, and Resolution (Cairo Declaration)" (Dipublico, 28–30 June 1993), para. 14, www.dipublico.org/100609/oau-declaration-on-a-mechanism-for-conflict-prevention-management-and-resolution-cairo-declaration/ (accessed 7 May 2020).
6 "OAU Declaration on a Mechanism for Conflict Prevention, Management, and Resolution (Cairo Declaration)," paras. 15–16.
7 "Report of the Secretary-General on the Establishment of a Mechanism for Conflict Prevention, Resolution, and Management," 31.
8 "OAU Declaration on a Mechanism for Conflict Prevention, Management, and Resolution (Cairo Declaration)," paras. 17–20.
9 Monde Muyangwa and Margaret A. Vogt, "An Assessment of the OAU Mechanism for Conflict Prevention, Management, and Resolution, 1993–2000" (New York: International Peace Academy, 2000), 9–10.
10 Muyangwa and Vogt, "An Assessment of the OAU Mechanism for Conflict Prevention, Management, and Resolution, 1993–2000," 19.
11 "Report of the Secretary-General on the Establishment of a Mechanism for Conflict Prevention, Resolution, and Management," 32.
12 "Provisional Agenda for the First Ministerial Ordinary Session of the Central Organ of the OAU Mechanism for Conflict Prevention, Management, and Resolution" (Organization of African Unity, 17–19 November 1993). AU Commission Archives.
13 Muyangwa and Vogt, "An Assessment of the OAU Mechanism for Conflict Prevention, Management, and Resolution, 1993–2000," 12.
14 Muyangwa and Vogt, "An Assessment of the OAU Mechanism for Conflict Prevention, Management, and Resolution, 1993–2000," 12.
15 Muyangwa and Vogt, "An Assessment of the OAU Mechanism for Conflict Prevention, Management, and Resolution, 1993–2000," 12–13.
16 "Introduction to the Report of the Secretary General to the 28th Ordinary Session of the OAU Assembly of Heads of State and Government," 13–15.
17 Muyangwa and Vogt, "An Assessment of the OAU Mechanism for Conflict Prevention, Management, and Resolution, 1993–2000," 11.

18 "Cases: Rwanda," The United States Holocaust Museum, www.ushmm.org/confront-genocide/cases/rwanda/rwanda-background (accessed 2 April 2017).

19 "Outgoing Code Cable: 11 January 1994," Frontline: The Triumph of Evil, www.pbs.org/wgbh/pages/frontline/shows/evil/warning/cable.html (accessed 3 April 2017).

20 "The UN's Response: 11 January 1994," Frontline: The Triumph of Evil, www.pbs.org/wgbh/pages/frontline/shows/evil/warning/unresponse.html (accessed 3 April 2017).

21 "100 Days of Slaughter: A Chronology of U.S./U.N. Actions," Frontline: The Triumph of Evil, www.pbs.org/wgbh/pages/frontline/shows/evil/etc/slaughter.html (accessed 3 April 2017).

22 "Rwanda – The Preventable Genocide: The Report of the International Panel of Eminent Personalities to Investigate the 1994 Genocide in Rwanda and the Surrounding Events" (Addis Ababa, Ethiopia: Organization of African Unity, 2000), 56–58. AU Commission Archives.

23 "Rwanda – The Preventable Genocide," 67.

24 "Rwanda – The Preventable Genocide," 153–54.

25 "Rwanda – The Preventable Genocide," xv.

26 "Rwanda – The Preventable Genocide," 83.

27 "Rwanda – The Preventable Genocide," xix.

28 "Ceasefire Agreement (Lusaka Agreement)," 10 July 1999, www.peaceagreements.org/view/319 (accessed 7 May 2020).

29 Muyangwa and Vogt, "An Assessment of the OAU Mechanism for Conflict Prevention, Management, and Resolution, 1993–2000," 13.

30 Jean Ping, "Keynote Address" (23 October 2008), www.responsibilitytoprotect.org/index.php/component/content/article/129-africa/1910-african-unions-commission-on-r2pkeynote-speech-by-chairperson-jean-ping (accessed 7 May 2020).

31 "Report of the Secretary-General on the Fundamental Changes Taking Place in the World and Their Implications for Africa: Proposals for an African Response," AHG/169 (XXVI) (Organization of African Unity, July 1990), 13–15. AU Commission Archives.

32 "Report of the Secretary-General on the Fundamental Changes Taking Place in the World and Their Implications for Africa," 4–8.

10

International conflict management after the end of the Cold War

As discussed in Chapter 1, many theories on norm creation and diffusion focus on the power of the international community, often led by western states or norm entrepreneurs, to influence other states to adopt progressive norms. For example, Sikkink and Finnemore advance the argument that norms reach a tipping point once they are accepted by enough actors and then eventually become internalized, and they also argue that the process of norm acceptance and internalization can be affected by not only the content of the norm but the type of states promoting it.[1] Risse puts forward the spiral model to explain the adoption of progressive norms in repressive states focusing on both top-down pressure from the international and bottom-up pressure from domestic groups that may be supported by international networks.[2] However, there has been a dearth of literature on norm creation in the Global South and Global South contributions to international norms, and this gap has only recently started to be addressed.[3] This book nests within this emerging literature and argues that the evolution of peace and security norms from the OAU to the AU was driven by forces within Africa and international pressure was not a determinant factor. This chapter discusses international peace and security developments in the 1990s to show that Africa was often developing new peace and security norms in tandem or ahead of international institutions. The purpose of this is to disprove arguments around the role of international pressure as well as arguments that place the transition as taking place predominantly during the post-Cold War period.

In the case of the evolution of norms at the regional level in Africa, Williams focuses on the internal contradictions of OAU policy as well as pressure from the international to conform to transnational liberal and human rights norms as the two most important factors that led to a change from non-interference under the OAU to non-indifference under the AU.[4] Specifically examining the role of international influence, Williams argues that a process of norm localization took place, with Africa drawing on the R2P doctrine, that was developed in the ICISS report and drew on the work of Francis Deng, and adapting it for the African regional context. Williams sees key events, notably Idi Amin's oppression and the Rwandan Genocide, which created local resonance with the principles and aims of R2P, and the inclusion of Article 4(h) in the AU Constitutive Act and the African endorsement of the 2005 UN World Summit Outcome Document demonstrate significant African regional support for R2P.[5] In this sense, Africa went through a process of localization in adopting Article 4(h) as it was drawn from the international but adapted to the regional needs.

I also argue that the impact of Amin's oppression and the Rwandan Genocide, along with other events, were vital for creating concern about atrocities and human rights and pushing reform. However, these events provoked reform attempts in the 1980s that continued throughout the 1990s and culminated in the creation of the AU. The inclusion of Article 4(h) in the AU Constitutive Act cannot represent a process of localization because its inclusion predates the release of the R2P report and the concept of sovereignty as responsibility comes out of the 1991 Kampala Forum and subsequent work by Francis Deng. This is evidenced by the timeline of normative change at the regional and international levels. As this chapter will show, Africa was ahead of the international community at many points during the 1990s when it came to advancing intervention, and the ICISS report had not yet been released when African leaders were debating the framework and principles of the AU. Examining the timeline and determining whether localization occurred gets to the heart of the issues around the capacity of regions to create and advance norms based on their own experiences and for their own purposes, and marginalized regions, in particular, are often overlooked when it comes to their contributions to regional, much less international, norms.

International practices

UN intervention in Iraq and Kuwait

Since the end of World War II, the UN Charter has steered global responses to conflict. The UN is guided by the principle of sovereignty, and Article 2(7) notes that the UN is not authorized to intervene in matters that are only within the domestic jurisdictions of states.[6] However, the Charter does allow the UN to intervene when a state commits an act of aggression or when the UNSC determines that a situation constitutes a threat to international peace and security. Chapter V gives the UNSC responsibility for maintaining international peace and security. Chapter VI covers the pacific settlement of disputes while Chapter VII deals with actions that can be taken with respect to breaches of peace. Chapter VII allows the UNSC to authorize sanctions, blockades, and non-consensual military interventions to address any situation it deems a threat to international peace.[7]

One of the primary tools used by the UN to maintain peace and security is peacekeeping. However, at least initially, peacekeeping was used only when there was a peace to keep and not as a peace enforcement mechanism. The three core principles of UN peacekeeping are consent of the parties, impartiality, and non-use of force except in self-defense or defense of the mandate.[8] The first peacekeeping mission began in 1948 when the UNSC approved the UN Truce Supervision Organization, which deployed UN military observers to the Middle East to monitor the truce between Israel and Arab states. Throughout the Cold War, the UN engaged in peacekeeping missions but to a lesser extent than it does today. Between 1948 and 1989 there were 18 peacekeeping missions.[9] During the Cold War period the UN was constrained because the US and the Soviet Union (now Russia) are permanent members of the UNSC with a veto. Both countries were engaged in proxy wars around the globe, and it was difficult for the UNSC to come to a consensus on when and where the UN should intervene. When peacekeeping missions were authorized it was typically a traditional peacekeeping mission meant to observe a ceasefire or peace agreement.

From 1991 through 2013, the UN authorized 51 peacekeeping missions.[10] This is in part due to the end of the Cold War and in part due to the shifting understanding of what constitutes a threat to international peace and security. As this chapter will show, refugee flows, humanitarian catastrophes, and civil wars moved away from being only under the purview of UN functional agencies to being discussed by the UNSC. As such, UN peacekeeping expanded beyond traditional missions authorized only under Chapter VI mandates, and the missions became multi-dimensional taking on a myriad of tasks, including implementing complex peace agreements, building institutions, disarming former combatants, and monitoring human rights.[11] One of the first examples of a UN-approved international intervention in the post-Cold War period is the invocation of the clause UN Charter aimed to deter crimes of aggression to defend Kuwait against an invasion by Iraq. The initial intervention approved by the UNSC to expel Iraq from Kuwait clearly fell under a traditional interpretation of the UN Charter that forbids crimes of aggression. Iraqi military forces invaded Kuwait on 2 August 1990. The UNSC met that day and determined that the invasion constituted a breach of international peace and demanded that Iraq withdraw its forces from Kuwait.[12] Subsequent resolutions throughout the latter half of 1990 continued to condemn Iraq and imposed sanctions and other punitive measures to try to compel Iraq to comply with UN demands for its withdrawal from Kuwait. Finally, in November 1990 the UN approved a coalition of states to use any necessary force to compel Iraq to comply with previous UNSC resolutions.[13]

Had the UN involvement ended after the expulsion of Iraqi troops from Kuwait it would have been a straightforward case of invoking the UN Charter to condemn and respond to an act of aggression. However, the UN went beyond its initial mandate to defend Kuwait's sovereignty when a humanitarian crisis began to unfold. The expulsion of Iraqi troops from Kuwait led to an unstable situation in Iraq. In early March 1991, Kurds in northern Iraq and Shiite Muslims in southern Iraq rebelled and initially were able to seize key cities. The government moved quickly to repress these rebellions using tanks and helicopters, and by mid-March the Iraqi government had regained control of their territory. However, fearing reprisals, Kurds and Shiites fled into the mountains along the borders of Turkey and Iran respectively. This created a humanitarian crisis as it was estimated that up to 1,000 people were dying every day from exposure and disease.[14] Civilians were left in an impossible situation of coming down from the mountains and facing the Iraqi military or dying from hypothermia.

In early April 1991, Turkey and Iran sent letters to the UNSC asking the body to take up the issue of the unfolding humanitarian catastrophe in order to prevent refugees from seeking sanctuary inside their borders. Both countries argued that the large number of refugees and scale of humanitarian crisis posed a legitimate threat to regional security and was therefore under the purview of the UNSC.[15] The UNSC did take up the issue, and on 5 April 1991, they adopted Resolution 688, which stated, "Gravely concerned by the repression of the Iraqi civilian population in many parts of Iraq … which led to a massive flow of refugees towards and across international frontiers and to cross-border incursions which threaten international peace and security in the region."[16] While the resolution also reaffirms a commitment to Iraq's sovereignty, territorial integrity, and political independence, it nonetheless condemns the repression of Iraqi civilians and designates the humanitarian consequences of that repression as a threat to international peace. It went on to demand that Iraq cease the repression of its citizens in Iraqi territory and insisted that humanitarian organizations be granted access to affected populations.[17] In this resolution we see an expansion of the issues taken up by the UNSC with the result being an evolving understanding of the situations that constitute threats to international security and thus necessitate an international response.

The adoption of Resolution 688 was not uncontested. Cuba, Yemen, and Zimbabwe voted against the resolution, and China and India abstained. These states argued that Iraq's repression of its own citizens was an internal situation and engaging the UNSC in a response could violate Article 2(7) of the UN Charter. These states maintained that UN agencies and not the

UNSC should respond to the humanitarian crisis.[18] Even though Resolution 688 did not explicitly authorize military action it did pave the way for military intervention on humanitarian grounds. Other than the case of condemning apartheid South Africa, it was also the first time the UNSC had demanded the improvement of an internal humanitarian situation on the grounds that it was a threat to international peace and security. There were efforts by the states that abstained or voted against the resolution to prevent it from being used as a precedent. The resolution was adopted under a Chapter VI and not a Chapter VII mandate, and the justification for adopting the resolution remained focused on the trans-boundary aspects of the situation and not a humanitarian imperative.[19]

In adopting Resolution 688, the UNSC created enough leeway to allow for a military response to protect refugees and enforce the provision of humanitarian aid. The UK publicly proposed creating humanitarian enclaves as a first step to get the Kurdish refugees down from the mountains. The US was initially reluctant to endorse this or any plan that involved American troops. However, due to domestic pressure from media coverage and concerns over international legitimacy, President Bush eventually authorized the use of US forces to respond to the crisis. In early April 1991, Iraq was told to not send any military forces north of the 36th parallel as that zone was being used distribute humanitarian supplies. On 16 April, President Bush announced that US military forces were establishing encampments in northern Iraq for refugees and that US action was motivated by humanitarian concerns. Overall, Operation Provide Comfort involved 5,000 American troops, 2,000 British troops, and 1,000 French troops guarding and sheltering approximately 60,000 Kurdish refugees. These nations stressed that this action was consistent with UN Resolution 688 and that UN would take over caring for the refugees as soon as possible.[20]

Perhaps more important than the immediate outcomes, is the precedent that Operation Provide Comfort did indeed set. The repression of Iraqi citizens was an internal issue even if it led to a situation where civilians were fleeing into neighboring states. There were many crises in the world that led to refugee flows, but this was the first time that one was designated by the UNSC as a threat to international peace and security. Comparatively, it is noteworthy that the August 1990 ECOWAS intervention in Liberia on humanitarian grounds precedes UNSC-approved action to address the Iraqi crisis by several months and, as discussed in Chapter 8, the ECOWAS intervention was later accepted if not endorsed by the UNSC. Thus, even though the UN precedent is important, it is not the first of its kind, and an African sub-regional organization helped to pave the way for an interventionist approach to a humanitarian crisis.

UN intervention in Somalia

Following Operation Provide Comfort, the UN emerged as more willing to approach internal humanitarian catastrophes as threats to international peace and security, but this would be a short-lived phenomenon. Another major humanitarian crisis of the early 1990s was the civil war and subsequent famine in Somalia. The strongman who had governed Somalia since 1969, Siad Barre, was deposed in January 1991. By November 1991 the country was engulfed in a brutal civil war as war lords fought to gain power. The fierce battle left many people dead and also decimated the country's agricultural and husbandry sectors. The devastation, coupled with a drought, led to a famine that killed approximately 350,000 people in 1992.[21] During the early stages of the civil war, the UN did not take strong action to address the growing crisis. Regional organizations had been involved, and the OAU and Arab League sent appeals directly to the parties to the conflict in December 1991 and January 1992 respectively. Noting these efforts and the growing humanitarian catastrophe the UNSC took up the issue and adopted Resolution 733 on 23 January 1992. The resolution states that the UNSC is gravely alarmed by the deterioration of the situation and its consequences for peace and security. It then goes on to impose a weapons embargo on Somalia under the authority of Chapter VII of the UN Charter and call upon all member states to contribute to humanitarian aid efforts.[22]

On 24 April 1992, UNSC Resolution 751 established the UN Operation in Somalia (UNOSOM) under the authority of the Secretary General. This operation was given very modest resources, and the resolution initially only allocated a deployment of 50 UN observers to monitor a ceasefire in Mogadishu. However, the resolution allowed in principle for the creation of a UN security force and called on all parties to work towards the cessation of hostilities that would allow for the delivery of humanitarian assistance.[23] Throughout the remainder of 1992, the UN struggled to offer a coherent and coordinated response to the unfolding tragedy. On 28 August, the UNSC adopted Resolution 755, which notes the UN is, "deeply disturbed by the magnitude of the human suffering caused by the conflict and concerned that the situation in Somalia constitutes a threat to international peace and security."[24] It authorized an increase in the troop strength of UNOSOM up to 3,500 peacekeeping personnel to ensure the delivery of relief supplies. The larger force was approved under Chapter VII, and even though it did not contain a specific provision allowing for the use of force, it was still authorized without the consent of the warring parties and clearly implied a threat of using force to deliver critical humanitarian aid as a matter of maintaining international peace and security. The issue now became backing up that threat of force with resources.[25]

Five-hundred UN peacekeepers arrived in September 1992, but they were equipped only for self-defense and unable to move beyond the airport due to a lack of security. The inability of the UN to deliver on its threat of force changed when the US government stepped forward offering 30,000 US troops for a UN mission in Somalia. The US notified the UN Secretary General of its offer of up to 30,000 troops to protect the delivery of humanitarian supplies in late November 1992. The offer was conditional on UN authorization and the mission being kept under US command. On 3 December 1992, the UNSC passed resolution 794. The resolution recognized the extraordinary situation and acknowledged it called for an immediate and exceptional response. It also clearly determined that the internal crisis constituted a threat to international peace and security because of, "the magnitude of the human tragedy caused by the conflict in Somalia, further exacerbated by the obstacles being created to the distribution of humanitarian assistance."[26]

The resolution authorized the US to create a mission as outlined in their offer to secure the environment under a Chapter VII mandate. Beyond authorizing a large mission to use force to deliver aid, this resolution is notable because it explicitly states that a situation entirely internal to a state constitutes a threat to international peace and security. There is no mention of trans-boundary consequences. It is also the first time that the UN authorized the use of force under Chapter VII to deliver humanitarian aid that was being obstructed by warlords within the country.

In contrast to Resolution 688 relating to Iraq, all states on the UNSC voted in favor of Resolution 794, including the African states on the Council, Cape Verde, and Zimbabwe.[27] This was a significant reversal for Zimbabwe, in particular, because it was one of three states to vote against Resolution 688. However, this was in line with the discussions that were happening in the wider continent. African states remained wary of outside intervention, but they also recognized the damage conflict was doing to their continent and sought a more proactive approach that prioritized African solutions but relied upon the UN in the event of a large-scale catastrophe.[28] The crisis in Somalia was such a catastrophe, and the OAU did not have the resources to manage it internally. Allowing the UN-approved intervention was in line with the protocol establishing the OAU Mechanism for Conflict Prevention, Management, and Resolution, adopted shortly after in July 1993, which mandated seeking UN assistance in situations where the OAU could not manage a conflict that had the potential to de-stabilize the region.[29]

The Unified Task Force (UNITAF) authorized by Resolution 794 was comprised predominantly of US troops with approximately 20 other states contributing smaller contingents. It began arriving in December 1992, and at its height was made up of about 37,000 troops under US command, authorized to use all necessary means to secure areas for humanitarian operations. The success of UNITAF is debatable. While it was able to ensure the delivery of some humanitarian aid, it was not able to operate in all areas or disarm warring parties who were obstructing the distribution of relief supplies.[30] The US was not interested in being drawn into a protracted operation. President Clinton was inaugurated in January 1993, and the US began pushing to withdraw their troops and for the UN to take over responsibility for operations in Somalia beginning in early 1993. On 26 March 1993, the UN adopted Resolution 814, which replaced both UNOSOM I and UNITAF with UNOSOM II under a Chapter VII mandate. The resolution stipulated that the mission, and more broadly the Secretary General's Special Representative in Somalia, take on a litany of tasks that went well beyond traditional peacekeeping, including assisting in the provision of aid, repatriation of refugees, promotion of political reconciliation, re-establishment of a Somali police-force, and finally creating hospitable conditions for civil society.[31]

The mandate for UNOSOM II represented a huge increase in the tasks peacekeeping missions take on, and UNOSOM II had great difficulty fulfilling its mandate. There was controversy over the methods used to enforce peace and pushback from Somali warlords who did not trust the UN. On 5 June 1993, 24 UN peacekeepers were killed and 57 were wounded as they tried to inspect an arms depot. Somali warlord Mohamed Aidid was blamed for the deaths of the peacekeepers, and the UN sought to bring him to justice by offering a reward and finally relying on US forces to capture him.[32] US Army Rangers and Delta Force were deployed to apprehend Aidid on 3 October 1993, but the mission did not go as planned. Two Blackhawk helicopters were shot down, leading to a protracted and bloody battle in the streets of Mogadishu where 500 Somalis and 18 Army Rangers were killed. The bodies of the Army Rangers were dragged through the streets and photos were broadcast across the globe leading to an immediate backlash in America. The tragedy became known as Black Hawk Down, and President Clinton responded by pulling all US troops out of Somalia by March 1994.[33] President Clinton also responded by signing Presidential Decision Directive 25 on the US Policy on Reforming Multilateral Peace Operations. This essentially restricts the involvement of US forces in peace-keeping missions to circumstances where there is a strong national-security interest.[34] Even after the US withdrawal, UNOSOM II would continue, with troops from India, Pakistan, Malaysia, and Egypt replacing American troops. However, it only ever achieved limited success and was eventually ended in February 1995.

Beyond the immediate impact in Somalia, Black Hawk Down had global ramifications. Prior to the Somalia debacle, the UNSC had been expanding the scope of situations it viewed as threats to international peace and security along with acceptable intervention practices. The ineffectiveness of the UN in Somalia combined with the public spectacle of peacekeeper deaths led the US to withdraw support for peacekeeping worldwide, and other western countries with powerful militaries became more reluctant to offer troops for peacekeeping missions. While the US continues to financially, and at times politically, support UN missions, the work of peacekeeping has been largely left to middle-power and developing countries. This led to a retrenchment in peacekeeping and willingness to intervene for several years in the mid-1990s, which coincided with some of the UN's most grievous failures.

UN failures in Rwanda and the former Yugoslavia

The Rwandan Genocide began on 6 April 1994, just five months after the Black Hawk Down incident in Mogadishu and days after the deadline for US troops to withdraw from Somalia. Interestingly, the day before the genocide began, the UNSC approved Resolution 909 authorizing an extension of the mandate of UNAMIR until 29 July 1994. As discussed in the last chapter, UNAMIR was established in October 1993 to help with the implementation of the OAU-supported Arusha Accords, which were meant to end the civil war between Hutu and Tutsi factions in the country. Resolution 909 noted the valuable contribution being made by UNAMIR to achieve peace in Rwanda while also noting concern about the deteriorating security situation. As such, the resolution also called for a review of the situation in Rwanda within six weeks.[35] The next day a plane carrying the Rwandan and Burundian presidents was shot down. Hutu extremists in the country took this as a signal, and the coordinated killings began within hours. The next UNSC resolution on Rwanda would not be passed until 21 April. The UN had known about the possibility for large-scale violence in Rwanda because of reports it had received from the UNAMIR Force Commander, and it had done nothing.[36] Then when the genocide began the UN actively sought to diminish its presence in the country.

Prior to the 21 April UNSC meeting, the UN Secretary General gave the Security Council members three options. The first option was a large force with a Chapter VII mandate, which had the power and resources to stop the genocide. The second option was to decrease the troop strength of UNAMIR to around 270 personnel and mandate them the act as an intermediary force between the two sides, and the final option was the complete withdraw of UNAMIR in the midst of the genocide.[37] In Resolution 912, the UNSC chose the second option. The resolution emphasizes that the Arusha Accords should remain central to the peace process in Rwanda and lamented the failure of the parties to adhere to the ceasefire. There was no mention of the one-sided nature of the killings. The resolution also raised concerns about the safety of UN personnel after the killing and desecration of Belgium peacekeepers and then authorized an adjustment to UNAMIR's mandate that essentially gutted the mission. Finally, it called upon the OAU and regional leaders to continue to work with the UN to resolve the crisis,[38] even though at this point there was no hope of a negotiated settlement, and the OAU did not have the resources or political will for a military intervention to stop the carnage.

The killing continued on a massive scale, and there was increasing pressure to act. Nearly one month later the UNSC met again and adopted Resolution 918 on 17 May 1994. There was still reluctance amongst many member states to name what was happening in Rwanda as genocide or to take responsibility for stopping the mass killing of civilians. In this regard it is telling when the resolution recalls, "in this context that the killing of members of an ethnic group with the intention of destroying such a group, in whole or in part, constitutes a crime punishable under international law."[39] The term genocide is not used. It is also telling that the resolution stresses that the people of Rwanda are ultimately responsible for reconciliation and reconstruction in their country. It does not speak of a threat to international peace and security despite enormous refugee flows like the situation in Iraq in 1991 as well as the catastrophic consequences for civilians. Resolution 918 does authorize an increased mandate and troop strength for UNAMIR. Under a Chapter VII mandate, it establishes a weapons embargo and allows UNAMIR to help refugees and civilians by creating secure humanitarian areas and using force within those areas to protect people.[40] This came too late though. UNAMIR's troop strength had already been drawn down to only 500 personnel, and the Secretary General found it difficult to secure additional troops from member states. UNAMIR eventually reached its full strength in October 1994, several months after the RPF had gained control of Rwanda and stopped the massacres. The unwillingness of the UN to act to protect Rwandan civilians even when it had troops on the ground left a poisonous legacy that undermined any confidence Africa had in the UN to effectively respond to conflict and humanitarian crisis on the African continent.[41] It is also a stark illustration of the peacekeeping and intervention retrenchment that occurred at the international level in the mid-1990s.

The UN's failure in Rwanda, coupled with its failure in the former Yugoslavia, would compel it to reassess how it responded to humanitarian disasters and conflicts that constituted a threat to international peace and security. The Socialist Federal Republic of Yugoslavia was created after

World War II and was comprised of six federal republics – Slovenia, Croatia, Bosnia-Herzegovina, Serbia, Montenegro, and Macedonia. While there was a history of tensions between the ethnic groups in the regions, President Tito sought to create a national Yugoslav identity and suppress tensions between the groups. However, when Tito died in 1981 tensions began to flair after the re-emergence of Serbian nationalism under the leadership of Slobodan Milosevic. There were calls from across several of the republics for independence and increasing calls from Serbian nationalists for a greater Serbia. In this context, Slovenia and Croatia declared independence in 1991. Slovenia was relatively ethnically homogenous, and attempts by the Yugoslav People's Army to militarily suppress independence failed after ten days. However, there was a significant Serbian population in Croatia, and Milosevic responded to Croatian independence by reminding the Serbs in Croatia of past abuses by Croats and promising them resources to defend themselves. In summer 1991, Serbian paramilitaries began conducting military campaigns to take control of key areas within Croatia, after which the conflict continued to progress.[42]

The UN did take up the issue of conflict in the former Yugoslavia in 1991. Resolution 713, adopted on 25 September, invokes Chapter VII to impose a weapons embargo on the former Yugoslavia. It also commends the European Community for its work to negotiate a peace accord as well as sending observers to oversee the implementation of a ceasefire. In this way the UN is engaging with the European Community in a similar way that it engaged with ECOWAS and their work to end the conflicts in Liberia and Sierra Leone. The resolution does not provide any mandate for UN intervention and instead relies on European efforts to address the crisis.[43] The possibility of a peacekeeping force was first discussed in late 1991. The government of Yugoslavia sent a letter to the President of the UNSC on 26 November 1991, and the UNSC met the next day. The body decided to consider the request for a peacekeeping mission and urged all parties to the conflict to come to an agreement to end fighting and support the deployment of a peacekeeping operation.[44] The mandate for a peacekeeping mission was not actually approved until several months later in February 1992.

Ceasefire agreements had already been signed, and the initial mandate for the UN Protection Force (UNPROFOR) under Resolution 743 was to help create the conditions necessary to reach a comprehensive peace agreement. However, as the conflict worsened despite negotiation efforts, it became clear that the UN needed to go beyond traditional peacekeeping in order to deliver humanitarian aid and ensure the security of civilians.[45] The UNSC remained engaged with the matter throughout 1992, but it did not take strong action until reports of torture and arbitrary detention of Muslim prisoners at Serb detention centers began to emerge in the media.[46]

Immediately after the media reports began to air, the UNSC adopted Resolution 770 on 13 August 1992 that noted deep concern about conditions in detention centers and, acting under a Chapter VII mandate, demanded access to any prison or detention facilities as well as access to ensure the delivery of humanitarian aid.[47] By casting it under a Chapter VII mandate the UNSC authorized all necessary means to deliver humanitarian aid. The resolution was welcomed by the host government, as it did not violate norms of sovereignty. However, it marked a point of increased UN activity to protect civilians in Bosnia.[48] Resolution 776 passed on 14 September 1992, authorizing an expansion of UNPROFOR's mandate and troop strength in Bosnia-Herzegovina and the use of force to protect humanitarian convoys if requested to do so by the International Committee of the Red Cross.[49] On 22 February 1993, the UNSC adopted Resolution 808 establishing an international tribunal for crimes against humanity. The resolution expressed, "grave alarm at continuing reports of widespread violations of international humanitarian law occurring within the territory of the former Yugoslavia, including reports of mass killings and the continuance of the practice of ethnic cleansing ... constitutes a threat to international peace and security."[50] This resolution is important because it specifically designates mass killings and ethnic cleansing even within states as a threat to international peace and security, and it establishes a mechanism to hold leaders who commit these crimes accountable at an international level. Note that this resolution was passed before Black Hawk Down, and similar language designating mass killings as a threat to international peace and security was not used in resolutions pertaining to Rwanda.

While the UN actions described above are important in demonstrating an evolution of intervention practices, one of the most important precedents and its accompanying consequences was the establishment of UN safe areas to protect civilians. Taking note of the 1948 Convention on the Prevention and Punishment of the Crime of Genocide and recognizing that UNPROFOR was acting under a Chapter VII mandate, the UNSC authorized the creation of a safe area that should be free of any armed attack around Srebrenica with Resolution 819 on 16 April 1993. The resolution also demanded an immediate withdrawal of Serb paramilitary units from Srebrenica.[51] Additional safe areas were added through subsequent resolutions but crucially none of them prescribed any response that could be taken if the safe areas were breached or attacked. UNPROFOR's mandate was renewed with Resolution 836 on 4 June 1993, and it was bolstered to try to address the critical weakness in the UN's efforts to protect civilians. The extended mandate called on UNPROFOR to deter attacks on UN designated safe areas and empowered them, "to take all necessary measures, including the use of force, in reply to bombardments against safe areas."[52]

As time went on and the failure in Somalia weighed on the international community, the UN found it difficult to match the action prescribed in earlier mandates to the resources required to fulfil them. In order to fully implement all the actions outlined in Resolution 836, the UN would need an additional 32,000 troops, but it was only able to secure an additional 3,500 troops. It allowed member states to provide air support to UN ground operations, and due to a lack of troops, the UN relied heavily on NATO airstrikes to enforce the mandate and repel Serb attacks in UN safe areas. The airstrikes were successful in halting an offensive against Gorazde but were unsuccessful in protecting civilians in many other areas. Notably, air strikes and UN forces were not able to protect Srebrenica, which fell in 1995. Within this area Muslim men and boys were systemically rounded up and killed, and it is estimated that at least 7,000 people were murdered.[53] The massacres at Srebrenica echoed the failures of the UN in Rwanda. A UN force was on the ground, but it was prevented from halting large-scale atrocities against civilians either because of a lack of political will, a lack of resources, or both.

Evolution of UN policy in the 1990s

The UN, like Africa, tried to reassess its approach to conflict management and peacekeeping in the early 1990s. In early 1992, the Secretary Council asked Secretary General Boutros Boutros-Ghali to prepare an analysis and a set of recommendations to improve preventative diplomacy, peacemaking, and peacekeeping. The Secretary General presented An Agenda for Peace in July 1992. The report acknowledged the changing international context and emphasized an essentially human security approach to international peace and security, further demonstrating the shift from a state security model to a human security model at both international and regional levels. Boutros-Ghali noted that a conviction had grown among UN member states that the UN had an opportunity to fulfil all aspects of its Charter by maintaining peace, advancing justice and human rights, and ensuring social progress.[54]

Boutros-Ghali acknowledged that the state is still the bedrock of the international system and sovereignty is crucial for the maintenance of the international system, but said, "the time of absolute and exclusive sovereignty, however, has passed; its theory was never matched by reality. It is the task of leaders of States to understand this and to find a balance between the needs of good internal governance and the requirements of an ever more interdependent world."[55] The report covers a range of options to promote international peace, including early warning, preventative diplomacy, peacemaking, and peacekeeping. While many of the proposed activities and approaches uphold traditional norms of sovereignty and host state consent, there is a robust section on military intervention. Boutros-Ghali advocated that being able and willing to use force as a last resort was the essence of collective security arrangements, and the UNSC must take timely action when peaceful means of failed. To do this he proposed creating a permanent UN force in addition to armed and expertly trained peace-enforcement units to respond to acts of aggression.[56]

Here it is again important to look at the timeline and the progression of ideas and practices at both the international and regional levels. In February 1992, the OAU Council of Ministers approved the Secretary General's request to set up a Division of Conflict Management. This was the first step in reforming the OAU conflict management structures in the early 1990s, and it built on past attempts and lessons. The July 1992 Report of the OAU Secretary General emphasized the gravity of conflict situations in Africa, the failures of past OAU efforts, and the need to reform.[57] The OAU Mechanism for Conflict Prevention, Management, and Resolution was formally established in June 1993. In examining how to set up this mechanism, OAU Secretary General Salim Ahmed Salim highlighted the debate that was happening within Africa about exceptional circumstances, such as the conflicts in Liberia and Somalia, that may necessitate the region becoming involved to stop egregious conflicts or atrocities before appealing to the international community.[58] Then there is, of course, ECOWAS efforts to respond to the conflict in Liberia by imposing a ceasefire and deploying a military intervention force in August 1990.[59] These debates and new practices were happening at the regional level, often before or in tandem with developments at the international level, and it is important to recognize the regional processes that were taking place and how they could have fed into the international processes and not simply how international processes trickle down to the regional level.

At the global level, the optimism of the 1992 Agenda for Peace report did not hold up in the new world order. The assumption had been that the UNSC would be a functioning body after the end of the superpower rivalry, but it would continue to be hampered by inconsistent political will and slow processes. When the UNSC was able to forcefully engage in attempts to enforce peace and protect civilians, the failures in Somalia, Rwanda, and Bosnia showed the constraints of military engagement. Boutros-Ghali issued a Supplement to the Agenda for Peace in 1995 on the 50th anniversary of the creation of the UN. The supplement acknowledged the complexities of the post-Cold War environment. It also discussed how peacekeeping has become more dangerous and expansive, as the UN is now dealing with more intra-state wars, which often entail a plethora of state-building and civilian protection activities well beyond simply monitoring borders and separating belligerents. After the experiences of Somalia,

Rwanda, and Bosnia, the 1995 Supplement speaks of resource constraints, the dangers of peacekeeping, and the pressure to take on unrealistic tasks. Boutros-Ghali stressed that while there have been new kinds of UN operations the mandates are still limited, and a conclusive end to a conflict must be sought through a negotiated settlement with the consent of the parties. He stated, "even though the use of force is authorized under Chapter VII of the Charter, the United Nations remains neutral and impartial between the warring parties, without a mandate to stop the aggressor (if one can be identified) or impose a cessation of hostilities."[60]

All in all, the 1995 Supplement was a far more cautious and restrained document than the original Agenda for Peace. It is clear that the experiences of the early 1990s had a dampening effect on the UN's political will and logistical ability to use force in intervening to protect civilians. The supplement emphasized the complexity of conflicts and the need for long-term development facilitated through UN functional agencies and regional involvement for burden sharing. Just as reform of peacekeeping and intervention was an iterative process at the regional level, so too was it an iterative process within the UN framework. The war in the former Yugoslavia re-started in the second half of the 1990s, and the impacts from the UN's failure in Somalia and Rwanda continued to be felt with the further deterioration of the Somali state and wars in the Democratic Republic of the Congo. In March 2000, UN Secretary Kofi Annan appointed a Panel on UN Peace Operations. The creation of this panel came on the heels of two critical reports in 1999 condemning UN failure to stop the genocide in Rwanda and to protect civilians in Srebrenica. The panel produced what would become known as the Brahimi Report, which was transmitted to UN member states in August 2000. The Brahimi Report put forward a comprehensive list of recommendations to reform and improve peacekeeping, and it emphasized the importance of political, financial, and operational support from member states in order for the UN to be a credible institution.[61] The recommendations touched on improving planning and deployment capacity, ensuring clear and feasible mandates, and redefining the relationship between the UNSC, UNDPKO, and troop contributing countries. The Report also emphasized the importance of developing a rapid response capacity as first recommended in the Agenda for Peace nearly a decade earlier.[62] The work of the panel was endorsed by the UNSC in Resolution 1318 in September 2000. The resolution was a declaration on ensuring an effective role for the UNSC in the maintenance of international peace and security. The UNSC pledged to give particular attention to peace and sustainable development in Africa and to pursue a number of actions to improve UN peacekeeping, such as crafting appropriate and feasible mandates, properly training and equipping UN peacekeeping personnel, consulting with troop-contributing countries, and upgrading the capacity of the UN to undertake peacekeeping.[63]

The emergence of the Responsibility to Protect

The above sections detailed the evolution of UN practice and policy leading up to the proposal of the R2P in 2001. After expanded missions in Iraq and Somalia, and then failures in Rwanda and Srebrenica, the UN was again faced with the possibility of atrocities. In 1999 there was grave concern in the UN about the situation in Kosovo, but the UNSC did not authorize military intervention to protect civilians due to a Russian veto threat as a permanent member of the UNSC. This led to NATO forces launching airstrikes in the spring of 1999 without UNSC authorization.[64] British Prime Minister Tony Blair defended NATO actions in Kosovo by arguing that the airstrikes were not based on any territorial ambitions but rather on values that cannot allow atrocities, and he stressed that the most urgent foreign policy problem the international community faced was identifying the circumstances when it was necessary and appropriate to intervene in other country's conflicts.[65] The conflict in Kosovo, along with past failures to protect civilians, led Secretary General Kofi Annan to issue a plea to the international community to find a way to address the persistent issue of when and how to intervene. In his September 1999 address to the General Assembly presenting his annual report, Annan spoke about the debate around intervention:

> Just as we have learned that the world cannot stand aside when gross and systematic violations of human rights are taking place, so we have also learned that intervention must be based on legitimate and universal principles if it is to enjoy the sustained support of the world's peoples. This developing international norm in favor of intervention to protect civilians from wholesale slaughter will no doubt continue to pose profound challenges to the international community. Any such evolution in our understanding of state sovereignty and individual sovereignty will, in some quarters, be met with distrust, skepticism, and even hostility. But it is an evolution we should welcome.[66]

In September 2000, the government of Canada with the support of several foundations announced the creation of the ICISS. The mandate of the Commission was to address the legal, moral, operational, and political aspects of the debate around humanitarian intervention and present a report to the Secretary General and wider international community. Twelve commissioners worked over the next year, and the R2P report was launched in December 2001.[67] R2P tries to codify responsibilities within the international community and simultaneously reaffirm sovereignty while providing parameters for humanitarian intervention. The basic principles affirm that the primary responsibility for protecting people within a state lies with the state, but when a state is unwilling or unable halt atrocities then there is an international responsibility to protect. The specific responsibilities endorsed by the Commission are the responsibility to prevent by addressing the causes of conflict and humanitarian crises, the responsibility to react to 'situations of compelling human need by appropriate measures', and the responsibility to rebuild, particularly if military intervention is undertaken.[68]

Following the report, the R2P concept was socialized through the international system and eventually taken up at the 2005 UN World Summit where it was endorsed in the Outcome Document.[69] Paragraphs 138 and 139 of the 2005 World Summit Outcome Document offer measured but clear support for the R2P while stressing that action to stop atrocities when peaceful means fail should be taken through the UNSC.[70] African countries offered critical support to R2P at the World Summit. The common African position on UN reforms, including R2P and the use of force, is articulated in the Ezulwini Consensus. The African region endorsed a responsibility of the international community to protect but was wary of instances where this obligation may be used as a pretext not to protect people but to undermine sovereignty. There was also an inclination to favor regional action even though the AU clearly saw a role for UN action and support. The African position stated, "It is imperative that Regional Organizations, in areas of proximity to conflicts, are empowered to take action. The African Union agrees that the intervention of Regional Organizations should be with the permission of the Security Council; although approval could be granted after the fact in circumstances requiring urgent action."[71] Even with these nuances engrained in the common African position, African countries voted to support the inclusion of paragraphs 138 and 139 in the World Summit Outcome Document.

R2P and more generally how the world should respond to atrocities is still a contested issue within the international community. As described in Chapter 2, many African states were wary of the invocation of R2P to justify air strikes in Libya in 2011. Skepticism of international efforts to address and punish atrocities has grown in Africa and other regions. For instance, following Libya, Brazil proposed the concept of Responsibility while Protecting to add some parameters to how R2P should be implemented by proposing more stringent criteria for military intervention and advocating for accountability from institutions that intervene.[72] There has also been discontent within Africa with the ICC, with several countries threatening withdrawal or even initiating withdrawal procedures from the ICC, and the question of mass withdrawal was raised at an AU Summit meeting in 2013.[73] In tandem with these developments, though, there have been developments within Africa, such as AU engagement in Burundi described in Chapter 2 and the trial of former Chadian dictator Hissène Habré under an African international justice mechanism, that have pushed forward African responses to atrocities.[74]

Comparing the international and the regional

It is critical to explore the timing of UN peacekeeping reform and the creation of R2P at the international level compared to similar developments at the regional level. Immediately after the end of the Cold War there was enthusiasm for more proactive UN responses to conflicts and atrocities. However, the failures in Somalia, Rwanda, and the former Yugoslavia, coupled with the complexity of multi-dimensional peacekeeping, led to a retrenchment in UN intervention as evidenced by the 1995 Supplement to the Agenda for Peace, which laid out a far more cautious picture of UN capacity and scaled back expectations for peacekeeping. In 1999, Secretary General Kofi Annan again called for an examination of how to approach peacekeeping and intervention eventually culminating in the development of R2P through the report of ICISS. The UN missions of the 1990s follow a similar pattern of surging forward and retreating back.

By comparison, the report on Fundamental Changes Taking Place in the World, which not only addressed the implications of the end of Cold War but also persistent regional challenges, was presented to the OAU in July 1990. This report highlighted the failures of African conflict management and eventually culminated in the creation of the OAU Conflict Management Division in 1992 and the Mechanism for Conflict Prevention, Management, and Resolution in 1993. ECOWAS deployed troops to Liberia against the wishes of the parties to the conflict and justified the action on the grounds of protecting civilians in August 1990, which was well before other commensurate international interventions. Finally, the 1991 CSSDCA and resulting Kampala Document outlining the interconnectedness of all African states and the links between security and development and the 1996 publication of *Sovereignty as Responsibility* (and book chapter in 1995) were years ahead of the formation of the ICISS following the humanitarian catastrophes in Rwanda and the former Yugoslavia and subsequent UN soul-searching.[75] As the next chapter will show, African leaders set the foundations for AU reform in September 1999, and the new AU Constitutive Act with its new norms grounded in human security was largely finalized in 2000 even though the AU did not officially replace the OAU until 2002.

The purpose of this chapter is not to diminish the evolution of intervention norms and practice at the international level. Rather it is to provide a baseline for comparison of norm evolution within the African region. Given that Africa undertook reforms throughout the 1980s and early 1990s, and set precedents before the international community that were later endorsed by the UN, and given that African initiatives and thinkers developed ideas which underpinned intervention reforms, Africa could not have gone through a process of adapting international norms when the OAU transitioned into the AU. Furthermore, given that the African regional organization began the process of reform well before the end of the Cold War, international pressure could not have been a determinant factor in pushing African leaders to pursue more robust mechanisms to manage conflict and atrocities on the continent. This volume analyzes how African peace and security norms developed, arguing that the pushes for reform largely came from within Africa, and proposes a theory of norm creation within regional institutions. It also lays out questions of how African regional institutions may have influenced international norms through external advocacy or coordinated member state efforts in international institutions. In this way, the volume argues that regions create regional norms based on experiences, advocacy, and mutually constituted ideas and interests, and there is significant capacity for regional organizations to contribute to international norm processes in ways that have previously not been recognized or explored.

Notes

1 Martha Finnemore and Kathryn Sikkink, "International Norm Dynamics and Political Change," *International Organizations* 52 (1998): 887–917.

2 Thomas Risse, "International Norms and Domestic Change: Arguing and Communicative Behavior in the Human Rights Area," *Politics and Society* 27, no. 4 (1999): 529–59.

3 Kathryn Sikkink, "Latin America's Protagonist Role in Human Rights," *International Journal on Human Rights* 12, no. 22 (2015): 207–18; Katharina P. Coleman and Thomas Kwasi Tieku, "African Actors in International Security: Four Pathways to Influence," in *African Actors in International Security: Shaping Contemporary Norms*, ed. Katharina P. Coleman and Thomas Kwasi Tieku (Boulder, CO: Lynne Rienner Publishers, 2018), 1–20; Eric Helleiner, "Principles from the Periphery: The Neglected Southern Sources of Global Norms," *Global Governance* 20, no. 3 (2014); Oliver Stuenkel, *Post-Western World: How Emerging Powers Are Remaking Global Order* (London: Polity Press, 2016).

4 Paul D. Williams, "From Non-Intervention to Non-Indifference: The Origins and Development of the African Union's Security Culture," *African Affairs* 106, no. 423 (2007): 266.

5 Williams, "From Non-Intervention to Non-Indifference," 275.

6 "Charter of the United Nations," 24 October 1945, www.un.org/en/charter-united-nations/index.html (accessed 30 September 2020).

7 "Charter of the United Nations."

8 "Principles of UN Peacekeeping," United Nations, https://peacekeeping.un.org/en/principles-of-peacekeeping (accessed 28 September 2020).

9 "List of Peacekeeping Operations 1948–2013" (United Nations), https://peacekeeping.un.org/sites/default/files/operationslist.pdf (accessed 28 September 2020).

10 "List of Peacekeeping Operations 1948–2013."

11 "Our History," United Nations, https://peacekeeping.un.org/en/our-history (accessed 28 September 2020).

12 "Resolution 660 (1990) of 2 August 1990" (United Nations, 2 August 1990), http://unscr.com/en/resolutions/660 (accessed 7 May 2020).

13 "Resolution 678 (1990) of 29 November 1990" (United Nations, 29 November 1990), http://unscr.com/en/resolutions/678, (accessed 28 September 2020).

14 Nicholas J. Wheeler, *Saving Strangers: Humanitarian Intervention in International Society* (Oxford: Oxford University Press, 2000), 141.

15 Wheeler, *Saving Strangers*, 142.

16 "Resolution 688 (1991) of 5 April 1991" (United Nations, 5 April 1991), http://unscr.com/en/resolutions/688 (accessed 7 May 2020).

17 "Resolution 688 (1991) of 5 April 1991."

18 Sophie Thomashausen, *Humanitarian Intervention in an Evolving World Order: The Cases of Iraq, Somalia, Kosovo, and East Timor* (Pretoria, South Africa: The Africa Institute of South Africa, 2002), 31.

19 Wheeler, *Saving Strangers*, 144–46.

20 Wheeler, *Saving Strangers*, 149–52.

21 Wheeler, *Saving Strangers*, 173–74.

22 "Resolution 733 (1992) of 23 January 1992" (United Nations, 23 January 1992), http://unscr.com/en/resolutions/733 (accessed 7 May 2020).

23 "Resolution 751 (1992) of 24 April 1992" (United Nations, 24 April 1992), http://unscr.com/en/resolutions/751 (accessed 7 May 2020).

24 "Resolution 775 (1992): Adopted by the Security Council at Its 3110th Meeting, on 28 August 1992" (United Nations, 28 August 1992), http://unscr.com/en/resolutions/775 (accessed 7 May 2020).

25 Wheeler, *Saving Strangers*, 178.

26 "Resolution 794 (1992): Adopted by the Security Council at Its 3145th Meeting, on 3 December 1992" (United Nations, 3 December 1992), http://unscr.com/en/resolutions/794 (accessed 7 May 2020).

27 Wheeler, *Saving Strangers*, 183–85.

28 "Report of the Secretary-General on the Establishment of a Mechanism for Conflict Prevention, Resolution, and Management," CM/1767 (LVII) (Organization of African Unity, 21-26 June 1993), 3. AU Commission Archives.

29 "OAU Declaration on a Mechanism for Conflict Prevention, Management, and Resolution (Cairo Declaration)" (Dipublico, 28–30 June 1993), para. 16, www.

dipublico.org/100609/oau-declaration-on-a-mechanism-for-conflict-preven
tion-management-and-resolution-cairo-declaration/ (accessed 7 May 2020).

30 Christine Gray, *International Law and the Use of Force* (Oxford: Oxford
University Press, 2004), 222–23.

31 "Resolution 814 (1993): Adopted by the Security Council at Its 3118th Meeting,
on 26 March 1993" (United Nations, 26 March 1993), http://unscr.com/en/reso
lutions/814 (accessed 7 May 2020).

32 Wheeler, *Saving Strangers*, 194–95.

33 Wheeler, *Saving Strangers*, 198–99.

34 "Presidential Decision Directive/NSC-25," 3 May 1994, https://fas.org/irp/
offdocs/pdd/pdd-25.pdf (accessed 7 May 2020).

35 "Resolution 909 (1994): Adopted by the Security Council at Its 3358th Meeting,
on 5 April 1994." (United Nations, 5 April 1994), http://unscr.com/en/resolu
tions/909 (accessed 7 May 2020).

36 "Outgoing Code Cable: 11 January 1994," Frontline: The Triumph of Evil,
www.pbs.org/wgbh/pages/frontline/shows/evil/warning/cable.html (accessed 3
April 2017); "The UN's Response: 11 January 1994," Frontline: The Triumph
of Evil, www.pbs.org/wgbh/pages/frontline/shows/evil/warning/unresponse.html
(accessed 3 April 2017).

37 Gray, *International Law and the Use of Force*, 229.

38 "Resolution 912 (1994): Adopted by the Security Council at Its 3368th Meeting,
on 21 April 1994" (United Nations, 21 April 1994), http://unscr.com/en/resolu
tions/912 (accessed 7 May 2020).

39 "Resolution 918 (1994): Adopted by the Security Council at Its 3377th Meeting,
on 17 May 1994" (United Nations, 17 May 1994), http://unscr.com/en/resolu
tions/918 (accessed 7 May 2020).

40 "Resolution 918 (1994)."

41 Gray, *International Law and the Use of Force*, 229–30.

42 Wheeler, *Saving Strangers*, 244–45.

43 "Resolution 713 (1991) of 25 September 1991" (United Nations, 25 September
1991), http://unscr.com/en/resolutions/713 (accessed 7 May 2020).

44 "Resolution 721 (1991) of 27 November 1991" (United Nations, 27 November
1991), http://unscr.com/en/resolutions/721 (accessed 7 May 2020).

45 Gray, *International Law and the Use of Force*, 218.

46 Wheeler, *Saving Strangers*, 251.

47 "Resolution 770 (1992): Adopted by the Security Council at Its 3106th Meeting,
on 13 August 1992" (United Nations, 13 August 1992), http://unscr.com/en/
resolutions/770 (accessed 7 May 2020).

48 Wheeler, *Saving Strangers*, 252.

49 "Resolution 776 (1992): Adopted by the Security Council at its 3114th meeting,
on 14 September 1992" (United Nations, 14 September 1992), http://unscr.com/
en/resolutions/776 (accessed 27 September 2020).

50 "Resolution 808 (1993): Adopted by the Security Council at Its 3175th Meeting,
on 22 February 1993" (United Nations, 22 February 1993), http://unscr.com/
en/resolutions/808 (accessed 7 May 2020).

51 "Resolution 819 (1993): Adopted by the Security Council at Its 3199th Meeting, on 16 April 1993" (United Nations, 16 April 1993), https://digitallibrary.un.org/record/164939?ln=en (accessed 7 May 2020).

52 "Resolution 836 (1993): Adopted by the Security Council at Its 3228th Meeting, on 4 June 1993" (United Nations, 4 June 1993), https://digitallibrary.un.org/record/166973?ln=en (accessed 7 May 2020).

53 Wheeler, *Saving Strangers*, 254–55.

54 Boutros Boutros-Ghali, "An Agenda for Peace: Preventative Diplomacy, Peacemaking, and Peace-Keeping," 17 June 1992, para. 3, www.un.org/ruleof law/files/A_47_277.pdf (accessed 29 September 2020).

55 Boutros-Ghali, "An Agenda for Peace," para. 17.

56 Boutros-Ghali, "An Agenda for Peace," paras. 42–44.

57 "Introduction to the Report of the Secretary General to the 28th Ordinary Session of the OAU Assembly of Heads of State and Government," CM/1706 (LVI) Part 1 (Organization of African Unity, 22 June-1 July 1992), 6–19. AU Commission Archives.

58 "Report of the Secretary-General on the Establishment of a Mechanism for Conflict Prevention, Resolution, and Management," 31.

59 "Decision A/DEC.1/8/90 on the Ceasefire and Establishment of an ECOWAS Ceasefire Monitoring Group for Liberia (ECOWAS Peace Plan)," 7 August 1990, www.peaceagreements.org/view/1305 (accessed 29 September 2020). "Decision A/DEC.2/11/90 Relating to the Adoption of the ECOWAS Peace Plan for Liberia and the Entire West African Sub-Region (ECOWAS Peace Plan)," 28 November 1990, www.peaceagreements.org/view/1310 (accessed 7 May 2020).

60 Boutros Boutros-Ghali, "Supplement to an Agenda for Peace," 25 January 1995, para. 19, https://digitallibrary.un.org/record/168325?ln=en (accessed 29 September 2020).

61 "Report of the Panel on United Nations Peace Operations" (United Nations, August 2000), www.un.org/en/ga/search/view_doc.asp?symbol=A/55/305 (accessed 7 May 2020).

62 Gray, *International Law and the Use of Force*, 239–41.

63 "Resolution 1318 (2000) Adopted by the Security Council at Its 4194th Meeting, on 7 September 2000" (United Nations, 7 September 2000), 2–3, http://unscr. com/en/resolutions/doc/1318 (accessed 7 May 2020).

64 Charles Cater and David M. Malone, "The Origins and Evolution of Responsibility to Protect at the UN," *International Relations* 30, no. 3 (2016): 279.

65 Tony Blair, "Doctrine of the International Community" (22 April 1999), www. globalpolicy.org/component/content/article/154/26026.html (accessed 7 May 2020).

66 Kofi Annan, "Secretary-General Presents His Annual Report to General Assembly," (20 September 1999), www.un.org/press/en/1999/19990920.sgsm 7136.html (accessed 7 May 2020).

67 International Commission on Intervention and State Sovereignty, "The Responsibility to Protect" (Ontario, Canada, December 2001), VII–VIII, http://responsibilitytoprotect.org/ICISS%20Report.pdf (accessed 7 May 2020).

68 International Commission on Intervention and State Sovereignty, XI.

69 Ekkehard Strauss, "A Bird in the Hand is Worth Two in the Bush," in *The Responsibility to Protect and International Law*, ed. Alex J. Bellamy, Sara E. Davies, and Luke Glanville (Boston: Martinus Njihoff, 2011), 28–29.

70 "2005 World Summit Outcome" (United Nations, 15 September 2005), paras. 138–139, http://responsibilitytoprotect.org/world%20summit%20outcome%20doc%202005(1).pdf (accessed 7 May 2020).

71 African Union Executive Council, "The Common African Position on the Proposed Reform of the United Nations: The Ezulwini Consensus" (African Union, 7–8 March 2005), 6, www.un.org/en/africa/osaa/pdf/au/cap_screform_2005.pdf (accessed 7 May 2020).

72 Marcos Tourinho, Oliver Stuenkel, and Sarah Brockmeier, "'Responsibility While Protecting': Reforming R2P Implementation," *Global Society* 30, no. 1 (2016): 138.

73 Christopher R. Rossi, "Hauntings, Hegemony, and the Threatened African Exodus from the International Criminal Court," *Human Rights Quarterly* 40, no. 2 (May 2018): 370–73.

74 Sofie A. E. Hogestol, "The Habre Judgement at the Extraordinary African Chambers: A Singular Victory in the Fight Against Impunity," *Nordic Journal of Human Rights* 34, no. 3 (2016): 147–56.

75 "The Kampala Document: Africa Moves to Launch a Conference on Security, Stability, Development, & Co-Operation in Africa," 19–22 May 1991, https://oldsite.issafrica.org/uploads/CSSDCA.PDF (accessed 7 May 2020); Francis Deng, "Reconciling Sovereignty with Responsibility: A Basis for International Humanitarian Action," in *Africa in World Politics: Post Cold War Challenges*, ed. John W. Harbeson and Donald Rothchild (Boulder, CO: West View Press, 1995); Francis M. Deng et al., *Sovereignty as Responsibility: Conflict Management in Africa* (Washington DC: Brookings Institute Press, 1996).

11

The advent of the African Union

Unlike the OAU, the AU was created through a multi-step process over several years. In July 1999, African Heads of State and Government decided to convene an extraordinary summit to discuss the political and economic integration of the continent. This was held in Sirte, Libya on 8–9 September and culminated in the Sirte Declaration. The declaration affirmed the intention of African leaders to establish a new organization – the AU – that would strengthen the unity of the continent and allow African states to achieve their economic goals while also eliminating the curse of conflicts in Africa, "which constituted a major impediment to the implementation of the development and integration agenda."[1] The Constitutive Act of the AU was negotiated at the ministerial level along with experts and then unanimously adopted by the OAU Assembly of Heads of State and Government at the Lomé Summit in July 2000. The Constitutive Act entered into force on 26 May 2001 when it had been ratified by two-thirds of the member states of the OAU after which there was a period of transition. The 38th ordinary session of the OAU Assembly in Durban, Africa on 8 July 2002 was the last summit of the OAU, and the new institution of the AU held its inaugural session on 9–10 July 2002.[2] The focus of this book is to trace the creation and evolution of norms within the African regional institution from the OAU leading up to the creation of the AU. It has shown how the regional organization got to the point of pursuing institutional transformation and normative change, and this chapter draws on the scholarship of Tieku and primary sources to illuminate the period immediately around the creation of the AU.

Creating the AU

The road to the AU

Leading up to the creation of the AU, there was a progression of documents and protocols that slowly formed and built up African conceptions of

human security, sovereignty as responsibility, and the links between security and development. The promulgation of documents again starts as far
back as the 1980s. Particularly important in this progression are the 1980
Lagos Plan of Action promoting development and cooperation, the 1981
Charter on Human and Peoples' Rights and accompanying establishment
of the African Human Rights Commission, the 1990 Charter on Popular
Participation placing the African citizen at the center of decision-making,
and the 1991 Treaty establishing the African Economic Community.[3] The
Cairo Agenda for Action was adopted in 1995 to again try to spur Africa's
social and economic development. It recognized that democracy, good
governance, peace, security, and justice were all essential components of
development, and it also that development is not possible without durable
peace. The agenda referred back to previous OAU initiatives, including the
1990 Report on Fundamental Changes Taking Place in the World, showing
how these initiatives built on past reforms.[4] Further declarations, including
the 1999 Algiers decision on unconstitutional changes of government and
the 2000 Solemn Declaration of the reconstituted Conference on Security,
Stability, Development and Cooperation, were also notable in the regional
context and fed into the process of creating the AU.[5]

The first step in the creation of the AU was the Sirte Declaration. It recalled
the ideals of the founding fathers of the OAU and pan-Africanist values of
unity, solidarity, and cohesion.[6] Those leaders gathered in Sirte agreed that
the continent needed to address the social, political, and economic realities
in Africa and as such agreed to establish a new union that would align with
the objectives of the OAU Charter and the Treaty establishing the African
Economic Community. The future continental organization would seek to
speed up implementation of economic integration and establish other features of continental unity, including a central bank, monetary union, court
of justice, and pan-African parliament. The leaders in Sirte also agreed to
hold a ministerial-level Conference on Security, Stability, Development and
Cooperation.[7] This shows the continuation of the ideas from the first conference in 1991 with the process to create the AU.

The next step in the creation of the AU was negotiating the Constitutive
Act. The Draft Treaty Establishing the African Union and Draft Protocol
to the Treaty Establishing the African Economic Community relating to
the Pan-African parliament were prepared by the OAU General Secretariat.
The drafts were examined and discussed by legal experts and parliamentarians at two meetings from 17–20 April 2000 in Addis Ababa and from
27–29 May 2000 in Tripoli. The draft was then considered by a ministerial
meeting from 31 May–2 June 2000, after which it was formally submitted
to the OAU Council of Ministers. From there the draft Constitutive Act
moved to the Assembly of Heads of State and Government where it was

adopted on 11 July 2000. The draft that was submitted to the Assembly was largely the draft that was adopted because the critical issues, such as the objectives, principles, and institutions of the AU, were worked out at the ministerial and expert levels.[8]

There are several key differences between the OAU Charter and the AU Constitutive Act. The purposes of the OAU focused on promoting unity and cooperation, defending the sovereignty and territorial integrity of member states, eradicating all forms of colonialism, and enabling international cooperation. The purposes of the AU, however, are far more encompassing and include not only defending member states and facilitating cooperation but promoting peace, good governance, human rights, and development, among other things. The principles of each organization are also different in critical ways. Article 3 of the OAU Charter affirms, "Respect for the sovereignty and territorial integrity of each State and for its inalienable right to independent existence,"[9] whereas Article 4 of the AU Constitutive Act affirms, "sovereign equality and interdependence among Member States of the Union (and) respect of borders existing on achievement of independence."[10] However, the Constitutive Act also adds several new principles, notably the right of the AU to intervene as a result of certain grave circumstances and respect for democratic principles, human rights, rule of law, and good governance.

The differences between the founding documents of the organizations are telling. The OAU was focused on shoring up the independence and sovereignty of member states and eradicating colonialism and white-minority regimes. The AU still seeks to protect its member states, but has taken on a much greater role in promoting peace, democracy, and development. As this book has shown, the OAU tried to support development and human rights issues through protocols and agreements, including the Lagos Plan of Action and Charter on Human and Peoples' Rights throughout the 1980s and 1990s, but it was not until the transition from the OAU to the AU that they were formally codified in the foundational documents of the organization. Additionally, while the AU still strives to respect sovereignty, it is no longer a principle of the organization. The principles of the AU only go so far as to respect sovereign equality and borders while also codifying a clear statement of sovereignty as responsibility in Article 4(h), allowing the AU to intervene in certain circumstances. Overall, Article 4 of the AU Constitutive Act significantly expands the principles of the organization by including recognized international law principles while incorporating new thinking among African states about how to manage the social, political, peace and security, and economic challenges facing the continent.[11]

Factors that shaped the creation of the AU

My argument relies on Tieku's scholarship to illuminate the positions of African leaders during the process to create the AU. Negotiations to draft the AU Constitutive Act were heavily influenced by leaders from Nigeria, South Africa, and Libya. After being a leading figure in creating the ALF and convening the Kampala Forum to discuss African security and development, President Olusegun Obasanjo fell from grace and was placed under house arrest in Nigeria by a political rival. However, he re-emerged onto the political scene and was once again elected president of Nigeria in 1999. In the same year, Thabo Mbeki was elected president of South Africa after Nelson Mandela stepped down. Simultaneously Colonel Muammar Gaddafi sought to rejuvenate pan-Africanism after many years of Libya being regionally and internationally isolated.[12] Obasanjo and Mbeki, in particular, were responsible for proposing reforms that shaped the peace and security transition from the OAU to the AU.

At the advent of the OAU, African leaders chose to codify non-interference, protection of state sovereignty and territoriality, and regional primacy. They chose to focus on protecting independent African states, ending all forms of colonialism, and facilitating cooperation. These decisions were influenced by a common understanding of pan-Africanism, events during the colonial period, advocacy by key leaders, and regional interests and values that were in part shaped by pan-Africanist ideas. At the advent of the AU, African leaders codified norms that embraced human security, allowed for interference in a limited set of circumstances, and promoted democracy and human rights. The focus of the organization significantly expanded to include forming a closer union, facilitating economic development, and addressing social and political challenges. The same factors that influenced the decisions at the creation of the OAU also influenced the decisions taken at the creation of the AU.

The continental understanding of the most important facets of pan-Africanism evolved over decades. Coming out of the colonial period, African leaders rallied around a conception of pan-Africanism that focused on solidarity, protecting African states, and the final liberation of the continent. In the 1990s, the final liberation of the continent had been achieved and African states were well-established, albeit still marginalized in the international system. However, African states had not been able to improve the lives of African people by facilitating development and managing conflict, nor had the continent been able to move towards a closer union. As such, the conception of pan-Africanism that African leaders embraced at the creation of the AU emphasized unifying the continent and improving the lives of Africans over simply protecting African states. This idea provided the framework for debate, while the beliefs of key leaders, events during the tenure of the OAU, and evolving regional interests and ideas helped to shape the outcomes.

Two key leaders who strongly influenced the discussions creating the AU were Thabo Mbeki and Olusegun Obasanjo. Mbeki was concerned that the international perception of the OAU protecting African dictators hurt its goal of achieving economic development, and he was most interested in transforming the international image of Africa in order to enhance investment and development. To do this Mbeki drew on the long history of pan-Africanism, calling on African states to conclude the work of earlier pan-Africanist movements and re-invent the African state to take its rightful place in international society. Mbeki proposed reforms that promoted democratic institutions and helped authoritarian regimes move toward democracy.[13] Obasanjo proposed reforms that drew heavily on the Kampala Forum and subsequent CSSDCA outcomes held in 1991. Obasanjo sought to further move Africa away from a state security approach to a human security approach that was multi-dimensional and acknowledged the interdependence of African states.[14] Specifically, he advocated that African leaders go beyond military considerations and embrace economic and social concerns. He also saw all African states as inseparably linked and pushed for a collective responsibility on security issues that did not allow African leaders to hide behind state sovereignty to commit abuses against their citizens.[15]

These proposals and their subsequent acceptance at the regional level did not evolve out of nowhere. The core features of the reforms were framed by a revised conception of pan-Africanism that had evolved over decades because of the impact of atrocities and violence conflicts and advocacy from leaders, such as Nyerere. The key events and advocacy that helped to drive a new understanding of pan-Africanism also helped to spur attempts at reform within the institutional confines of the OAU. However, African leaders were still constrained by the normative framework of their regional institution, and there were not yet fully developed ideas to replace strict non-interference and protection of state sovereignty. The ideas to replace the old tenets of the OAU were developed through the Kampala Forum, Deng's theory of sovereignty as responsibility, and advocacy by other key actors, including OAU Secretary General Salim.

Furthermore, the continental interests had evolved during the nearly four decades of the OAU's existence. Economic development and self-sufficiency began to emerge as a regional interest in the early 1980s with the adoption of the Lagos Plan of Action. This coincided with the emergence of reforms that promoted human rights. The emerging regional interests were influenced by the evolving pan-Africanist ideas demonstrating how ideas and interests were mutually constitutive throughout the OAU period. In early 1990s the OAU fulfilled its primary regional goal of eradicating colonial and white-minority regimes when apartheid finally ended in South Africa. Yet the proliferation of conflicts, notably the Rwandan Genocide and subsequent wars in the Democratic Republic of the Congo, continued to severely hamper economic development goals and Africa's international reputation.

Institutional transformation and the creation of the AU

At an institutional level, transformation followed Blyth's hypotheses of institutional creation and reform. Fundamentally, ideas reduce uncertainty, as well as shape expectations, by acting as an interpretive framework for how political systems work.[16] Pan-Africanism is the idea that African leaders drew upon when crafting their institutions. At the creation of the OAU, pan-Africanism provided an interpretation of the international political system that highlighted the vulnerability of African states after years of domination and inconsistency in the standards applied to western and colonized states. This shaped the expectations of African leaders who then constructed an institution and pursued policies that primarily sought to protect African states from domination and eradicate all forms of colonialism. However, ideas, just like institutions, can evolve. Throughout the tenure of the OAU, the common conception of pan-Africanism evolved from focusing on liberation and cooperation to focusing on improving African lives and unity. This re-shaped the expectations of African leaders, who moved away from focusing only on African state security to embracing the importance of human security.

Ideas need to lead the way on institutional change, and are the blueprints that actors can use to contest and re-shape existing institutions. It is effective to use ideas to attack existing institutions because the existing structure and policies are all a result of the ideas that underpin the institution. Thus, the ideas are a crucial weapon in attacking and restructuring institutions.[17] After the conflict and atrocities of the 1970s, Nyerere attacked the idea of strict non-interference and absolute protection of state sovereignty. The events and the advocacy from Nyerere and others helped to undermine the ideas that were the basis of the OAU. However, once an existing idea has been discredited, new ideas will need to act as blueprints to guide institutional transformation.[18]

The ideas that underpinned the new normative and institutional framework of the AU were not fully developed in the early 1980s. While Nyerere offered critiques of existing ideas, the concepts of human security and sovereignty as responsibility needed to be fully developed to guide institutional transformation. These ideas were developed in the African context in the late 1980s and throughout the 1990s by several African policy-makers and scholars. Following on the AFL initiative, Francis Deng, with other scholars, articulated a clear vision for the theory that could underpin the principles put forward in the Kampala Document. Deng et al. sought to put forward a vision that worked within the confines of state sovereignty while also creating space for intervention if states failed to meet their obligations. They argued that states have accountability to both domestic and international constituencies. Domestically, state leaders must provide for the minimum needs of their people and ensure the maintenance of peace and security. Internationally, states are accountable to other states because conflict and instability is not typically contained by borders. In addition, states have a responsibility to the global community to cooperate in order to assist or check other states that have been unable to fulfil the obligations of sovereignty.[19]

Because of the timing of the creation of the AU in the post-Cold War period and around the emergence of R2P it makes sense to acknowledge international dynamics. However, focusing on these dynamics instead of looking at the longer and deeper process of evolution that created the opportunity for institutional and normative transformation is under determinant. The timing of the R2P report in comparison with the development of the AU Constitutive Act, African precedents throughout the preceding two decades, and the early African regional support for R2P clearly indicate an African regional position on intervention norms that pre-dated the development of international norms. The creation of norms within regional institutions at both the advent of the OAU and the AU was premised on pan-Africanist ideas that helped to shape regional interests and values, the influence of critical events, and advocacy by key leaders.

Notes

1 "Sirte Declaration" (African Union, 8–9 September 1999), para. 6, https://archives.au.int/handle/123456789/2475 (accessed 7 May 2020).
2 Tiyanjana Maluwa, "The Transition from the Organization of African Unity to the African Union," in *The African Union: Legal and Institutional Framework*, ed. Abdulqawi A. Yusef and Fatsah Ouguergouz (Leiden: Martinus Njihoff, 2012), 31–32.
3 "AU in a Nutshell," African Union, https://au.int/en/au-nutshell (accessed 7 May 2020).
4 "Relaunching Africa's Economic and Social Development: The Cairo Agenda for Action" (Organization of African Unity, 1995), para. 10.
5 "AU in a Nutshell."
6 "Sirte Declaration," para. 3.

7 "Sirte Declaration," para. 8.
8 Maluwa, "The Transition from the Organization of African Unity to the African Union," 39–40.
9 "Organization of African Unity Charter," 25 May 1963, https://au.int/en/trea ties/oau-charter-addis-ababa-25-may-1963 (accessed 7 May 2020).
10 "Constitutive Act of the African Union," 26 May 2001, https://au.int/en/trea ties/constitutive-act-african-union (accessed 7 May 2020).
11 Maluwa, "The Transition from the Organization of African Unity to the African Union," 43.
12 Thomas Kwasi Tieku, "Explaining the Clash and Accommodation of Major Actors in the Creation of the African Union," *African Affairs* 103, no. 411 (2004): 251.
13 Tieku, "Explaining the Clash," 255.
14 Tieku, "Explaining the Clash," 256.
15 Tieku, "Explaining the Clash," 256.
16 Mark Blyth, *Great Transformations: Economic Ideas and Institutional Change in the Twentieth Century* (New York: Cambridge University Press, 2002), 35–37.
17 Blyth, *Great Transformations*, 39.
18 Blyth, *Great Transformations*, 40.
19 Francis M. Deng, Sadikiel Kimaro, Terrence Lyons, Donald Rothchild, and I. William Zartman, *Sovereignty as Responsibility: Conflict Management in Africa* (Washington DC: Brookings Institute Press, 1996), xvii.

12

Conclusions

Findings

This book proposes an argument to augment our understanding of how regional organizations contribute to international society by analyzing the process of norm creation and evolution and the subsequent institutional and policy manifestations at the regional level in Africa. It has examined why the OAU chose specific norms in 1963 that manifested in a non-interference conflict management policy and what led the AU to codify different norms in the early 2000s that led to a non-indifference conflict management policy. In 1963, the regional organization adopted norms that entrenched protection of state sovereignty and territorial integrity, non-interference, and regional primacy leading to a conflict management policy that prioritized non-interference above stopping violent conflict. The AU formally replaced the OAU in 2002 after years of negotiation and transition. While the regional organization maintained many OAU norms, new AU norms place an emphasis on sovereignty as responsibility and human security instead of only state security, and include a norm that allows for interference in the internal affairs of a member state in the event of war crimes, crimes against humanity, and genocide. This change resulted in the non-indifference conflict management policy that has empowered the organization to respond more forcefully and consistently to violent conflict. Contrary to explanations that focus on the dynamics of the post-Cold War era or the influence of the international community, this book has argued that norm creation and evolution from the OAU to the AU was largely internally driven.

Norm creation at the regional level is driven by ideas that in turn help to shape regional interests and values and is further influenced by the impact of key events and advocacy by prominent leaders. At the creation of the OAU in 1963, pan-Africanist ideas helped to shape regional interests and values that prioritized protecting nascent African states, carving out space for Africa in the international community, and liberating the continent. This set the parameters of the debate within the regional organization, and

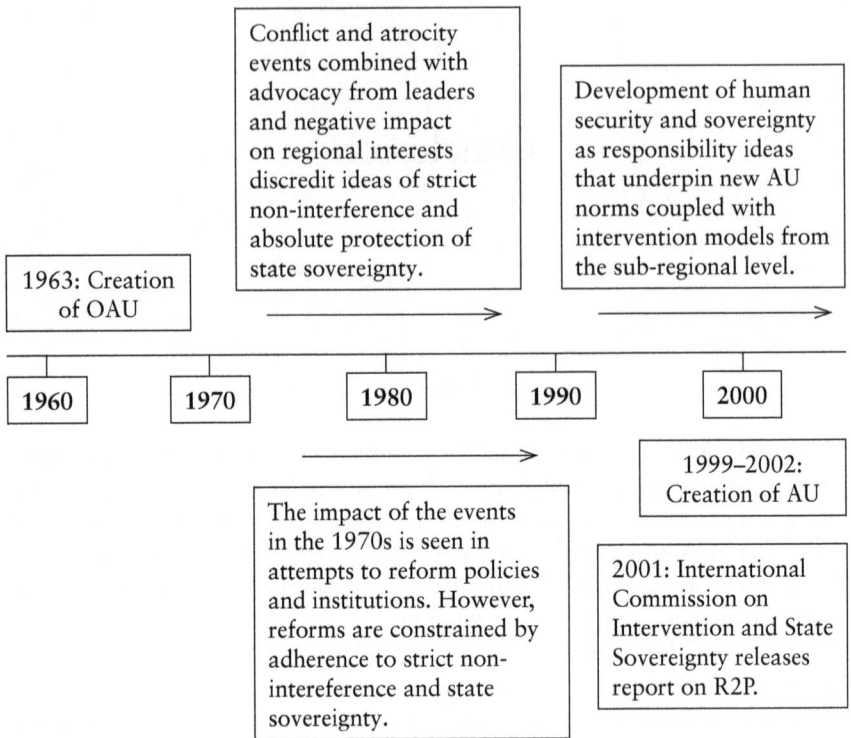

Figure 3 Process from the Organization of African Unity to the African Union

the events leading up to and after independence as well as advocacy from key leaders culminating in the OAU Charter that codified protecting state sovereignty and territoriality, non-interference, and regional primacy. The same factors that led to the creation of OAU norms led to the evolution of the regional organization and the codification of new norms under the AU. OAU norms began to be discredited and pan-Africanist ideas and regional interests and values evolved throughout the tenure of the OAU due to the impact of events and advocacy by leaders. As demonstrated in the time-line in figure 3, the OAU norms began to be discredited with the conflict and atrocities of the 1970s. The region attempted reform in the 1980s, but the ideas that would underpin new norms and guide institutional and policy change were not yet fully developed. Concepts around human security and sovereignty as responsibility developed in the 1980s and throughout the 1990s with ideological innovations from Salim Ahmed Salim, the Kamala Forum, and Francis Deng, among others. It is these ideas that supported the codification of a new human security norms in the AU Constitutive Act.

The creation of the OAU

The OAU was created in the immediate post-independence era. The events leading up to independence, advocacy by independence leaders, and regional interests and values all underpinned pan-Africanist ideas explaining why the OAU codified specific norms. Pan-Africanism helped to shape the parameters of the debate by providing points of common focus around the need to foster solidarity, ensure the final liberation of the continent, protect African statehood, and promote Africa's place in the world. In the immediate independence era the regional interests included protecting nascent African states and eradicating colonial and white-minority regimes from the continent, which aligned with pan-Africanist themes. Ideas and interests were mutually constitutive in this case as each helped to shape and justify the other.

The norms chosen at the creation of the OAU were not simply the regional institution adopting the prevailing international norms because there were no other options. There was advocacy by many prominent leaders, and there was a robust debate at the OAU founding conference. For instance, there was a proposal from Kwame Nkrumah to create a political union of African states, whereas Haile Selassie and other leaders advocated for a progressive path to unity.[1] While the OAU did codify norms protecting state sovereignty that aligned with international norms, it added to and adapted existing international norms in two important ways. First, it pushed a norm of racial equality in the international system and linked state legitimacy and a right to non-interference with accepting in principle racial equality and self-determination norms. This linking was implicit at the foundation of the OAU with the creation of the Liberation Committee to fund and support movements with the aim of overturning white-minority and colonial regimes while enshrining non-interference in the internal affairs of OAU member states. The link between the applicability of non-interference norms and state acceptance of principles of racial equality and self-determination became explicit through the 1969 Lusaka Manifesto.[2]

Secondly, the OAU strengthened the existing international norm giving regions a place in international affairs. Chapter VIII of the UN Charter gives space to regional arrangements and allows regions to enforce UNSC mandates. However, the OAU went further than simply pushing for Africa to have a role in the global community. Nkrumah and other leaders pushed the OAU to codify non-intervention and a commitment to non-alignment.[3] The regional organization also consistently pushed for primacy in handling conflicts and other issues on the continent. The OAU built up its capacity to engage with the international community as a regional unit through the African Group at the UN, and the region was largely successful at keeping

African conflicts off the UNSC agenda for several decades while still pushing UN action against the apartheid regime.

Tracing the process of norm creation at the advent of the OAU shows that it aligns in some ways with subsidiarity. However, the OAU did not adopt norms solely out of fear of outside domination. Instead, it sought to protect independent member states from any threats of interference – both from outside powers and from within the continent. OAU norms protected state sovereignty and territoriality and sought to keep international actors from interfering by pressing for regional primacy, but there was also fear of subversion from other African states, which was reflected in the OAU norms prohibiting subversive activities and more general non-interference. This shows the complexity of OAU norms by highlighting multiple motivations based on regional experiences with colonialism and domination and with conflicts and interference from other African states in the immediate independence era.

The gradual shift from the OAU to the AU

In the immediate post-independence era, liberating the continent, protecting the security of new African states, and asserting Africa's role in the world were the top priority interests of the region. However, the events of the 1960s and 1970s would hinder work to achieve these interests as well as economic development interests that emerged later in the tenure of the OAU. The destruction from the Nigerian-Biafran civil war and the atrocities of Amin and Bokassa damaged the ability of African states to condemn the atrocities of apartheid South Africa. Coupled with advocacy from African leaders, particularly President Nyerere, the catastrophic human toll of these events and negative impacts on regional interests forced some leaders to re-evaluate the primacy of state sovereignty and strict non-interference no matter the cost, and these ideas were gradually discredited.

In the 1980s, the OAU undertook institutional fixes without changing its foundational norms. These fixes included supporting a multilateral peacekeeping mission to resolve an internal conflict in Chad, a failed attempt to create a Political Security Council, and adopting the African Charter on Human and Peoples' Rights. However, transformative change did not happen at this juncture because the ideas that would underpin such a change were not fully developed. At a basic level, ideas enable actors to interpret the environment around them and this informs institutional construction.[4] The ideas that underpinned the OAU were being discredited, but new ideas had to emerge to guide normative and institutional change before a new institution could emerge. The result was limited institutional reform, which conformed to existing norms or failed attempts at reform that were seen throughout the 1980s and early 1990s.

An idea to replace strict non-interference while maintaining state sovereignty came with the slow development of human security and sovereignty as responsibility. Both concepts began to emerge in the 1980s through the linking of conflict and development outcomes. They were further developed through the CSSDCA in Kampala in 1991 and by Francis Deng in his volume on sovereignty as responsibility published in 1996. In the late 1990s, Obasanjo and Mbeki used these ideas to push for reforms that led to the construction of a new organization with new norms prioritizing human security and sovereignty as responsibility. The AU preserved non-interference but carved out exceptions in certain circumstances thus underpinning an entirely new and more robust institution and conflict management framework known as non-indifference. The same factors that shaped the creation of OAU norms shaped the creation of AU norms. Pan-Africanists ideas, which had evolved over the tenure of the OAU, influenced regional interests, and coupled with advocacy by key leaders and the impact of critical events, these factors led to the creation of new AU norms.

Theoretical contribution

The theoretical findings of this book are three-fold. First, the processes of norm creation and evolution at the regional level in Africa were driven by ideas and other factors, notably interests, events, and the influence of leaders. Pan-Africanist ideas guided discussions and set the parameters of debate, and the outcomes of the debate about which norms the region should choose were influenced by events, the experiences and beliefs of leaders, and regional interests. The interests of the region were underpinned by pan-Africanist ideas. In this way ideas and interests are mutually constitutive both from the standpoint of how each is constructed but also from the standpoint of how each influences decisions on norm creation and evolution.

Beyond demonstrating the power of ideas coupled with other factors to shape regional norms, institutions, and policies, this book demonstrates the agency of regions, particularly marginalized regions, to create norms based on their collective experiences and for their own purposes. While the OAU codified the prevailing norms of the international system, they did so with the specific intention of protecting their nascent states, and they also added to existing norms in new ways. At the advent of the AU, the African region again adopted norms based on their own experiences and for their own purposes. At both the advent of the OAU and the AU, the factors determining norm creation were pan-Africanist ideas that helped to shape regional interests coupled with the influence of critical events and advocacy by leaders, and international pressure was not a determinant factor. This book has demonstrated that international relations must have theoretical frameworks that allows for regional organizations to create norms independent of outside pressure or events and instead prioritize factors internal to the region.

Finally, this book has shown the importance of ideas in driving institutional creation and transformation.[5] Pan-Africanist ideas of solidarity, liberating the continent, and carving out space for Africa in the global community acted as a blueprint for independence era leaders when they met to create the OAU. These ideas, along with other factors, drove the codification of OAU norms that protected nascent African states through non-interference and shoring up state sovereignty and territoriality. These norms had to be discredited by critical events and advocacy by key leaders and new ideas had to emerge to guide institutional creation. Thus institutional transformation took place after an alternative idea was put forward to act as a blueprint to guide the deconstruction of the OAU and the reconstruction of the AU in its place. This concept of institutional transformation explains why the AU was created in the 2000s and not in the 1980s. The ideas of human security and sovereignty as responsibility were not yet fully developed to guide institutional creation.

What is at stake?

The broader implication of my argument is that the role of regions in the international order, particularly the African region, has been undertheorized and under-acknowledged. This book has explored Africa's role in creating and promoting norms based on its own experiences and for its own purposes. Some scholars, notably Acharya, have proposed how regions play a role in norm creation in their own region through localization or subsidiarity. Acharya has also proposed the concept of norm circulation to demonstrate a multi-agency and multi-step process of norm diffusion. In this conception, no matter the point of initiation, norms go through a complex process of feedback, resistance, and repatriation, which feed into their formation and acceptance at multiple levels.[6] In this way regions and other agents contribute to the creation and dissemination of norms.

Acharya argues this concept can be used to help explain the emergence of the R2P norm with particular attention paid to the contributions from Africa. There is significant evidence that R2P drew on a number of sources, including the idea of sovereignty as responsibility as well as human rights and Just War debates. Particularly important in the formulation of R2P was sovereignty as responsibility as developed by Francis Deng following the 1991 Kampala Forum.[7] Yet, despite important contributions from the regional level, the inclusion of Article 4(h) in the AU Constitutive Act prior to the official release of the R2P report, and advocacy by some African leaders around the idea of responsible sovereignty throughout the 1990s, R2P is typically seen as a western norm that is credited to the work of ICISS.[8] Beyond not receiving credit for regional contributions, in the case of progressive norms, such as R2P, Global South regions are often seen as having norms foisted upon them by cosmopolitan Global North states or transnational networks of norm entrepreneurs instead of contributing to the active construction of norms.

R2P is just the most recent example of regional contributions to norm processes. Even as far back as the immediate post-independence era, African states were making contributions to the international community. The African Group at the UN and their allies were successful in expanding the membership of UN bodies, partnering with UN functional agencies, and patrolling the UN agenda to limit international discussion of regional issues. Africa carved out space for itself in international institutions and shaped the agendas of those institutions. Furthermore, Africa helped to create and advance norms of racial equality and regional primacy in the global community and then used these norms to promote African regional interests.

The norm of racial equality emerged after advocacy from a variety of actors. Yet there is little analysis of how this norm came to be taken for granted in the international system, its origins, or which actors fed into it. Racial equality was promoted by pan-Africanists during the colonial period when white colonial powers dominated black African states while claiming superior governing capacity. When independence arrived, African states demanded the eradication of the last remnants of colonial and white-minority regimes on their continent, and African leaders linked the legitimacy of states and respect for their sovereignty to acceptance in principle of self-determination and racial equality norms. These norms underpinned a policy that promoted non-interference in independent African states whilst allowing the OAU to fund liberation movements and impose sanctions for internal policies. The diffusion of a norm of racial equality also motivated state, regional, and international protest against South Africa's internal policies of racial segregation over a period of decades. Protests manifested in condemnations from the global community and sanctions even from those states with interests in maintaining diplomatic, economic, and security ties with South Africa.[9]

It also should not be taken for granted that the OAU would automatically advocate for a norm of racial equality. South Africa was a powerful state, which controlled entry points to the continent. It sought dialogue with the OAU, and other independent African states could have gained tremendously from trade and economic cooperation with South Africa. South Africa had powerful military resources that it deployed against other states in the southern African sub-region, which could have been avoided through dialogue. Why then did the OAU not negotiate with South Africa to reap significant economic benefits and avoid conflict? It was a non-starter, and states that even suggested cooperation were condemned because of pan-Africanist principles of solidarity. Africa constructed its interests in terms of adherence to regional foundational principles and not solely in terms of material interests. The overriding argument here is that regions have choices in the norms they adopt, and they adopt norms based on their own experiences and for their own purposes. Beyond acknowledging the role that regional organizations play in creating and promoting norms, scholarship must also seek to explain how regional organizations develop norms. They are not pre-determined by the international system but are chosen because of ideas endorsed by the region and influenced by events, political leaders, and regional interests.

The lack of scholarship on how regions create and promote norms has implications for how global politics is structured and practiced, as well as our understanding of it. The under-acknowledgment of regional organizations in norm processes has negative outcomes when promoting and practicing new norms. When R2P was invoked to justify the NATO intervention in Libya in 2011, many African states condemned the intervention out of concern that R2P was being used to justify regime change. Coming from a history of domination, African and other former colonized states believed that R2P was not used as a last resort to save civilian lives but rather as another tool for domination by powerful states to remove an unpopular leader. As a result, support for R2P has waned in a region where it was previously very strong. Additionally, Brazil proposed Responsibility while Protecting to clarify when use of force should be used and shape the boundaries of when and how R2P should be implemented.[10]

When marginalized regions are not given credit for their contributions to international norms, the norms then seem to be owned and imposed by powerful states. Furthermore, when states raise legitimate concerns about domination through the implementation of these norms the concerns are viewed as illegitimate balking that undermines human rights. This in turn undermines the norm, whereas if marginalized regions were viewed as credible actors in creating and shaping norms, there would be benefits at all levels. The international would gain more knowledge about ideas and practices that have worked at regional levels and their potential application at the international level, and regional organizations would have more agency to create and shape global norms.

To fully understand the impact of regions in the creation, contestation, and promotion of norms there must be increased research and theorizing in two areas. First, little is understood of the influence of regions on states and on the international. The question should not always be how the international influences the regional but rather how regional organizations influence the international. In the case of states, how does the regional organization influence the internalization of norms by states? It is clear that not all states within Africa have embraced human security or sovereignty as responsibility. However, the AU Commission has acted as a leader within the region to promote these concepts, build up institutional capacity, and push member states to embrace them. What impact, if any, has the bureaucracy of the regional body had in promoting these norms amongst member states, or is it always the member states that control the organization? Furthermore, there needs to be more research on the mechanisms and conditions through which regional organizations contribute to norm processes. Why do some ideas from the regional level resonate at the international level and others do not? Must regions work through international organizations and with powerful states to promote norms or is there space for regions to act as norm entrepreneurs in their own right?

Finally, there needs to be additional research on how regions develop their own norms. This book used process-tracing methodologies to theorize the processes through which African regional institutions created norms and how these norms evolved. However, there is not a guiding theory that has been tested in all regions to explain regional norm creation, which is not driven by fear of outside domination or pressure from powerful states and transnational networks. This book has shown the importance of events that specifically impacted the region and the collective understanding of regional ideas – in this case pan-Africanism, key leaders, and regional interests as critical aspects of regional level norm creation and promotion. Further work must be done to apply this to other regional contexts to understand the extent to which these factors were unique to Africa or whether there is broader theoretical applicability.

In sum, there is a piece of the puzzle missing in our understanding of norm processes. The dynamic role regional organizations can play in creating and promoting norms at the regional level and their contributions to the international must be recognized. Regions occupy an odd space in the international order. Regions operate within themselves to find collective principles and policies and function both internally to manage relationships amongst member states and externally to promote their agenda to the international community. Thus it can be difficult to trace processes and influence at multiple levels. However, despite the complexities and inconsistencies within regional politics, the role of regional organizations, particularly those in marginalized regions, must be recognized and theorized in order to give us a full picture of how norms are produced, accepted, and ultimately practiced.

Notes

1 "1963 Statements His Excellency Kwame N'Krumah, President of the Republic of Ghana," in *Celebrating Success: Africa's Voice over 50 Years (1963–2013)* (Addis Ababa: African Union Commission, 2013), 34–41; "1963 Statements His Imperial Majesty Haile Selassie I, Emperor of Ethiopia," in *Celebrating Success*.

2 "The Lusaka Manifesto on Southern Africa Proclaimed by the Fifth Summit Conference of East and Central African States" (Government of the United Republic of Tanzania, 14–16 April 1969), para. 9, http://reference.sabinet.co.za/webx/access/journal_archive/00020117/33.pdf (accessed 7 May 2020).

3 Amitav Acharya, "Norm Subsidiarity and Regional Orders: Sovereignty, Regionalism, and Rule-Making in the Third World," *International Studies Quarterly* 55, no. 1 (2011): 115.

4 Mark Blyth, *Great Transformations: Economic Ideas and Institutional Change in the Twentieth Century* (New York: Cambridge University Press, 2002), 36–37.

5 Blyth, *Great Transformations*.

6 Acharya, "The R2P and Norm Diffusion: Towards a Framework of Norm Circulation," *Global Responsibility to Protect* 5 (2013), 471.

7 Acharya, "The R2P and Norm Diffusion," 472.

8 Acharya, "The R2P and Norm Diffusion," 467 and 474–76.

9 Audie Klotz, *Norms in International Relations: The Struggle Against Apartheid* (London: Cornell University Press, 1995), 165.

10 Cristina G. Stefan, "On Non-Western Norm Shapers: Brazil and the Responsibility While Protecting," *European Journal of International Security* 2 (2016): 96–97.

Bibliography

"100 Days of Slaughter: A Chronology of U.S./U.N. Actions." Frontline: The Triumph of Evil. www.pbs.org/wgbh/pages/frontline/shows/evil/etc/slaughter. html (accessed 3 April 2017).

"1963 Statements His Excellency Ahmadou Ahidjo, President of the Federal Republic of Cameroon." In *Celebrating Success: Africa's Voice over 50 Years (1963–2013)*, 11–15. Addis Ababa, Ethiopia: African Union Commission, 2013.

"1963 Statements His Excellency Ahmed Ben Bella, Prime Minister of Algeria." In *Celebrating Success: Africa's Voice over 50 Years (1963–2013)*, 7–8. Addis Ababa, Ethiopia: African Union Commission, 2013.

"1963 Statements His Excellency Alhaji Abubakar Tafawa Balewa, Prime Minister of the Federation of Nigeria." In *Celebrating Success: Africa's Voice over 50 Years (1963–2013)*, 79–82. Addis Ababa, Ethiopia: African Union Commission, 2013.

"1963 Statements His Excellency Félix Houphouët-Boigny, President of the Republic of Ivory Coast." In *Celebrating Success: Africa's Voice over 50 Years (1963–2013)*, 49–55. Addis Ababa, Ethiopia: African Union Commission, 2013.

"1963 Statements His Excellency François Tombalbaye President of the Republic of Chad." In *Celebrating Success: Africa's Voice over 50 Years (1963–2013)*, 19–20. Addis Ababa, Ethiopia: African Union Commission, 2013.

"1963 Statements His Excellency Fulbert Youlou, President of Congo (Brazzaville)." In *Celebrating Success: Africa's Voice over 50 Years (1963–2013)*, 21–25. Addis Ababa, Ethiopia: African Union Commission, 2013.

"1963 Statements His Excellency Gamal Abdel Nasser, President of the United Arab Republic." In *Celebrating Success: Africa's Voice over 50 Years (1963–2013)*, 110–15. Addis Ababa, Ethiopia: African Union Commission, 2013.

"1963 Statements His Excellency Kwame N'Krumah, President of the Republic of Ghana." In *Celebrating Success: Africa's Voice over 50 Years (1963–2013)*, 34–41. Addis Ababa, Ethiopia: African Union Commission, 2013.

"1963 Statements His Excellency Léopold Sédar Senghor." In *Celebrating Success: Africa's Voice over 50 Years (1963–2013)*, 85–88. Addis Ababa, Ethiopia: African Union Commission, 1963.

"1963 Statements His Excellency Modibo Keita, President of Mali." In *Celebrating Success: Africa's Voice over 50 Years (1963–2013)*, 69–72. Addis Ababa, Ethiopia: African Union Commission, 2013.

"1963 Statements His Excellency Philibert Tsiranana, President of the Malagasy Republic." In *Celebrating Success: Africa's Voice over 50 Years (1963–2013)*, 61–68. Addis Ababa, Ethiopia: African Union Commission, 2013.

"1963 Statements His Excellency Sékou Touré, President of the Republic of Guinea." In *Celebrating Success: Africa's Voice over 50 Years (1963–2013)*, 42–48. Addis Ababa, Ethiopia: African Union Commission, 2013.

"1963 Statements His Imperial Majesty Haile Selassie I, Emperor of Ethiopia." In *Celebrating Success: Africa's Voice over 50 Years (1963–2013)*, 1–6. Addis Ababa, Ethiopia: African Union Commission, 2013.

"The 1975 Treaty of the Economic Community of West African States," 28 May 1975. Archiving and Documentation Division, Communications Directorate, ECOWAS Commission.

"2005 World Summit Outcome." United Nations, 15 September 2005. http://responsibilitytoprotect.org/world%20summit%20outcome%20doc%20 2005(1).pdf (accessed 7 May 2020).

"3207 (XXIX). Relationship between the United Nations and South Africa." United Nations, 30 September 1974. https://digitallibrary.un.org/record/189829 (accessed 7 May 2020).

Aaronson, Michael. "The Nigerian Civil War and Humanitarian Intervention." In *The History and Practice of Humanitarian Intervention and Aid in Africa*, edited by Bronwen Everill and Josiah Kaplan, 176–96. New York: Palgrave Macmillan, 2013.

Aboagye, Lt. Colonel Festus B. *ECOMOG: A Sub-Regional Experience in Conflict Resolution, Management, and Peacekeeping in Liberia*. Accra, Ghana: Seco Publishing Limited, 1999.

Acharya, Amitav. "Norm Subsidiarity and Regional Orders: Sovereignty, Regionalism, and Rule-Making in the Third World." *International Studies Quarterly* 55, no. 1 (2011): 95–123.

———. "The R2P and Norm Diffusion: Towards a Framework of Norm Circulation." *Global Responsibility to Protect* 5 (2013): 466–79.

———. *Whose Ideas Matter? Agency and Power in Asian Regionalism*. New York: Cornell University Press, 2009.

Adeniran, Tunde. "Pacific Settlement Among African States: The Role of the Organization of African Unity." Kano, Nigeria: Nigerian Institute of International Affairs, 1980.

Aderinwale, Ayodele. "The Conference on Security, Stability, Development and Cooperation in Framework and the Role of Regional Institutions." In *Peace, Human Security and Conflict Prevention in Africa*, edited by Moufida Goucha and Jakkie Cilliers, 59–68. Pretoria, South Africa: Institute for Security Studies, 2001.

"African Charter on Human and Peoples' Rights," 1986. www.achpr.org/legalin struments/detail?id=49 (accessed 7 May 2020).

"African Union Abandons Plans to Send Peacekeepers to Burundi." *BBC*, 31 December 2015. www.bbc.co.uk/news/world-africa-35454893 (accessed 7 May 2020).

African Union Commission. *African Union Handbook 2015*. Addis Ababa, Ethiopia: African Union Commission and New Zealand Ministry of Foreign Affairs, 2015.

African Union Executive Council. "The Common African Position on the Proposed Reform of the United Nations: The Ezulwini Consensus." African Union, 7–8 March 2005. www.un.org/en/africa/osaa/pdf/au/cap_screform_2005.pdf (accessed 7 May 2020).

Ageron, Charles-Robert. *Modern Algeria: A History from 1830 to the Present.* London: C. Hurst & Co. Ltd, 1991.

"Agreement with the Sudanese Parties on the Modalities for the Establishment of the Ceasefire Commission and the Deployment of Observers in the Darfur," 28 May 2004. www.peaceagreements.org/view/92 (accessed 7 May 2020).

Ajala, Adekunle. *Pan-Africanism: Evolution, Progress, and Prospects.* New York: St. Martin's Press, 1973.

Amate, C. O. C. *Inside the OAU: Pan-Africanism in Practice.* New York: St. Martin's Press, 1986.

"Amendments to the Charter and the Protocol of the Commission of Mediation, Conciliation and Arbitration." CM/334, Organization of African Unity, August 1970. AU Commission Archives.

Anghie, Antony. *Imperialism, Sovereignty and the Making of International Law.* Cambridge: Cambridge University Press, 2005.

Annan, Kofi. "Secretary-General Presents His Annual Report to General Assembly." Presented at the UN General Assembly, 20 September 1999. www.un.org/press/en/1999/19990920.sgsm7136.html (accessed 7 May 2020).

"The Atlantic Charter – Declaration of Principles Issues by the President of the United States and the Prime Minister of the United Kingdom," 14 August 1941. www.nato.int/cps/en/natolive/official_texts_16912.htm (accessed 7 May 2020).

"AU in a Nutshell." African Union. https://au.int/en/au-nutshell (accessed 7 May 2020).

Avant, Deborah D., Martha Finnemore, and Susan K. Sell. "Who Governs the Globe?" In *Who Governs the Globe?*, edited by Deborah D. Avant, Martha Finnemore, and Susan K. Sell, 1–32. Cambridge: Cambridge University Press, 2010.

Badmus, Isiaka A. *The African Union's Role in Peacekeeping: Building on Lessons from Security Operations.* New York: Palgrave Macmillan, 2015.

Beach, Derek, and Rasmus Brun. *Process-Tracing Methods: Foundations and Guidelines.* Ann Arbor, MI: University of Michigan Press, 2013.

Bellamy, Alex J. *The Responsibility to Protect: A Defense.* Oxford: Oxford University Press, 2015.

"Biography of Dr. Salim Ahmed Salim." United Nations, April 2002. www.un.org/News/dh/hlpanel/salim-salim-bio.htm (accessed 7 May 2020).

Blair, Tony. "Doctrine of the International Community." Chicago Economic Club, 22 April 1999. www.globalpolicy.org/component/content/article/154/26026.html (accessed 7 May 2020).

Blyth, Mark. *Great Transformations: Economic Ideas and Institutional Change in the Twentieth Century.* New York: Cambridge University Press, 2002.

Borgen, Christopher J. "Transnational Tribunals and the Transmission of Norms: The Hegemony of Process." *George Washington International Law Review* 39, no. 1 (2007): 685–764.

Boutros-Ghali, Boutros. "An Agenda for Peace: Preventative Diplomacy, Peacemaking, and Peace-Keeping," 17 June 1992. www.un.org/ruleoflaw/files/A_47_277.pdf (accessed 29 September 2020).

———. "Supplement to an Agenda for Peace," 25 January 1995. https://digitallibrary.un.org/record/168325?ln=en (accessed 29 September 2020).

"Cases: Rwanda." The United States Holocaust Museum. www.ushmm.org/confront-genocide/cases/rwanda/rwanda-background (accessed 2 April 2017).

Cater, Charles and David M. Malone. "The Origins and Evolution of Responsibility to Protect at the UN." *International Relations* 30, no. 3 (2016): 278–97.

"Ceasefire Agreement (Lusaka Agreement)," 10 July 1999. www.peaceagreements.org/view/319 (accessed 7 May 2020).

Cervenka, Zdenek. *The Unfinished Quest for Unity: Africa and the OAU*. London: Julian Friedmann Publishers Ltd, 1977.

"Charter of the United Nations," 24 October 1945. www.un.org/en/charter-united-nations/index.html (accessed 30 September 2020).

Checkel, Jeffrey T. "Mechanisms, Processes, and the Study of International Institutions." In *Process Tracing: From Metaphor to Analytic Tool*, edited by Jeffrey T. Checkel and Andrew Bennett, 74–97. New York: Cambridge University Press, 2015.

Clapham, Christopher. *Africa and the International System: The Politics of State Survival*. Cambridge: Cambridge University Press, 1996.

Coleman, Katharina P., and Thomas Kwasi Tieku. "African Actors in International Security: Four Pathways to Influence." In *African Actors in International Security: Shaping Contemporary Norms*, edited by Katharina P. Coleman and Thomas Kwasi Tieku, 1–20. Boulder, CO: Lynne Rienner Publishers, 2018.

"Communique of the Peace and Security Council of the African Union (AU) at Its 557th Meeting Held on 13 November 2015, Adopted the Following Decision of the Situation in Burundi." African Union, 13 November 2015. www.peaceau.org/uploads/psc-557-comm-burundi-12-11-2015.pdf (accessed 7 May 2020).

"Constitutive Act of the African Union," 26 May 2001. https://au.int/en/treaties/constitutive-act-african-union (accessed 7 May 2020).

Conteh-Morgan, Earl. "The Politics and Diplomacy of the Liberian Peace Process." In *Peacekeeping in Africa*, edited by Karl P. Magyar and Earl Conteh-Morgan, 32–51. London: Macmillan Press Ltd, 1998.

"Convention Governing the Specific Aspects of Refugee Problems in Africa." Organization of African Unity, 20 June 1974. https://au.int/en/treaties/oau-convention-governing-specific-aspects-refugee-problems-africa (accessed 23 September 2020).

"Council of Ministers Thirty-Fifth Ordinary Session from 18–28 June 1980: African Charter of Human and Peoples' Rights." CM/1068 (XXXV), Organization of African Unity, 18–28 June 1980. AU Commission Archives.

Cronje, Suzanne. *The World and Nigeria*. London: The Anchor Press Ltd, 1972.

Darkwa, Linda. "Humanitarian Intervention." In *African Actors in International Security: Shaping Contemporary Norms*, edited by Thomas Kwasi Tieku and Katharina P. Coleman, 21–38. Boulder, CO: Lynne Rienner Publishers, 2018.

Dear, I.C.B. and M.R.D. Foot, eds. "Brazzaville Conference." In *The Oxford Companion to World War II*. Oxford: Oxford University Press, 2003. www.ox

fordhandbooks.com/view/10.1093/law/9780199640133.001.0001/law-978019 9640133-e-35 (accessed 7 May 2020).

"Decision A/DEC.1/8/90 on the Ceasefire and Establishment of an ECOWAS Ceasefire Monitoring Group for Liberia (ECOWAS Peace Plan)," 7 August 1990. www.peaceagreements.org/view/1305 (accessed 7 May 2020).

"Decision A/DEC.2/11/90 Relating to the Adoption of the ECOWAS Peace Plan for Liberia and the Entire West African Sub-Region (ECOWAS Peace Plan)," 28 November 1990. www.peaceagreements.org/view/1310 (accessed 7 May 2020).

Deng, Francis. "Reconciling Sovereignty with Responsibility: A Basis for International Humanitarian Action." In *Africa in World Politics: Post Cold War Challenges*, edited by John W. Harbeson and Donald Rothchild, 295–310. Boulder, CO: West View Press, 1995.

Deng, Francis M. and I. William Zartman. *A Strategic Vision for Africa: The Kampala Movement*. Washington DC: Brookings Institute Press, 2002.

Deng, Francis M., Sadikiel Kimaro, Terrence Lyons, Donald Rothchild, and I. William Zartman. *Sovereignty as Responsibility: Conflict Management in Africa*. Washington DC: Brookings Institute Press, 1996.

Dersso, Solomon. Interview with Dr Solomon Dersso, Commissioner, African Commission on Human and Peoples' Rights. Interview by Kathryn Nash, 29 March 2016.

———. "The Quest for Pax Africana: The Case of the African Union's Peace and Security Regime." *African Journal on Conflict Resolution* 12 (2012): 11–49.

Desgrandchamps, Marie-Luce. "Dealing with 'Genocide': The ICRC and the UN during the Nigeria-Biafra War, 1967–70." *Journal of Genocide Research* 16, no. 2–3 (2014): 281–97.

"Development of the Community – The First Five Years." Lagos, Nigeria, 1981.

"Draft Agenda for the Eighteenth Ordinary Session of the Assembly of Heads of State and Government." AHG/101 (XVIII) Rev. 1, Organization of African Unity, 24–27 June 1981. AU Commission Archives.

"Draft Agenda for the Thirty-Fifth Ordinary Sessions of the Council of Ministers." CM/1039 (XXXV) Rev. 1, Organization of African Unity, 18–28 June 1980. AU Commission Archives.

Dumor, E.K. *Ghana, OAU, and Southern Africa: An African Response to Apartheid*. Accra, Ghana: Ghana Universities Press, 1991.

"Economic Community of West African States (ECOWAS): Revised Treaty," Economic Community of West African States, 24 July 1993. Archiving and Documentation Division, Communications Directorate, ECOWAS Commission.

"Economic Community of West African States Protocol on Non-Aggression." Economic Community of West African States, 20 April 1978. http://documen tation.ecowas.int/download/en/legal_documents/protocols/Protocol%20on%20 Non-aggression.pdf (accessed 7 May 2020).

"ECOWAS: Achievements, Challenges, and Future Prospects." Lagos, Nigeria, n.d.

Engel, Ulf and Joao Gomes Porto. "The African Union's New Peace and Security Architecture: Toward an Evolving Security Regime." In *Regional Organizations in African Security*, edited by Fredrik Soderbaum and Rodrigo Tavares, 14–28. New York: Routledge, 2011.

Esedebe, P. Olisanwuche. *Pan-Africanism: The Idea and Movement, 1776–1991*, second edition Washington DC: Howard University Press, 1994.

Eslava, Luis, and Sundhya Pahuja. "Between Resistance and Reform: TWAIL and the Universality of International Law." *Trade Law and Development* 3, no. 103 (Spring 2011): 104–30.

Finnemore, Martha and Kathryn Sikkink. "International Norm Dynamics and Political Change." *International Organizations* 52 (1998): 887–917.

Furley, Oliver and Roy May. "Tanzania's Military Intervention in Uganda." In *African Interventionist States*, edited by Oliver Furley and Roy May. Aldershot: Ashgate Publishing Limited, 2001.

Gaulle, Charles de. "Speech Made by General de Gaulle at Opening of Brazzaville Conference." Presented at the Brazzaville Conference, Brazzaville, 30 January 1944. www.charles-de-gaulle.org/pages/stock-html/en/the-man/home/speeches/sp eech-made-by-general-de-gaulle-at-the-opening-of-the-brazzaville-conference-on-january-30th-1944.php (accessed 7 May 2020).

Gordon, Jacob. *African Leadership in the Twentieth Century: An Enduring Experiment in Democracy*. Lanham, MD: University Press of America, 2002.

Gray, Christine. *International Law and the Use of Force*. Oxford: Oxford University Press, 2004.

Hailey, Lord, Franklin D. Roosevelt, and Winston S. Churchill. "The Colonies and the Atlantic Charter." *Journal of The Royal Central Asian Society* 30, no. 3–4 (1943): 233–46.

Hall, Peter A. "Conclusion: The Politics of Keynesian Ideas." In *The Political Power of Economic Ideas: Keynesianism Across Nations*, edited by Peter A. Hall, 361–92. Princeton, NJ: Princeton University Press, 1989.

Hammad, Salah. Interview with Ambassador Salah Hammad, Senior Human Rights Expert, Department of Political Affairs, African Union Commission. Interview by Kathryn Nash, 5 April 2016.

Hardie, Frank. *The Abyssinian Crisis*. London: B.T. Batsford Ltd, 1974.

Heerten, Lasse and A. Dirk Moses. "The Nigeria-Biafra War: Postcolonial Conflict and the Question of Genocide." *Journal of Genocide Research* 16, no. 2–3 (2014): 169–203.

Helleiner, Eric. "Principles from the Periphery: The Neglected Southern Sources of Global Norms." *Global Governance* 20, no. 3 (2014): 359–60.

Hogestol, Sofie A.E. "The Habre Judgement at the Extraordinary African Chambers: A Singular Victory in the Fight Against Impunity." *Nordic Journal of Human Rights* 34, no. 3 (2016): 147–56.

Hoskyns, Catherine. "The Part Played by the Independent African States in the Congo Crisis July 1960–December 1961," 30–50. Wiesneck: Gutenbergdruckerei Robert Oberkirch, 1963.

Hovet, Thomas. "Effect of the Africa Group of States on the Behaviour of the United Nations." In *Africa and International Organization*, edited by Yassin El-Ayouty and Hugh C. Brooks, 11–17. The Hague: Martinus Njihoff, 1974.

Howard, Peter and Reina Neufeldt. "Canada's Constructivist Foreign Policy: Building Norms for Peace." *Canadian Foreign Policy Journal* 8, no. 1 (2000): 11–38.

"Humanitarian Ceasefire Agreement on the Conflict in Darfur," 8 April 2004. www.peaceagreements.org/view/647 (accessed 7 May 2020).

Imobighe, Thomas Akhigbe. *The OAU (AU) and OAS in Regional Conflict Management: A Comparative Assessment.* Ibadan, Nigeria: Spectrum Books Limited, 2003.

Ingebritsen, Christine. "Norm Entrepreneurs: Scandinavia's Role in World Politics." *Cooperation and Conflict: Journal of Nordic International Studies Association* 37, no. 1 (2002): 11–23.

"International Coalition for the Responsibility to Protect." *Accounting for the African Union Response in Libya: A Missed Opportunity?* blog, 13 September 2011. http://icrtopblog.org/2011/09/13/accounting-for-the-african-union-au-response-to-libya-a-missed-opportunity/ (accessed 7 May 2020).

International Commission on Intervention and State Sovereignty. "The Responsibility to Protect." Ontario, Canada. December 2001. http://responsibilitytoprotect.org/ICISS%20Report.pdf (accessed 7 May 2020).

"Introduction to the Report of the Secretary General to the 28th Ordinary Session of the OAU Assembly of Heads of State and Government." CM/1706 (LVI) Part 1, Organization of African Unity, 22 June–1 July 1992. AU Commission Archives.

Jeng, Abou. *Peacebuilding in the African Union: Law, Philosophy, and Practice.* Cambridge: Cambridge University Press, 2012.

Jennings, Eric T. *Free French Africa in World War II: The African Resistance.* New York: Cambridge University Press, 2015.

Jorgensen, Jan Jelmert. *Uganda: A Modern History.* London: Croom Helm Ltd, 1981.

"The Kampala Document: Africa Moves to Launch a Conference on Security, Stability, Development, & Co-Operation in Africa," 19–22 May 1991. https://oldsite.issafrica.org/uploads/CSSDCA.PDF (accessed 7 May 2020).

Karbo, Tony. "Conclusion." In *The Palgrave Handbook of Peacebuilding in Africa*, edited by Tony Karbo and Kudrat Virk, 455–65. London: Palgrave Macmillan, 2018.

Katzenstein, Peter J. "Introduction: Alternative Perspectives on National Security." In *The Culture of National Security: Norms and Identity in World Politics*, edited by Peter J. Katzenstein, 1–32. New York: Columbia University Press, 1996.

Killingray, David. "Labour Mobilisation in British Colonial Africa for the War Effort, 1939–46." In *Africa and the Second World War*, edited by David Killingray and Richard Rathbone, 68–96. London: Palgrave Macmillan, 1986.

Klotz, Audie. *Norms in International Relations: The Struggle Against Apartheid.* London: Cornell University Press, 1995.

Koga, Kei. *Reinventing Regional Security Institutions in Asia and Africa: Power Shifts, Ideas, and Institutional Change.* London: Routledge, 2017.

Krisch, Nico. "International Law in Times of Hegemony: Unequal Power and the Shaping of the International Legal Order." *The European Journal of International Law* 16, no. 3 (2005): 369–408.

Kufuor, Kofi Oteng. *The African Human Rights System: Origin and Evolution.* New York: Palgrave Macmillan, 2010.

Kuper, Leo. *Genocide: Its Political Use in the Twentieth Century.* New Haven, CT: Yale University Press, 1981.

"Lagos Plan of Action for Economic Development of Africa 1980–2000." Organization of African Unity, 28–29 April 1980. www.resakss.org/node/6653 (accessed 7 May 2020).

Lemarchand, René. *Burundi: Ethnic Conflict and Genocide*. New York: Woodrow Wilson Center Press, 1994.

Levitt, Jeremy. "African Interventionist States and International Law." In *African Interventionist States*, edited by Oliver Furley and Roy May, 15–50. Aldershot: Ashgate Publishing Limited, 2001.

"List of Peacekeeping Operations 1948–2013." United Nations. https://peacekeep ing.un.org/sites/default/files/operationslist.pdf (accessed 28 September 2020).

Lloyd Axworthy. "RtoP and the Evolution of State Sovereignty." In *The Responsibility to Protect: The Promise of Stopping Mass Atrocities in Our Time*, edited by Jared Genser and Irwin Cotler, 3–16. Oxford: Oxford University Press, 2012.

"The Lusaka Manifesto on Southern Africa Proclaimed by the Fifth Summit Conference of East and Central African States." Government of the United Republic of Tanzania, 14–16 April 1969. http://reference.sabinet.co.za/webx/ access/journal_archive/00020117/33.pdf (accessed 7 May 2020).

Maluwa, Tiyanjana. "The Transition from the Organization of African Unity to the African Union." In *The African Union: Legal and Institutional Framework*, edited by Abdulqawi A. Yusef and Fatsah Ouguergouz, 25–52. Leiden: Martinus Njihoff, 2012.

Mamdani, Mahmood. *Imperialism and Fascism in Uganda*. London: Heinemann Educational Books Ltd, 1983.

Mays, Terry. *Africa's First Peacekeeping Operation: The OAU in Chad 1981–1982*. Westport: Praeger Publishers, 2002.

Mazrui, Ali A. *Towards a Pax Africana: A Study of Ideology and Ambition*. Chicago, IL: University of Chicago Press, 1967.

M'Bayo, Tamba E. "W.E.B. Du Bois, Marcus Garvey, and the Pan-Africanism in Liberia, 1919–1924." *Historian* 66, no. 1 (2004): 19–44.

Meo, Nick. "Libya: Jacob Zuma Accuses Nato of Not Sticking to UN Resolution." *The Telegraph*, 14 June 2011. www.telegraph.co.uk/news/worldnews/afri caandindianocean/libya/8575984/Libya-Jacob-Zuma-accuses-Nato-of-not-stic king-to-UN-resolution.html (accessed 7 May 2020).

Mezu, S. Okechukwu. "Introduction: The Philosophy of Pan-Africanism." In *The Philosophy of Pan-Africanism: A Collection of Papers on the Theory and Practice of the African Unity Movement*, edited by S. Okechukwu Mezu, 15–20. Washington DC: Georgetown University Press, 1965.

Moore, Jennifer. *Humanitarian Law and Action Within Africa*. Oxford: Oxford University Press, 2012.

Murithi, Tim. "Briefing: The African Union at Ten: An Appraisal." *African Affairs* 111, no. 445 (2012): 662–69.

———. "The Role of the African Peace and Security Architecture in the Implementation of Article 4(h)." In *Africa and the Responsibility to Protect*, edited by Dan Kuwali and Frans Viljoen, 139–51. New York: Routledge, 2014.

Muyangwa, Monde and Margaret A. Vogt. "An Assessment of the OAU Mechanism for Conflict Prevention, Management, and Resolution, 1993–2000." New York: International Peace Academy, 2000.

Mwakikagile, Godfrey. *Nyerere and Africa: End of an Era*. Pretoria, South Africa: New Africa Press, 2009.

Mwanasali, Musifiky. "From Non-Interference to Non-Indifference: The Emerging Doctrine of Conflict Prevention in Africa." In *The African Union and Its Institutions*, edited by John Akokpari, Angela Ndinga-Muvumba, and Tim Murithi, 41–62. Auckland Park: Jacama Media Ltd, 2008.

Ndlovu-Gatsheni, Sabelo J. "Pan-Africanism and the International System." In *Handbook of Africa's International Relations*, edited by Tim Murithi, 21–29. New York: Routledge, 2014.

Nyerere, Julius. "Without Unity There Is No Future for Africa." *New African*, May 2013.

"OAU Conflict Management Review: Echoes from Liberia." Addis Ababa, Ethiopia, n.d. AU Commission Archives.

"OAU Declaration on a Mechanism for Conflict Prevention, Management, and Resolution (Cairo Declaration)." Dipublico, 28–30 June 1993. www.dipublico. org/100609/oau-declaration-on-a-mechanism-for-conflict-prevention-manageme nt-and-resolution-cairo-declaration/ (accessed 7 May 2020).

"OAU Review 1963–1968: Special Issue – Fifth OAU Summit – Algiers Sept 1968." Organization of African Unity, September 1968. AU Commission Archives.

Odesanya, Justice M.A. "Report of the President of the Commission of Mediation, Conciliation and Arbitration." CM/172/Add. 2, Organization of African Unity, September 1967. AU Commission Archives.

Ofodile, Anthony Chukwuka. "The Legality of ECOWAS Intervention in Liberia." *Columbia Journal of Transnational Law* 32 (1994–1995): 381–418.

Okeke, Jide Martyns. "United in Challenges? The African Standby Force and the African Capacity for the Immediate Response to Crises." In *Future of African Peace Operations: From the Janjaweed to Boko Haram*, edited by Cedric De Coning, Linnea Gelot, and John Karlsrud, 90–104. London: Zed Books Ltd, 2016.

"Organization of African Unity Charter," 25 May 1963. https://au.int/en/treaties/ oau-charter-addis-ababa-25-may-1963 (accessed 7 May 2020).

O'Toole, Thomas. *The Central African Republic: The Continent's Hidden Heart*. Aldershot: Gower Publishing Company Limited, 1986.

"Our History," United Nations, https://peacekeeping.un.org/en/our-history (accessed 28 September 2020).

"Outgoing Code Cable: 11 January 1994." Frontline: The Triumph of Evil. www. pbs.org/wgbh/pages/frontline/shows/evil/warning/cable.html (accessed 3 April 2017).

Padmore, George. *Africa and World Peace*. London: Frank Cass and Company Limited, 1972.

———. *History of the Pan-African Congress*. London: The Hammersmith Bookshop Ltd, 1963.

———. *Pan-Africanism or Communism: The Coming Struggle for Africa*. London: Dobson Books Limited, 1956.

Pan, Jashobanta. "African Union's Intervention in Sudan: Importance and Effectiveness." *Insight on African* 2, no. 2 (2010): 113–27.

Parsons, Timothy. "The Military Experiences of Ordinary Africans in World War II." In *Africa and World War II*, edited by Judith A. Byfield, Carolyn A.

Brown, Timothy Parsons, and Alawad Sikainga, 3–23. New York: Cambridge University Press, 2015.

Peter, Chris Maina. *Human Rights in Africa: A Comparative Study of the African Human and People's Rights Charter and the New Tanzanian Bill of Rights.* London: Greenwood Press, 1990.

Ping, Jean. "Keynote Address." Presented at the Round-Table High-Level Meeting of Experts on the Responsibility to Protect in Africa, Addis Ababa, Ethiopia, 23 October 2008. www.responsibilitytoprotect.org/index.php/component/content/article/129-africa/1910-african-unions-commission-on-r2pkeynote-speech-by-chairperson-jean-ping (accessed 7 May 2020).

Pitts, Michelle. "Sub-Regional Solutions for African Conflict: The ECOMOG Experiment." *Journal of Conflict Studies* 19, no. 1 (1999). https://journals.lib.unb.ca/index.php/JCS/article/view/4379/5057 (accessed 7 May 2020).

Porto, Joao Gomes and Ulf Engel. "The African Peace and Security Architecture: An Evolving Security Regime?" In *Africa's New Peace and Security Architecture: Promoting Norms, Institutionalizing Solutions*, edited by Ulf Engel and Joao Gomes Porto, 143–60. Surrey: Ashgate Publishing Limited, 2010.

Powell, Anita. "Burundian President Slammed Over AU Threats." *Voice of America*, 31 December 2015. www.voanews.com/content/burunid-nkurunziza-african-union-au-threats/3125705.html (accessed 7 May 2020).

Power, Jonathan. *Like Water on Stone: The Story of Amnesty International.* Boston: Northeastern University Press, 2001.

"Presidential Decision Directive/NSC-25," 3 May 1994. https://fas.org/irp/offdocs/pdd/pdd-25.pdf (accessed 7 May 2020).

Price, Richard. "A Genealogy of the Chemical Weapons Taboo." *International Organization* 49, no. 1 (1995): 73–103.

———. "Syria and the Chemical Weapons Taboo." *Journal of Global Security Studies* 4, no. 1 (2019): 37–52.

"Principles of UN Peacekeeping." United Nations. https://peacekeeping.un.org/en/principles-of-peacekeeping (accessed 28 September 2020).

"Protocol A/SP. 3/5/81 Relating to Mutual Assistance on Defence." Economic Community of West African States, 29 May 1981. Archiving and Documentation Division, Communications Directorate, ECOWAS Commission.

"Protocol of the Commission of Mediation, Conciliation and Arbitration." *International Legal Materials* 3, no. 6 (1964): 1116–24.

"Provisional Agenda for the Fifth Ordinary Session of the Central Organ of the OAU Mechanism for Conflict Prevention, Management, and Resolution," Organization of African Unity, 30 May 1994. AU Commission Archives.

"Provisional Agenda for the First Ministerial Ordinary Session of the Central Organ of the OAU Mechanism for Conflict Prevention, Management, and Resolution." Organization of African Unity, 17–19 November 1993. AU Commission Archives.

"Provisional Agenda for the Fourteenth Extra-Ordinary Session of the Central Organ of the OAU Mechanism for Conflict Prevention, Management, and Resolution," Organization of African Unity, 13 July 1994. AU Commission Archives.

"Provisional Agenda for the Fourth Ordinary Session of the Assembly of Heads of State and Government," AHG/27, Organization of African Unity, September 1967. AU Commission Archives.

"Provisional Agenda for the Second Ordinary Session of the Assembly of Heads of State and Government." AHG/5, Organization of African Unity, October 1965. AU Commission Archives.

"Provisional Agenda for the Third Ordinary Session of the Assembly of Heads of State and Government." AHG/13, Organization of African Unity, November 1966. AU Commission Archives.

"Relaunching Africa's Economic and Social Development: The Cairo Agenda for Action." Organization of African Unity, 1995.

"Report of the Administrative Secretary-General of the Commission of Mediation, Conciliation and Arbitration." CM/924 (XXXI), Organization of African Unity, July 1978. AU Commission Archives.

"Report of the Administrative Secretary-General of the OAU: A Review of the Years 1963–1968." CM/212, Organization of African Unity, September 1968. AU Commission Archives.

"Report of the Administrative Secretary-General on the Commission of Mediation, Conciliation and Arbitration." CM/315, Organization of African Unity, February–March 1970. AU Commission Archives.

"Report of the Administrative Secretary-General on the Co-Ordination of Africa's Defence System." CM/655 (XXV), Organization of African Unity, 18–27 July 1975. AU Commission Archives.

"Report of the Administrative Secretary-General on the Third Session of the Defence Commission." CM/340 (XV), Organization of African Unity, August 1970. AU Commission Archives.

"Report of the Panel on United Nations Peace Operations." United Nations, August 2000. www.un.org/en/ga/search/view_doc.asp?symbol=A/55/305 (accessed 7 May 2020).

"Report of the Secretary General on the Proposal for the Establishment of a Political Security Council." CM/1118 (XXXVI), Organization of African Unity, 23 February–1 March 1981. AU Commission Archives.

"Report of the Secretary-General on the Establishment of a Mechanism for Conflict Prevention, Resolution, and Management." CM/1767 (LVII), Organization of African Unity, 21–26 June 1993. AU Commission Archives.

"Report of the Secretary-General on the Fundamental Changes Taking Place in the World and Their Implications for Africa: Proposals for an African Response." AHG/169 (XXVI), Organization of African Unity, July 1990. AU Commission Archives.

"Resolution 504 (1982) of 30 April 1982." United Nations, 30 April 1982. https:// undocs.org/S/RES/504(1982) (accessed 7 May 2020).

"Resolution 660 (1990) of 2 August 1990." United Nations, 2 August 1990. http:// unscr.com/en/resolutions/660 (accessed 7 May 2020).

"Resolution 678 (1990) of 29 November 1990." United Nations, 29 November 1990. http://unscr.com/en/resolutions/678 (accessed 7 May 2020).

"Resolution 688 (1991) of 5 April 1991." United Nations, 5 April 1991. http:// unscr.com/en/resolutions/688 (accessed 7 May 2020).

"Resolution 713 (1991) of 25 September 1991." United Nations, 25 September 1991. http://unscr.com/en/resolutions/713 (accessed 7 May 2020).

"Resolution 721 (1991) of 27 November 1991." United Nations, 27 November 1991. http://unscr.com/en/resolutions/721 (accessed 7 May 2020).

"Resolution 733 (1992) of 23 January 1992." United Nations, 23 January 1992. http://unscr.com/en/resolutions/733 (accessed 7 May 2020).

"Resolution 751 (1992) of 24 April 1992." United Nations, 24 April 1992. http://unscr.com/en/resolutions/751 (accessed 7 May 2020).

"Resolution 770 (1992): Adopted by the Security Council at Its 3106th Meeting, on 13 August 1992." United Nations, 13 August 1992. http://unscr.com/en/resolutions/770 (accessed 7 May 2020).

"Resolution 775 (1992): Adopted by the Security Council at Its 3110th Meeting, on 28 August 1992." United Nations, 28 August 1992. http://unscr.com/en/resolutions/775 (accessed 7 May 2020).

"Resolution 788 (1992): Adopted by the Security Council at Its 3138th Meeting." United Nations, 19 November 1992. http://unscr.com/en/resolutions/788 (accessed 7 May 2020).

"Resolution 794 (1992): Adopted by the Security Council at Its 3145th Meeting, on 3 December 1992." United Nations, 3 December 1992. http://unscr.com/en/resolutions/794 (accessed 7 May 2020).

"Resolution 808 (1993): Adopted by the Security Council at Its 3175th Meeting, on 22 February 1993." United Nations, 22 February 1993. http://unscr.com/en/resolutions/808 (accessed 7 May 2020).

"Resolution 814 (1993): Adopted by the Security Council at Its 3118th Meeting, on 26 March 1993." United Nations, 26 March 1993. http://unscr.com/en/resolutions/814 (accessed 7 May 2020).

"Resolution 819 (1993): Adopted by the Security Council at Its 3199th Meeting, on 16 April 1993." United Nations, 16 April 1993. https://digitallibrary.un.org/record/164939?ln=en (accessed 7 May 2020).

"Resolution 836 (1993): Adopted by the Security Council at Its 3228th Meeting, on 4 June 1993." United Nations, 4 June 1993. https://digitallibrary.un.org/record/166973?ln=en (accessed 7 May 2020).

"Resolution 866 (1993): Adopted by the Security Council at Its 3281st Meeting." United Nations, 22 September 1993. http://unscr.com/en/resolutions/866 (accessed 7 May 2020).

"Resolution 909 (1994): Adopted by the Security Council at Its 3358th Meeting, on 5 April 1994." United Nations, 5 April 1994. http://unscr.com/en/resolutions/909 (accessed 7 May 2020).

"Resolution 912 (1994): Adopted by the Security Council at Its 3368th Meeting, on 21 April 1994." United Nations, 21 April 1994. http://unscr.com/en/resolutions/912 (accessed 7 May 2020).

"Resolution 918 (1994): Adopted by the Security Council at Its 3377th Meeting, on 17 May 1994." United Nations, 17 May 1994. http://unscr.com/en/resolutions/918 (accessed 7 May 2020).

"Resolution 1318 (2000) Adopted by the Security Council at Its 4194th Meeting, on 7 September 2000." United Nations, 7 September 2000. http://unscr.com/en/resolutions/doc/1318 (accessed 7 May 2020).

"Resolution 1973 (2011): Adopted by the Security Council at Its 6498th Meeting, on 17 March 2011." United Nations, 17 March 2011. www.undocs.org/S/RES/1973%20(2011) (accessed 7 May 2020).

"Resolutions Adopted by the Fifth Ordinary Session of the Assembly of Heads of State and Government Held in Algiers," Organization of African Unity, 13–16 September 1968. https://au.int/sites/default/files/decisions/9517-assembly_en_13_16_september_1968_assembly_heads_state_government_fifth_ordinary_session.pdf (accessed 7 May 2020).

"Resolutions Adopted by the First Conference of Independent African Heads of State and Government Held in Addis Ababa, Ethiopia, from 22 to 25 May 1963." Organization of African Unity, 22–25 May 1963. https://au.int/sites/default/files/decisions/32247-1963_cias_plen_2–3_cias_res_1–2_e.pdf (accessed 7 May 2020).

"Resolutions Adopted by the First Ordinary Session of the Assembly of Heads of State and Government in Cairo, UAR, From 17 to 21 July 1964." Organization of African Unity, 17–21 July 1964. https://au.int/sites/default/files/decisions/9514-1964_ahg_res_1-24_i_e.pdf (accessed 7 May 2020).

"Resolutions Adopted by the Sixth Ordinary Session of the Assembly of Heads of State and Government Held in Addis Ababa." Organization of African Unity, 6–10 September 1969. https://au.int/sites/default/files/decisions/9518-assembly_en_6_10_september_1969_assembly_heads_state_government_sixth_ordinary_session.pdf (accessed 7 May 2020).

"Resolution on Chad Adopted by the Assembly of Heads of States and Government of the Organization of African Unity, Meeting in Its Seventeenth Ordinary Session in Freetown, Sierra Leone from 1–4 July 1980." AHG/ Res. 101 (XVII), Organization of African Unity, 1–4 July 1980. AU Commission Archives.

"Resolutions and Declarations Adopted by the Fourth Ordinary Session of the Assembly of Heads of State and Government Held in Kinshasa," Organization of African Unity, 11–14 September 1967. https://au.int/sites/default/files/decisions/9516-assembly_en_11_14_september_1967_assembly_heads_state_government_fourth_ordinary_session.pdf (accessed 7 May 2020).

"Resolving Conflicts in Africa: Implementation Options," 1993. AU Commission Archives.

Risse, Thomas. "International Norms and Domestic Change: Arguing and Communicative Behavior in the Human Rights Area." *Politics and Society* 27, no. 4 (1999): 529–59.

Rossi, Christopher R. "Hauntings, Hegemony, and the Threatened African Exodus from the International Criminal Court." *Human Rights Quarterly* 40, no. 2 (2018).

"Rwanda – The Preventable Genocide: The Report of the International Panel of Eminent Personalities to Investigate the 1994 Genocide in Rwanda and the Surrounding Events." Addis Ababa, Ethiopia: Organization of African Unity, 2000. AU Commission Archives.

Sakwe, Etane Ebokely Benjamin. "African States: Settlement of Political Disputes: The Role of the Organization of African Unity, 1963–1979, a Historical Review and Speculative Analysis." ETD Collection for AUC Robert W. Woodru Library, Paper 2187, 1980. AU Commission Archives.

Sikkink, Kathryn. *Evidence for Hope: Making Human Rights Work in the 21st Century*. Princeton, NJ: Princeton University Press, 2017.

————. "Latin America's Protagonist Role in Human Rights." *International Journal on Human Rights* 12, no. 22 (2015): 207–18.

Simpson, Brad. "The Biafran Secession and the Limits of Self-Determination." *Journal of Genocide Research* 16, no. 2–3 (2014): 337–54.

"Sirte Declaration." African Union, 8–9 September 1999. https://archives.au.int/handle/123456789/2475 (accessed 7 May 2020).

Stefan, Cristina G. "On Non-Western Norm Shapers: Brazil and the Responsibility While Protecting." *European Journal of International Security* 2 (2016): 88–110.

Straus, Scott. "Darfur and the Genocide Debate." *Foreign Affairs* 84, no. 1 (2005): 123–33.

Strauss, Ekkehard. "A Bird in the Hand is Worth Two in the Bush." In *The Responsibility to Protect and International Law*, edited by Alex J. Bellamy, Sara E. Davies, and Luke Glanville, 25–58. Boston: Martinus Njihoff, 2011.

Stuenkel, Oliver. *Post-Western World: How Emerging Powers Are Remaking Global Order*. London: Polity Press, 2016.

"Supplementary Budget of the Commission of Mediation, Conciliation and Arbitration of the Organization of African Unity." CM/219, Organization of African Unity, September 1968. AU Commission Archives.

Thakur, Ramesh. "The Use of International Force to Prevent or Halt Atrocities: From Humanitarian Intervention to the Responsibility to Protect." In *The Oxford Handbook of International Human Rights Law*, edited by Dinah Shelton. Oxford: Oxford University Press, 2013. www.oxfordhandbooks.com/view/10.1093/law/9780199640133.001.0001/law-9780199640133-e-35 (accessed 7 May 2020).

Thomas, Caroline. *New States, Sovereignty, and Intervention*. Aldershot: Gower Publishing Company Limited, 1985.

Thomashausen, Sophie. *Humanitarian Intervention in an Evolving World Order: The Cases of Iraq, Somalia, Kosovo, and East Timor*. Pretoria, South Africa: The Africa Institute of South Africa, 2002.

Thompson, Vincent Bakpetu. *Africa and Unity: The Evolution of Pan-Africanism*. London: Longman Group Ltd, 1969.

Tieku, Thomas Kwasi. "Explaining the Clash and Accommodation of Major Actors in the Creation of the African Union." *African Affairs* 103, no. 411 (2004): 249–67.

Titley, Brian. *Dark Age: The Political Odyssey of Emperor Bokassa*. Liverpool: Liverpool University Press, 1997.

Toga, Dawit. Political Analyst, Peace and Security Department, Conflict Management Division, African Union Commission. Interview by Kathryn Nash, 1 April 2016.

Tourinho, Marcos, Oliver Stuenkel, and Sarah Brockmeier. "'Responsibility While Protecting': Reforming R2P Implementation." *Global Society* 30, no. 1 (2016): 134–50.

"The UN's Response: 11 January 1994." Frontline: The Triumph of Evil. www.pbs.org/wgbh/pages/frontline/shows/evil/warning/unresponse.html (accessed 3 April 2017).

"Universal Declaration of Human Rights," 10 December 1948. www.un.org/en/universal-declaration-human-rights/ (accessed 7 May 2020).

"Universal Declaration of Human Duties." CM/966 (XXXIII) Add. 1, Organization of African Unity, July 1979. AU Commission Archives.

"Verbatim Record: Council of Ministers First Committee (Political): Third Session – Afternoon Session." CM (III) (1) SR.2, Organization of African Unity, 14 July 1964. AU Commission Archives.

Walraven, Klaas Van. *Dreams of Power: The Role of the Organization of African Unity in the Politics of Africa 1963–1993*. Surrey: Ashgate Publishing Limited, 1999.

Walraven, Klaas van. "Heritage and Transformation: From the Organization of African Unity to the African Union." In *Africa's New Peace and Security Architecture: Promoting Norms and Institutionalizing Solutions*, edited by Ulf Engel and Joao Gomes Porto, 31–56. Surrey: Ashgate Publishing Limited, 2010.

Westad, Odd Arne. *The Global Cold War*. Cambridge: Cambridge University Press, 2005.

Wet, Erika de. "The Evolving Role of ECOWAS and the SADC in Peace Operations: A Challenge to the Primacy of the United Nations Security Council in Matters of Peace and Security?" *Leiden Journal of International Law* 27 (2014): 353–69.

Wheeler, Nicholas J. *Saving Strangers: Humanitarian Intervention in International Society*. Oxford: Oxford University Press, 2000.

Wilkins, Gregory L. *African Influence in the United Nations, 1967–1975: The Politics and Techniques of Gaining Compliance to UN Principles and Resolutions*. Washington DC: University Press of America, 1981.

Williams, Paul D. "The African Union's Peace Operations: A Comparative Analysis." In *Regional Organizations in African Security*, edited by Fredrik Soderbaum and Rodrigo Tavares, 29–50. New York: Routledge, 2011.

———. "From Non-Intervention to Non-Indifference: The Origins and Development of the African Union's Security Culture." *African Affairs* 106, no. 423 (2007): 253–79.

———. "IPI Global Observatory." *Special Report: The African Union's Coercive Diplomacy in Burundi* (blog), 18 December 2015. http://theglobalobservatory. org/2015/12/burundi-african-union-maprobu-arusha-accords/ (accessed 7 May 2020).

Index

Lightning Source UK Ltd.
Milton Keynes UK
UKHW030358120322
399945UK00003B/136